Books by Richard Bangs and Christian Kallen

RIDING THE DRAGON'S BACK   (1989)

ISLANDS OF FIRE, ISLANDS OF SPICE   (1988)

PATHS LESS TRAVELLED   (Editors; 1988)

SOBEK'S ADVENTURE VACATIONS   (1986)

RIVERGODS   (1985)

1,000 ADVENTURES   (1984)

THE ADVENTURE BOOK   (1983)

RIDING
THE
DRAGON'S
BACK

RIDING THE DRAGON'S BACK

The Race
to Raft
the
Upper
Yangtze

RICHARD
BANGS
AND
CHRISTIAN
KALLEN

Atheneum

New York

1989

Atheneum
Macmillan Publishing Company
866 Third Avenue, New York, N.Y. 10022
Collier Macmillan Canada, Inc.

Library of Congress Cataloging-in-Publication Data
Bangs, Richard, 1950–
    Riding the dragon's back : the race to raft the upper Yangtze / Richard Bangs and Christian Kallen.
    p.   cm.
    ISBN 0-689-11932-1
    1. Yangtze River Watershed (China)—Description and travel. 2. Rafting (Sports)—China—Yangtze River Watershed. 3. Bangs, Richard, 1950–   —Journeys—China—Yangtze River Watershed.
I. Kallen, Christian.   II. Title.
DS793.Y3B36   1989
915.1'20458—dc20   89-15086   CIP

Macmillan books are available at special discounts for bulk purchases for sales promotions, premiums, fund-raising, or educational use. For details, contact:

Special Sales Director
Macmillan Publishing Company
866 Third Avenue
New York, N.Y. 10022

Designed by Erich Hobbing

10 9 8 7 6 5 4 3 2 1

Printed in the United States of America

Contents

viii   Contents

Author's Note

We were able to interview nearly everyone connected with the Sino–USA Upper Yangtze River Expedition, and have done our best to present an accurate portrayal of the challenges faced, successes achieved, and disappointments endured by the team. One important point of view is incomplete, however—that of Ken Warren, organizer and leader of the expedition. Public materials and forums, including newspaper and magazine articles, slide lectures, and press conferences, did provide some insight into his perspective. However, when we approached him directly, he declined the opportunity to present his version of details and issues associated with his expedition. We regret this, but nonetheless feel the reader will here find the most comprehensive report currently available on all five major Yangtze River expeditions of the mid-1980s.

Additionally, we should attempt to clarify any confusion that may result from the binary authorship of this work, in contrast to the first-person singular narrative form, most noticeably in the latter half of the book. The primary voice is that of Richard Bangs, the "I" of the tale; Christian Kallen's voice is not silent, but hopefully harmonious. This renders the book truly Taoist in execution: Out of the One comes the Two; out of the two comes this book, and from this book the diverse readers who make our efforts worthwhile.

Acknowledgments

This book is itself a bit like the river it features, in that it appears as a final result, impressive in size and laden with freight, the lustrous product of a single entity. There is little indication of the trouble upstream, the rapids, shoals, and canyons traversed to reach the end, to say nothing of the tributaries that feed the whole. But unlike the mute mature Yangtze, we can give credit to those who contributed, the many people and organizations who augmented the tiny trickle of an idea so that it grew to become the final product you hold in your hands. This is necessarily an inconclusive list of the myriad talents that went into this book; to those of you not mentioned here, please know that we thank you for your efforts in helping to create a work whose whole is not necessarily greater than the sum of its parts.

Since the actual expedition that formed the cornerstone of *Riding the Dragon's Back* was organized and executed by SOBEK Expeditions, our primary thanks should go to them, both the corporate entity and the individuals who compose it. Foremost among the latter is John Yost, whose lifelong interest in China helped fuel the fires of longing and ambition that resulted in this book, and whose energy made the trip possible. Helping hands were lent by Dr. Helen Clyatt Yost, who put together the medical kits and kept the candle burning; John Kramer, the SOBEK equipment manager; Paul Henry, the controller who desperately tried and finally succeeded in keeping the finances under control, along with Joyce Helmbrecht and Melanie Tan, the bookkeepers who supported those efforts; Laura Taylor, who supervised the ticket writing; Nigel Dabby, who traveled to China to help negotiate the permit; Sloan Smith and Johannes Tan, who organized the photography; Leslie Jarvie, who kept things humming in our absence; and Peter Buchanan, our attorney.

Second only to this front line of supporters are the various corporations and concerns that donated equipment to make the SOBEK Great Bend of the Yangtze Expedition possible. This list must include Avon Inflatables and Achilles Riverboats for their state-of-the-art river rafts; AlpineAire Foods for their freeze-dried delights; Canham Frames; Carter Oars; Cascade Designs for their dry bags and Therm-a-rest sleeping pads; Coleman for their Peak One stoves, lamps, and sleeping bags; Colorado Kayak Supply, which supplied Stohliquist Dry Suits; The North Face for tents and sleeping bags; Converse Rubber Company for shoes; ExtraSport for life jackets and river wear; Gerber Knives; Gull Oars; JVC for the videocamera that documented the expedition; Minolta for the cameras that took many of the photos in this book; Nikon for its waterproof ActionTouch cameras; *National Geographic* magazine for supplying and developing film; Oakely sunglasses; O'Neill Wetsuits and Body Glove for on-river wear; Pelican waterproof cases; Perception for Joel Fogel's yellow kayak; Solarts for their solar recharger; Sony Corporation of America for waterproof Walkmans; Tekna for flashlights; Teva for the boatman's favorite river shoe; Thule car racks; Ultra-Flex Oars; Uvex for sunglasses; Whitewater Manufacturing for dry bags; and the airlines that lent their technology and support services to the members of this expedition, including United Airlines, Singapore Airlines, and CAAC for domestic flights within China.

Other individuals who lent their personal assistance include Kevan and Alex Khanamirian, who made extra efforts to find the right sponsors, as did Suzanne Jordan, Nancy McClesky, and Elizabeth Wimbrow; Bill Graves of *National Geographic* magazine, who supported our efforts over the long years it took to reach the Long River; Rick Laylin of United Airlines, who has always been an advocate of our most outlandish projects; Ambassador Robert Yost, who interceded on our behalf when things were looking bleak; Ann Cassidy, who provided her Lake Tahoe retreat as a writing den; and Yanthie Indrakusuma, who helped process the endless manuscript revisions.

We also want to thank the Explorers Club of New York for their sanction and flag, and Janet Baldwin at their library for her assistance in research. Other research assistance was lent by John Leedam, Arlene Belasco Kallen, and Marti Morec. Special thanks are also due to Steve Goldsmith of Odyssey Tours; Tovya Wager of Asian Pacific Adventures; Kent Madin of Boojum Expeditions; Sam Moore for his scouting hike into Tiger's Leap Gorge; Jeff Chop of the 1985 National Geographic Source of the Yangtze Expedition, who leant his thesis, videos, and recollections; and Diana Kendrick, who supplied us with information from the State Department. Jim Abrams of the Associated Press Beijing office was particularly helpful, as was Dewey Pendergrass of the American Embassy in China. Other assistance in diplomacy was provided by Governor Lamm of Colorado, Senator Laxalt of Nevada, Senator Cranston of California, the Institute of East Asian Studies at Berkeley, the US–China Friendship Association, the National Council for US–China Trade, and Xie Fie, cultural attaché at the Embassy of the People's Republic of China, Washington, DC.

In China, our particular gratitude is extended to Zheng Fengrong, manager of China International Sports Travel, and her associates at CIST including Tsao Hong Jun, Wang Fu Zhao, Qu Yin Hua, Sixiang Luo, and Cao Huiying. Shi Zhan Chun and Hu Lin of the Chinese Mountaineering Association were also of great assistance. Special gratitude is due Lu Mei of Beijing, not only for her translation of *Drift* by Dai Shan Kui, which provided the basis for chapters 5 and 12, but also for her continued generous efforts on our behalf. Jiang Jiang, currently of Provo but clearly a river lover at heart, also provided a parallel translation of *Drift*, to our deepest appreciation.

As a work of research as well as recollection, this volume would not be possible without source information as it appeared in *Sports Illustrated*, *USA Today*, *Outside*, *Backpacker*, the *San Francisco Chronicle* and *San Francisco Examiner*, the *Los Angeles Times*, the *Minneapolis Star & Tribune Sunday Magazine*, the *Portland Oregonian* and *Portland Examiner*, the *Idaho Statesman*, the *Yakima Herald-Republic*, the *News-Review*, Roseburg, Oregon, the *Eugene Register-Guard*, *Willamete Week*, *Range Finder*, *NOLS Currents*, and *River Runner* and *Canoe* magazines. Several Chinese publications also proved invaluable, including *China Sports Magazine*, *China Reconstructs*, the *China Daily* and the *South China Morning Post*. In addition, our thanks go to the people at the American Wilderness Alliance, Friends of the River, the Northwest Rafters Association, and to Bob Woodward at *Adventure Travel* magazine. Our gratitude also to the Sino–USA Upper Yangtze River Expedition, many of whose members found time to speak with us at great length and with great insight.

On a more intimate level, our appreciation extends to our agent, Howard Morhaim, as well as to Judy Kern, Evan Oppenheimer, and Richard Constantine at Atheneum. Finally, the travels and travails that resulted in *Riding the Dragon's Back* were well borne by our respective helpmates, Pam Roberson and Kathryn Sieck, without whose support our efforts might seem bleak indeed.

To the River of Dreams

Let me journey down
On the great river . . .
'twixt gorges of the hills.
—YU-PE-YA'S LUTE

Yes, the Amazon and Nile are longer; the Zaire carries more water. But somehow, the Yangtze is the flow that rules, the stream that evoked a rush of reverence among explorers of the past and the geologists, ethnologists, hydraulic engineers, and river runners of today. Rising from the Qinghai-Tibetan plateau, it careens and sweeps more than 3,900 miles, spinning through twelve of China's twenty-nine provinces, falling 17,660 feet before spilling into the East China Sea near Shanghai. It accepts over seven hundred major tributaries, drains a fifth of China's land area, supports a third of the country's population. Its lower half has seen the rise and fall and resurrection of kingdoms and dynasties for twenty-three centuries, and its gorges and basins have been among the major avenues of trade in Asia since the times of the Roman Empire. But the upper half of the Yangtze has been a cipher, an unknown land of myth and mystery, an enigma protected by the world's deepest canyons, bathed by some of the world's biggest rapids. After all other rivers had been run, all other canyons penetrated and explored, the Yangtze remained *aqua incognita*: the last emperor of wild rivers.

Beginning in the late 1960s, river rafting gave a new lease on life to the universal spirit of adventure. Inflatable rafts made of tough, abrasion-resistant synthetic materials, designed to ride over the biggest waves, with storage space for a fortnight of food and a six-pack of people, yet weighing just one hundred pounds each, became the Volkswagen of exploration. The biggest, the smallest, the most remote, and the most glamorous rivers were navigated—the Blue Nile, the Euphrates, the Ganges, the Indus, the headwaters of the Amazon and the mighty Zambezi. But the Yangtze was the brass ring, the prize that eluded the most determined adventurers. For wildwater connoisseurs, running the Yangtze had been a dream for decades. It seeped into conversations around campfires; it evoked images of liquid thunder, of secret lamaseries clinging to streaked limestone cliffs, of gorges thin as a glacier crevasse, of jade-laced mountains draped by eternal snows.

Oddly, it was neither geography nor hydraulics that kept the Yangtze forbidden, but politics. The river was in the heart of perhaps the world's most xenophobic nation, the People's Republic of China. Since 1949, when the Communists under Mao Zedong and Zhou Enlai had wrested power away from Chiang Kai-shek's Kuomintang, mainland China had become a land of riddles. First the influence of the Western democracies was cast off, then the advice of the only other major Communist country in the world, the Soviet Union, was banished from the ancient land. Finally, with the Cultural Revolution of 1966–76, it seemed that China was excluding even its own history and traditions from its present, cutting itself off from its roots. Until the Bamboo Curtain rose, there was little hope of ever seeing the Yangtze's wildest water.

It was then a supreme irony that it was not earnest negotiation or border wars that finally opened up China, but sports—specifically Ping-Pong. In 1972, the United States Table Tennis Association sponsored the visit of a team from the People's Republic, the first cultural exchange between the two countries since 1945. The "Red Chinese" responded to their warm welcome by extending an invitation for the American team to visit China, with the result that the first official American visitors to China in three decades were not diplomats, but sportsmen.

Less than a year later Richard Nixon was toasting Zhou Enlai in Beijing, and the slow progress toward official relations had begun. Finally the Cultural Revolution ended—the Ten Years of Chaos, as it is now known in China—and reason began to prevail. Official diplomatic relations were established between the United States and the People's Republic in 1979, but fully a year earlier the first group of American tourists was allowed to visit China. The Chinese government, while keen to experiment with tourism and its attendant infusion of hard currency, wanted to dip a cautious toe in such capitalist-tinged waters, and looked to its ideological allies for support. Since Ethiopia had recently undergone a Chinese-style Communist revolution, and an air link was already established between the two countries, China asked Ethiopian Airlines to help organize some initial tours to the Middle Kingdom.

By luck, SOBEK Expeditions, the adventure travel company I co-owned, had been running rafting tours to Ethiopia's Omo River since 1973, so the airline turned to us to recruit American tourists. I helped lead a group of fifty that started in California, winged to Rome, flew down to Addis Ababa, over to Bombay, then across the great mountains and plains of China, in the pitch of darkness: we were told the government wouldn't allow daylight flights for fear of spying through the windows.

It was a city tour—Shanghai, Guangzhou (Canton), Hangzhou, and Beijing. In Beijing, I left a museum tour early, got lost in streets where no passerby spoke English and no sign was recognizable, but finally made my way to the Tienanmen Square headquarters of CITS, China International Travel Service, our hosts. There I slapped down a stack of rafting brochures on the desk of the highest official I was allowed to see, a Mrs. Hu Muying, properly dressed in gray chinoiserie. I took a deep breath and asked the big question, "How about the Yangtze?" I held on to the last sound as though I didn't want ever to let it go.

Her nod was vacant. There is rarely a no in China. Instead, they serve tea. Looking at Mrs. Hu Muying was like looking at the Chinese emperor in the Marguerite Yourcenar story: "beautiful, but blank, like a looking-glass placed too high, reflecting nothing except the stars and the immutable heavens." It was clear rafting was something entirely new to my host, and she raised her thick eyebrows at the photographs of rubber boats pitching through haystacks of whitewater. After much consideration, she suggested I put my request in the form of a written proposal and send it along after my return to the United States.

So began an eight-year correspondence. I would pen eloquent entreaties, and cite the lofty potential for furthering world peace through rafting. Silence was the usual response. It was maddening, as it seemed with each passing month new regions of China were opened to tourism and new activities were allowed. By the dawn of the 1980s, the news was thick of treks being offered, mountain climbing permits being issued—yet nothing when it came to rafting. I thought perhaps they saw through my carefully crafted attempts at lifting the desire to dip oars in the river of dreams to a higher plane. But I kept trying.

Then, in early 1982, a telex clacked into the SOBEK offices in Angels Camp, California. It was from the Chinese Mountaineering Association, stating it now had the authority to issue a permit to raft the upper Yangtze. Might we be interested in accepting an invitation? Amidst the whoops and cries of self-congratulation, someone typed a telex back: "Yes, we would be only too happy to accept such an invitation and raft the upper Yangtze. Please send details and costs."

For days we heard nothing. I imagined a phalanx of abacuses spinning overtime, working out every last *feng*. Then, at last, a week after the first surprise telex, another pecked its way into our lives. "You may raft the upper Yangtze for a fee of one million dollars." It went on to explain the fee included several hotel nights and transportation to and from the river. Communists, perhaps, but certainly the most audacious of profiteers.

Needless to say, it was a fee beyond SOBEK's resources. But not everyone's. ABC TV's long-running Sunday television series "The American Sportsman" was stretching for more spectacular material, and the first descent of the upper Yangtze appealed to executive producer John Wilcox. The previous fall we had produced an episode featuring the first descent of the Zambezi with Wilcox, and our relations were good; so he contacted the Chinese directly and began negotiations. In April 1982 he called me and said everything was a go, and asked SOBEK to outfit the expedition. His plan was to take John Denver on the expedition as the star of his show; during a quiet stretch of river he would sing his then-current hit, "Shanghai Breezes." Wilcox asked if I would fly to China in August to nail down arrangements.

Three weeks before my scheduled departure another telex arrived, this one announcing that our Yangtze expedition was canceled because of denials from provincial authorities. Perhaps as a consolation prize, the Chinese Mountaineering Association (CMA) offered to let us go rafting on a river they had picked out, the Jian Jun Guo, a glacier-fed stream that spills off Mount Bogda near Urumqi in Xinjiang (northwesternmost China), bubbles for about twenty miles, then feeds into Tian Chi, Heaven's Pool, a locally popular tourist attraction. The area was politically unsensitive, it had become a popular trekking destination, and the river, if it could be called that, was so small as to pose virtually no threat to life or limb. The CMA offered a combination trek/river trip for the comparative bargain of four thousand dollars per person. At least it would be the first river rafting trip in China, and we took the proffered bait.

Even though both lead time and the river were short, we thought it might help pave the way to the Yangtze. With a few phone calls, we were able to recruit four clients, including a sixty-two-year-old Washington State hops farmer named Gerrit Schilperoort. Because of the size of the undertaking, we could only afford to send one representative from

SOBEK, and John Yost, who had never been to China though he majored in Chinese studies at Wesleyan University, lobbied for and got the spot. I stayed behind and supervised the office.

The trip took place the last two weeks of August 1982 and was marred by minor problems, such as the CMA forgetting to bring the promised tents, and one of the clients becoming so ill she had to stay in a hotel rather than being able to trek or raft. But most of all, the river was a disappointment. "There was no river, just an obstacle course," John Yost complained. They managed to float a tiny raft for three hours, through an area scenically unimpressive, in water so shallow they had to get out and push about half the time. It may have been the first river-rafting expedition in China, but it was a dud.

For the next four years we continued to negotiate with the Chinese, trying to convince them of the veracity of Laffer's Curve, the cornerstone of Reaganomics—that by lowering the price, more people would raft their rivers, and they would make more money. Perhaps, they seemed to acknowledge, but there would be only one "first descent," and as they had done well selling "first ascents" of their major mountain peaks to foreigners, they were going to hold out for a hefty fee for the Yangtze. Over the passing years their price came down, but they made it clear that at a minimum they expected several hundred thousand dollars for the first foreign try at the Yangtze.

Meanwhile, we had been hearing rumors of another whitewater rafter who was lobbying hard for the right to run the Yangtze. Ken Warren of Tualatin, Oregon, had run two major tributaries of the Ganges, and one descent had been filmed for ABC under the aegis of John Wilcox. But as far as we knew, that was the extent of his overseas experience. He owned a small Oregon rafting company, with such rivers as the Snake, the Owyhee, and the Deschutes on the menu; but dozens of companies ran those rivers, while SOBEK had made nearly thirty first descents on international rivers over the past decade, including such classics as the Blue Nile, the Indus, the Euphrates, the Bío-Bío, Chile's biggest river, and the Zambezi in south-central Africa. Smug in that knowledge, perhaps feeling superior, we felt there was no way Warren would be granted a permit before SOBEK.

We had not accounted for two things: Ken Warren's zeal and the power of money. In 1986, Warren and his sponsors forked over $325,000 to the China Sports Service to fulfill his own dream of being the first on the river's uppermost reaches. He quickly assembled a crew and a raft of product sponsors, informed the press of his ambitious plans, and took off for the headwaters of the Yangtze. Ironically, the fairy godfather the Oregon rafter found to underwrite his attempt was none other than television producer John Wilcox, eager to make a comeback into network showcasing following the cancellation of "The American Sportsman."

Warren's goal was ambitious—to run the upper 1,900 miles of the Yangtze, from its reputed source on the southwestern slopes of Mount Geladandong in the Tanggula Mountains, to Yibin in Sichuan, the heretofore uppermost reach of traditional navigation on the waters of the Yangtze. It would be an expedition to end all expeditions, as major a river effort as had been mounted in this century. Privately, we doubted Warren's ability to come close to attaining his goal, but there it was—he had won first shot at the long-sought prize, to raft the Yangtze.

Then came a new twist. The Yangtze is, in so many ways, the defining river of Chinese civilization, and the young people of China—on the rebound from the effects of the Gang of Four—took offense at these efforts by outsiders to conquer the dragon stream. Just as Chinese climbers had claimed first ascents on the country's highest mountains before allowing outsiders to climb them, so Chinese rafters demanded the opportunity to run the Yangtze first. It became an issue of national pride, a test of the phoenix China that had risen from the ashes of the Cultural Revolution. First a solitary rafter made an ill-fated attempt, then a semi-official government team, and finally a series of spontaneous young Chinese rafting squads headed for the headwaters to beat the Americans down the river. The race was on—a dangerous, dramatic, and altogether adventurous race to run the Yangtze, to ride the dragon from its snowy lair to the muddy banks of the sea.

Some called it the last great river run on the planet; others called it impossible, a killer. Its allure was unarguable, and the competition between Ken Warren and the Chinese had all the drama of the race to the Poles. Many wanted to get there, some to see and experience it before it was too late, before the modern world brought irrevocable change to this far corner; others to be a part of a last, great first; some just for curiosity, and others for the glory.

During the summer of 1986, while Ken Warren and the Chinese teams raced down the increasingly wild waters of the Yangtze, SOBEK's permit to run the river remained active. With Ken Warren officially taking the "first descent" slot, however, the price to SOBEK dropped to just over $100,000, with an additional $10,000 fee if we wanted to film the expedition. While the price finally sounded reasonable, it was still beyond our means. We realized we might have to raise the money by selling places on the expedition to qualified people, probably clients from past trips. The SOBEK trip down the Yangtze would thus become in part a commercial venture, and not an expedition in the purest sense.

In a way this was appropriate. SOBEK Expeditions is, after all, a business, running adventure travel tours on seven continents, from climbing Aconcagua in Argentina to rafting the Zambezi in Zambia. Many of SOBEK's thirty-some first descents had turned into commercially viable operations, offered to the public at large. The Zambezi provided the classic example: the southern African river had first been extensively surveyed by David Livingstone, whose journey down its length was interrupted by the stupendous breach in the landscape he called Victoria Falls. In 1981, SOBEK undertook the challenge of running the previously unnavigated stretch of the Zambezi below the Falls, an exploit which had never before been considered possible—and which was videotaped by John Wilcox for ABC television. Five years later, commercial operations on the Zambezi totaled nearly a quarter of a million dollars annually, with over five thousand people experiencing the Zambezi's whitewater each year.

Perhaps as a consequence of our company's reputation, we found ourselves in negotiation not with China Sports Service (CSS), the agency that backed Warren, but with a related group called Chinese International Sports Travel (CIST). The boards of the two agencies have members in common, but while CSS is concerned with expeditions (such as high-altitude mountain climbs), CIST is oriented to tourism (such as bicycle tours). Still, if CIST wanted to back an expedition, there was nothing to prevent them: CSS had no lock on mountain climbs, treks, or even first descents.

We continued to hope we could find financial backing for our Yangtze trip without going to clients. We asked *National Geographic* to underwrite the expedition, but they had already committed to Warren and demurred. We tried to find corporate sponsorship, asking Kodak, DuPont, and others to lend name and resources to our adventure. No takers. With John Wilcox officially backing Ken Warren's trip, we sought film deals with other sources, even going so far as to approach the major studios for the possibility of a feature—*Indiana Jones on the River of Golden Sands*, perhaps. Again, no luck. Our only recourse was to sell seats on the trip to our clients, preferably ones who had been on extreme rafting trips and could handle the uncertainty and physical challenges of the upper Yangtze. It was a risky route, no doubt: the majority of SOBEK's exploratory expeditions over the years had been conducted with a crew of proven professionals. Yet the only way we could afford to pay the Chinese price tag was to open the door to deeper pockets and hope for the best. Whether or not the Yangtze would provide the same opportunities as the Zambezi remained to be seen.

While the notion of running from source to sea has romantic appeal, SOBEK set its sights on a much more practical route, a three-hundred-mile section of the Yangtze called the Great Bend in northwest Yunnan Province. Here, as the river pitches south towards Vietnam, it makes a sharp turn back on itself, pierces a range of mountains that reach toward nineteen thousand feet, arcs up to the Sichuan border, then traces another hairpin turn and once more slides southward. Finally, it veers back in a last sharp curve to run almost due east on its long final march to the sea. At places its south-flowing waters are but twenty miles from its northward currents, but the two are separated by massive glacial-sculpted peaks. The landscape promised to be exotic, imposing; the river was certain to be a challenge.

The Great Bend, though in the "Forbidden Zone" and unvisited by Westerners since 1949, was legendary for its rugged beauty, its steep canyons, its soaring peaks, and most especially for Hutiaoxia, Tiger's Leap Gorge. Legend has it that a tiger fleeing from a hunter came to the edge of this gorge and found it so narrow that in a single bound he flew across the foaming waters to safety on the other side. Botanist and ethnologist Joseph Rock had wandered through the gorge in 1925, and proclaimed it "by far the finest of all the gorges in Yunnan," within which the river "becomes a mad torrent flowing through a terrifying gorge." Rock negotiated a narrow mule trail, at some points 2,500 feet above the river, that winds through the twelve-mile-long canyon, and described what he saw in the August 1926 issue of *National Geographic*:

> The Yangtze flows at 6,000 feet elevation where it enters the gorge, and as the peaks of the range which it pierces as with a giant's sword are more than 19,000 feet in height, the gorge is approximately 13,000 feet in depth.
>
> In many places the river is only 20 yards in width and is one continuous series of cascades and rapids. The actual depth of the water must be enormous, for the vast placid stream is here compressed into a narrow ribbon of white foam.
>
> The cliffs rise steeply on both sides, culminating in jagged crags and pinnacles, and above these tower the ice-crowned peaks of the Likiang snow range.

We were granted an October launch date, as our research showed the water would be relatively low, well after the summer snow melt and the monsoon rains of July and August, while the daily temperatures would still be hospitable. With the help of Los Angeles–based Odyssey Tours and an enterprising kayaker from Kentucky, Sam Moore, we pulled together cast and crew for a fall 1986 Great Bend expedition. As Ken Warren and company were unpacking their gear in Golmud, we were packing ours at our warehouse in Angels Camp.

Through the ensuing months of 1986, as the Chinese and Warren pursued their dreams down the Yangtze, we watched with not-altogether-detached interest. Although our start date was set for October, four months after Warren began his descent from the headwaters, and five months after the Chinese, I entertained a fantasy: the inexperienced but patriotic Chinese would have difficulties in the first few hundred miles of river, and slowly would be overtaken by the more experienced Warren team. Both would arrive at Tiger's Leap Gorge weeks behind schedule, in late October—just when SOBEK was launching its long-sought descent of the same gorge. Now that would be a real race, I told myself, a keen contest of whitewater skills on a river of dreams, set in the soaring limestone peaks of China.

Until then, there was nothing to do but wait, scour the papers for word of the expeditions ahead of us, and consider what made the Yangtze the centerpiece of these powerful ambitions, competitions, and fantasies, bizarre even in the often strange and exotic world of adventure.

PART ONE

1986 — The Year of the Tiger

CHAPTER ONE

The Yangtze in History

The River flows to
the East.
Its waves have
washed away all
the heroes of history.
—SU TUNG P'O

The largest nation on earth, China finds its wellsprings not in the might of its dynasties, nor in the archives of its literature, but in the villages of its countryside. Here, land-rooted families base their lives and traditions on the slow cycles of the season: the planting and harvesting, the monsoon and the calm, the flood and the drought. Changes in the centuries-old patterns of society have come from beyond the Great Wall, brought by the horse-borne warriors of the steppes, or the European barbarians who traded in demoralization. Yet outside the swirling eddies of history, the constant return of summer, winter, fall, and spring remains the durable current behind all change. This is a country whose history resembles nothing so much as the alternately turbulent and placid course of a mighty river.

That river is the Yangtze. Even more than the Huang Ho (Yellow River), along whose course many of the early dynasties were formed, the Yangtze has virtually described the country—it has divided north from south, it has defined empires and defied emperors, it has slaughtered millions and fed many more. The country lives in dreaded dependence on its cycles of flood and drought, plenty and scarcity. And while the farmers and merchants of the land are indebted to these nurturing cycles, they are forever fearful of the river's ancient, capricious rages. In its fickle necessity, the river resonates with the central mythic image of

3

China—the dragon, the winged lizard who rules the heavens, the very image of supernatural willfulness. While the mandarins bowed before the Dragon Throne, the peasants have known that it is along the length of the Yangtze that the dragon's lair has truly been found.

Much of the recent writing on China has emphasized the baffling nature of the country today. Whether Orville Schell or Paul Theroux, Mark Salzman or Peter Jenkins, the visitor is alternately puzzled, reassured, comforted, and confounded by many aspects of China—the headlong retreat from the recent Cultural Revolution, the seemingly baseless confidence of its newest economic goals, the virtual erasure of old Beijing and its replacement by a city whose skyline is besieged by monstrous cranes, invaders from a parallel universe of machinery. Still, some things, as the saying goes, remain the same. One of these is the Yangtze. The facts remain unchanged, unchangeable. Historic events are matters of record, and even the legends of the Yangtze have become hardened and polished by repetition and revision into gemstones of truth.

To this vast store of detail and lore is now added the recent history of the taming of the uppermost waters of the Yangtze, during the years from 1985 to 1987, by adventurers who sought to achieve a last great first—the navigation of the river from its headwaters to the East China Sea. There were loners like Yao Maoshu, rebels like Jiehu Arsha, and obsessed adventurers like Ken Warren. Whatever their motivation, these driven individuals and divided teams found themselves caught up in a race to conquer an unconquerable opponent, a race to ride the dragon, to tame the mighty Yangtze.

Within China, the Yangtze is primarily known as the Chang Jiang, the Long River. This is the lower half, the navigable stretch from Shanghai to Yibin, the port town nearly two thousand miles upstream; this is the two thousand miles that pass through and create history in China. Above Yibin, the river is the River of Golden Sands, the Jinsha Jiang, a tumultuous thousand-mile-long tributary whose wild waters reflect the bandit-ridden heritage of its remote tribes. When it reaches into Qinghai Province and the Tibetan Plateau, the Jinsha Jiang becomes known as the Tongtian Ho—the River to Heaven, whose crystalline waters nourish the nomads at the farthest reach of the Celestial Kingdom. Taken together, this tripartite beast we call the Yangtze is more than just a river: in baldly quantitative terms alone, it is virtually a cosmic force.

Third in length among the world's rivers, the Yangtze's 3,960 miles place it just 200 miles longer than the Mississippi-Missouri, 200 miles behind the two champion distance runners, the Nile and the Amazon. Water volume at its mouth is the world's fourth greatest, averaging 1.2 million cubic feet per second; its annual total of 244 cubic miles of water bears with it some 300 million tons of alluvial soil, which adds one square mile of land to its delta every sixty-four years. Combined with the lesser outflow of the Huang Ho, these two Chinese rivers discharge in every year almost as much soil as all the rivers in North and South America combined—four times as much as it took to build the Great Wall. It is a river of such enormity that, as Paul Theroux noted, "All Yangtze statistics are hopelessly huge and ungraspable; they obscure rather than clarify."

Like any monster, the Yangtze is also unpredictable, dangerous, a killer. One of the century's most devastating natural disasters took place in 1931, when six enormous flood waves swept down the Yangtze to destroy twenty-three sets of dams and dykes, flooding more than 35,000 square miles of land. Some 40 million people were left homeless, the economy of China was devastated; some observers speculated that at least 140,000 people drowned, and perhaps a million people altogether lost their lives as a direct or indirect result of that year's flood. Several major cities along the Yangtze—including the capital of the Republic of China, Nanjing, and the industrial center Wuhan—were underwater for weeks. Yet the 1931 flood was only one of three enormous floods in this century, and over a thousand recorded between 206 B.C. and the present. Deep in the chronicles of China's history there is the great flood of 2297 B.C., when the Huang Ho as well as the Chang Jiang overflowed their banks and turned the North China Plain into a vast lake for years.

Aside from the periodic catastrophic floods that plague the Yangtze Basin, the annual spring floods are far from benevolent. The flood season usually begins in March or April and can last for more than half the year, as long as eight months. Water levels fluctuate along the Yangtze an *average* of 65 feet between low water and high water levels; in the Three Gorges region of Hubei Province, the annual flood stage can be up to 175 feet—some say as much as 275 feet—above low water levels. Here the river is only about 600 feet wide, but it is also some 500 to 600 feet deep, even during nonflood months—giving the Yangtze title as the world's deepest river.

But the river which taketh away also giveth. In part because of the vast amounts of alluvium that flooding leaves behind, the million-square-mile Yangtze River Basin is one of the world's most fertile regions. Below the Three Gorges near Yichang, the course of the Yangtze levels out and meanders across the most industrially and agriculturally developed area in China. Monsoons—the moisture-bearing summer winds of Asia—bring over forty inches of rainfall each year, but in the Yangtze Basin a series of lakes and tributary river channels regulate the seasonal rising and falling of the river. Weather conditions in this temperate coastal climate are ideal for a growing period of up to eleven months a year; according to local climatic conditions, two or even three crops may be harvested in some areas. Cotton, wheat, barley, corn, beans, and other more modern crops are grown here, in addition to that staple of China's diet, rice—a mind-boggling 70 percent of the country's rice. This is truly the proverbial rice bowl of China, and fully a third of China's billion-plus population lives in the Yangtze River Basin.

Over the centuries, it has been the Huang Ho or Yellow River that has often seemed most central to China's history. Its 2,900-mile length arches through the heartland of China, witness to the rise and fall of dynasties since the mythical Yellow Emperor, Huang Ti, of 2600 B.C. But a thousand miles longer, and nearly twenty times greater in flow, the Yangtze's influence on China's history and imagination is correspondingly greater. Its coils encircle the Middle Kingdom in a deadly embrace, its serpentine course winds from high snowy lair to muddy wallow. The comparison with the dragon is not facile, but apt: the dragon in China is a monster, yes, but a life-giving, order-preserving monster.

The *I Ching* or Book of Changes is the classic text of Taoist prophecy—said to be the product of the fertile insight of Fu Hsi, legendary inventor of writing as well as, perhaps coincidentally, boat travel. The book is built from the basis of the first hexagram, six solid lines, heaven over heaven, "the Creative"; the creative totem of China is the Dragon. "In China the dragon has a meaning altogether different from that given it in the Western world," noted Richard Wilhelm in his translation of the Book of Changes. "The dragon is a symbol of the electrically charged, dynamic, arousing force that manifests itself in the thunderstorm. In winter this energy withdraws into the earth; in the early summer it becomes active again, appearing in the sky as thunder and lightning. As a result the creative forces of the earth begin to stir again."

The first extant representations of the dragon in China's history are on the Oracle Bones in use during the Shang Dynasty from over a thousand years B.C., the same bones that provided the root symbolism of the I

Ching. These divination tools show some 120 representations of the dragon—evidence that the idea of the dragon is more ancient still, so ancient that some nonscientific souls have speculated that the image of the *lung* (old style; currently spelled *long*)—with its huge head, gaping mouth, elongated body, coiled tail, and scales—might derive from extinct flying reptiles. Far more likely is that the image represents a kind of chimera, a creature composed of diverse parts of known animals: the head of a lion, body of a goat, and tail of a snake, as in the Greek myth of Bellerophon.

Another possible source for the dragon image is less preposterous than pterosaurs—the crocodile. Witness the common characteristics of the two: an enormous mouth, two rows of huge teeth, clearly marked scales, four clawed feet, a long tail, and the ability to live both on land and water. Wherever in China were there crocodiles but along the Yangtze? While today there are only about five hundred of the Yangtze alligator—a relatively small, eight-foot creature of Anhui Province—in the past no fewer than seventeen genera of crocodilians lived in China. Most of them have been extinct for millennia, but one—the twenty-foot-long saltwater crocodile of the Yangtze rivermouth—was killed off only a few centuries ago.

This enormous creature probably began to lose his battle with time upon his first encounter with the tidal fishermen of his habitat, near the town of Chaozhou in the Yangtze's coastal region. The many huge man-eating crocs so endangered people's lives and property that 1,200 years ago the prefectural governor of the Tang Dynasty issued an "ultimatum" to the crocodiles, telling them they must move or he would have hunters kill them with poison arrows. During the Northern Sung Dynasty (960–1279) that followed, people threw quicklime into the waters to poison the reptiles. By the end of the Ming Dynasty (1644) the saltwater crocodile was extinct.

A common local name for today's alligator in China is "earth dragon"; the saltwater crocodile was called the "flood dragon." An ancient text indicates that in the days of the Yellow Emperor there were specialists qualified to keep and breed dragons, but it seems likely that they were husbanding crocodiles rather than dragons four millennia ago.

Whether or not the dragon is "descended" from the crocodile in an imaginative way, it is quite possible that a tribal group, quite probably from the Yangtze River coastal region, adopted the saltwater crocodile as their totem. The local deity, revered for his very fearsomeness, over time and distance grew in influence as well as in size: his long tail lengthened, his teeth grew larger, the threat became greater. The dragon became identified with creativity, the productive forces of nature, and hence with springtime, when the dragon was said to emerge from the waters and ascend to the skies to announce the return of nature's energies.

Even today the biological reflects the philosophical: the emergence of the mud-covered Yangtze alligator from hibernation corresponds with the coming of spring. But the dragon's natural dwelling is not in the water, nor on the muddy shores like his earthly counterpart, but in the sky: it is, as one commentator has elegantly stated, a cosmic manifestation, which appears only as a prelude to vanishing.

It was under the Ch'u Empire of the middle and lower Yangtze, which flowered in the fourth and third centuries B.C., that this most compelling of Chinese images reached its modern form. The Ch'u unified the mammalian and reptilian styles of the oracle bones and local representations into a simplified yet energetic image, one which became identical with Chinese royalty and power. It was during this time that Confucius went to the seat of the Ch'u Empire to meet with Lao-tzu, founder of the rival school of Taoism. Confucius told his disciples, "The dragon's ascent into heaven on the wind and the clouds is something which is beyond my knowledge. Today I have seen Lao-tzu, who is perhaps like a dragon."

During the Han Dynasty that followed, the dragon became most powerfully identified with imperial power when the Emperor Kao-tze claimed to be descended from a dragon. But another thousand years passed before the Yuan Dynasty of 1271–1368 attempted to restrict the dragon exclusively to imperial use. Despite the death penalty for breach of this edict, multiple transgressions took place, to the extent that the emperor finally agreed to reserve representations of the imperial dragon to those creatures having five claws instead of four (should you find a footprint). In Chinese diplomacy, the emperor's robes were called *lung-p'ao*, his bed the *lung-ch'uang*, and his seat the *lung-tso*—the Dragon Throne.

Despite the Yangtze's vast importance to China's history and economy, it has always been—and to some extent remains today—a barrier as much as a bond. It is bridged for trains or motor vehicles in only seven places: at the major cities of Shanghai, Nanjing, Wuhan, and Chongqing, as well as the smaller passages at Yidu (near Yichang), Yibin, and Dukou. There are no significant crossings above Dukou, in Sichuan Province, for the upper third of the river's length. Smaller bridges are found in more remote areas, some of them suitable for occasional truck traffic, but most only of value for people on foot or pack animals. Consult a map of the United States, count the twenty-eight major highway crossings of the Mississippi between Baton Rouge and Minnesota, and you'll get an idea of the relative simplicity of Chinese life.

By contrast, river traffic on the Yangtze is both plentiful and of undisputed historical significance. There has been trade up the Yangtze and its tributaries for well over two thousand years, possibly longer—the Oracle Bones are filled with ideograms for boats, boatbuilding, and river trade. The junks that plied its waters when Marco Polo lingered by the Yangtze's riverside would not look out of place among today's fleets. Classical legends attribute the birth of the junk to Fu Hsi, one of the great rulers of the mythic period, himself the offspring of a nymph and a rainbow.

Curiously, although boats throughout Asia seem to have their origin in the dugout canoe—it's true of Burma, Indonesia, and the Philippines—in China the story may be different. The word for boat, sampan, is derived from san pan, meaning three planks, or a raft. The upturned bow and stern apparently evolved from the bamboo raft, itself the most natural way of transporting building materials downstream.

From the port of Shanghai inland, there is extensive cargo and passenger traffic over nearly 35,000 navigable river miles; "No other river in the world," suggested G. R. G. Worcester, the former river inspector for Chinese maritime customs during the Nationalist period, "provides such an ideal natural network of waterways, whereby the most distant parts of the country are accessible." The cities of Nanjing, Wuhan, and even Chongqing, 1,700 miles upstream, are major ports. The tri-city industrial complex of Wuhan (Hanyang, Hankou, and Wuchang) is over 700 miles from the South China Sea, but enormous tankers of ten-thousand-ton displacement make this a regular stop. Smaller craft of up to two thousand tons can reach Yichang, but then, abruptly, the Three Gorges intervene—still the most celebrated river gorge system in the world, as ancient as it is spectacular.

Over three millennia ago, according to Chinese legend, the great emperor Yu, who became the god of floods and flood control (no mean province in an agrarian country), sat on a mountaintop near Fengjie deciding the direction of rivers. But the mountains intervened and contested Yu-wang's orders. Finally the wizard Wu-tze took Yu-wang's side, and with a mighty blast of breath cleft the mountains and allowed the river to flow through Wind Box Gorge, at just over four miles the shortest of the three gorges. The old emperor Yu thenceforth decided to take matters into his own hands, and hacked out the rest of the gorges with an ax. (Geologists, ever the spoilers of mythology, claim the gorges have been eroded from the rising walls of limestone in the past 250 million years.)

Although today cargo ships can pass through the relatively quiet waters of the gorges, rendered navigable by dynamite and dredging following the Communist Revolution, in centuries past the 405-mile stretch between Yichang and Chongqing, then known as the Upper River, was strenuously navigated by junks towed upriver by teams of "trackers." The back-breaking crux of the route was the 118 miles of Qutang, Wu, and Xiling gorges (formerly Ch'u-t'ang, Wu, and Hsi-ling).

Travel up this dangerous stretch of river has been a part of Chinese life for untold centuries. The ancient river runners who alternately sailed and towed their junks up the gorges left high and low water marks, with instructions and warnings for each level, carved in the walls of the gorges. In 763 A.D., during a low-water year, carved fish were revealed on a newly exposed rock, clearly indicating the even greater antiquity of river traffic in the region. The reason for this traffic was no doubt the same two millennia ago as it was earlier this century—trade. "The commerce of this rich section of China is sufficient to cause mariners to undertake the very hazardous voyage," wrote Lieutenant Commander A. W. Ashbrook of the U.S. Navy in 1930. By that time, he continued, there were "two British, one American, one Japanese, one French, one German and several Chinese companies operating steamers" through the gorges.

At the beginning of the century, before the advent of motorized travel on the Yangtze, foreign visitors who made this trip through the Three Gorges told of a journey aboard creaking junks, the vessel of choice on the rivers of China. Junks—the name comes from the Chinese word *chwan*, signifying the keelless sailing ship favored in river traffic— boasted one to three masts, each of a single sturdy piece of wood; they were up to 120 feet long, with accommodations for crew on deck, and storage for as much as ninety tons of goods. Each large cargo junk was accompanied by teams of from twenty to eighty trackers, who hauled on tow ropes to lever the boat upstream by brute strength over the stubborn, dangerous rapids. Inspector Worcester tabulated some seventy-two rapids in the 350 miles between Yichang and Chongqing, nearly all of them in the first 150 miles upstream from Yichang. Although each junk carried its crew of trackers on board, hundreds if not thousands more lived within the gorges themselves ("nearly always stark naked," according to Lieutenant Commander Ashbrook), ready to hire out for the labor of hauling the heaviest ships through the most dangerous rapids.

Their work was always noted with amazement by those who ventured through the gorges, including novelist John Hersey, whose short but memorable A *Single Pebble* tells of a journey through the Three Gorges:

> These laborers fascinated me, and I had the habit of sitting by the hour observing them, while they scrambled from rock to rock on the riverbank, straining frightfully at their halters and dividing their heavy work evenly between them; or while they moved slowly, step by chanted step, along a level towing bund; or while they crept lynx-footed along a ledge on the wall of one of the gorges, hauling the clumsy junk against the powerful current. Their work had a long tradition behind it, as the fluted places on obstructing boulders proved, where tow ropes had dragged across the rocks for so many centuries that they had worn grooves—stone filed away by braided bamboo! The trackers, doing the work of animals, sustained their hard hours by listening to antique melodies and fantasies which the head tracker constantly sang as he, too, tugged at the top end of the towline. They marked time for his songs with a repeated unison cry at the moment when all of them together planted each footstep: "Ayah! . . . Ayah! . . ." (New York: Alfred A. Knopf, 1956)

The journey between Yichang and Chongqing took from twenty days to two months. Writing in the March 1948 *National Geographic,* W. Robert Moore said, "Roughly, one out of every ten junks is badly damaged on the trip between Ichang and Chungking. One in twenty is totally wrecked. Occasionally even a steamer piles up on the rocks." A tracker was not expected to lead a long life; but this was China, and life was cheap.

As with other occupations in China, even the junkman had his patron diety. This was Yang Tai, a historical pirate from the Southern Sung Dynasty of nine hundred years ago, who boasted that the imperial government couldn't capture him "unless they could fly and come from the air." His remote domain in the gorges of the Upper River persisted for many years, though he was eventually captured. In his honor temples along the river and nearly all junks trading on its waters had wooden prayer scrolls dedicated to him; and prior to a journey upstream from Yichang, a special ceremony was offered to him, marked by the sacrifice of a cock and the sprinkling of its blood on the bow to assure a safe journey.

Daily life along the Yangtze focused on the river, which became literally the center of the universe for its citizens. Small floating hotels serviced the traveler who wished only a berth for the night outside the closed walls of the riverside cities; floating kitchens served hot meals to traveler and laborer alike. There were even floating theaters on barges in the Upper River, bringing the formalized classic style of Chinese theater to the smallest villages. As Worcester noted, "The junkman's call has descended for generations from father to son; sometimes a junk has been sailed by three or more generations of *loadah* [shipmasters]." The rapids pilot, too, was a hereditary position, and it must be believed that the backbreaking work of the tracker was also a job passed, however unwillingly, from broken father to brash young son. Entire clans were thus generated and deceased with the scent and sound of the river suffusing every living moment.

In 1898, the first steam-powered boat made the trip up river, commanded by English merchant Archibald Little, cutting the travel time between Yichang and Chongqing to less than three weeks. Regular steam service was started by river customs inspector Cornell Plant in 1909. After the Communists came to power in 1949, they dredged and dynamited the river's course throughout much of its length, particularly in the gorges, further easing the travail of travel. Today, a number of government-run ships make the passage in three days. The Chinese are quick to point out that the river now handles a dozen times more goods than it did in preliberation years, and the once dangerous gorges now claim few casualties.

In addition to the extensive trade, thousands of Chinese and foreign tourists alike take the commercial cruise up or down the Yangtze gorges each year, looking for an experience of the past, hoping to find a wonder of the world that will not disappoint them. They board one of six ships designated for foreign tourists, or one of the many steamers in the Jianghan fleet—formerly called Dongfanghong, "The East is Red," and still commonly known by that name. Although the hundred-plus miles of the gorges float by at the comparatively blinding speed of seventeen miles an hour, the ancient sights are for the most part still there: the Meng Liang Staircase, reputedly carved 1,800 years ago during the fabled Three Kingdoms period; the mountain of Wu, said to be inhabited by witches; and Goddess Peak, a thirty-five-foot-high stone pillar atop a mountain, the youngest and fairest of twelve fairies who guide ships along the river.

However one travels through the gorges, the scenery remains remarkable. Worcester, who virtually lived on the Yangtze for many years while carrying out his duties as a river inspector (a period interrupted by his serving for "three apprehensive years" in a Japanese prison camp), wrote glowingly of Wind Box Gorge, the most dramatic of the Three Gorges, in his 1966 survey of rivercraft, *Sail and Sweep in China:*

> The river here is silent and shrouded in gloom, the steep limestone cliffs rise sheer from the water, culminating in pinnacles and battlements of eccentric shape over 700 feet high. Their ragged walls are rich with colour, either from their own metallic surfaces of copper or purple or greenish from the hue of the undergrowth and of occasional pines or bamboos clinging to inaccessible clefts and ledges. In spring an unbelievable wealth of colour is provided by a profusion of wild azalea, while in autumn the turning leaves give yet another aspect, flaming from every shade of yellow into russet and dull purple red, and mosses and ferns add their vivid note of green in the crannies. Tortuous ravines [abound], whence drop small vertical waterfalls which in the rainy season become bounding torrents. No words can possibly do justice to the stupendous grandeur of the Upper Yangtze at any time of the year.

Any look at China that fails to take into view its considerable history—twenty-three centuries of documented rule, plus another ten centuries of dynasties that survive in legend—runs the risk of suggesting the earth's largest nation is somehow equivalent to all others. It is not: it is the oldest continuous civilization on the planet, and has been responsible for so many technical, scientific, political, and finally cultural revolutions that all other countries seem strangely naïve by comparison. By the same token, it is easy to get lost in the steady succession of emperors, who march across the centuries since the Chou conquered the Huang Ho valley about a thousand years B.C. From that point forward a multiplicity of dynasties and kingdoms, punctuated by periods of warfare and political chaos, make a quick reading of Chinese history hopelessly confusing.

Although most of the earliest kingdoms had their capital either at Luoyang or Changan, near present-day Xian, both on the Huang Ho, the influence of the Huang Ho empires was determined by how successfully they extended their influence southward across the snaking course of the Yangtze. China was formed from the conquest—and assimilation—of the Yangtze-based Ch'u by the Yellow-based Ch'in two centuries before Christ. The Ch'in crushed the feudal kingdoms of eastern Asia, and under Ch'in Shih Huang Ti, first emperor of the Ch'in Dynasty, China itself was created—as the very name suggests.

Isolated ramparts of protection against the barbarian nomads of the north were joined together, and the 1,400-mile Great Wall came into being. Ch'in armies marched west to the borders of Tibet, south across the Yangtze into southern China, and on to the Tonkin kingdom of Southeast Asia. The Ch'in laid the foundations for the empires that succeeded it, setting up administrative and governmental structures that survived into the twentieth century. During those few years between 221 and 207 B.C. the Ch'in created the provinces and built the roads linking them that are still in use today, and set up remote imperial posts to connect the capital with its outlying areas of control.

But Shih Huang Ti was hardly a benevolent despot. He ordered the unification of "the hundred schools of thought" into one by such methods as reducing many styles of writing to one, burning a large part of the collected literature of preceding generations, and executing scholars who disagreed with his point of view. He ruled with an iron hand and taxed with an open palm; his death was largely unmourned and his body had to be returned to the capital under cover, for fear of a general revolt. Despite its glories, the Ch'in Dynasty lasted but twenty years—it collapsed eight years after Shih Huang Ti died, and the four-hundred-year dynasty of the Western Han began.

There are many rulers in Chinese history like Shih Huang Ti, cruel yet effective men who forged the unwieldy nation. Then, too, there are the gentler souls who have occupied the Dragon Throne, whose mark on history may be no less lasting. During the Sung Dynasty of imperial China's maturity, a brief thousand years ago, the emperor Hui Tsung ruled China in a very different way, from 1101 to 1115. Within his palace Hui Tsung had nearly four thousand ladies at his service, with whom he staffed what may have been the world's first department store, a market within the Forbidden City itself run by the emperor's concubines, women in waiting, and female attendants. "For the first time in history ministers of state found themselves buying rare delicacies from beauties upon whom it would previously have cost them their lives to gaze," noted John Blofeld in *The Chinese Art of Tea*.

Aside from his obvious affection for female companionship, Hui Tsung had an obsession with the technology and etiquette of tea, which only three centuries earlier—recent by Chinese standards—had become the standard beverage of the Middle Kingdom. The emperor even authored a classic text, *Ta Kuan Ch'a Lun*, on the art and science of brewing tea, especially the floral, refreshing white-leaf tea, picked in the dewy predawn hours by country maidens. Sad to say, the emperor's aesthetic interests proved insufficient to governance, and he was forced to abdicate in the face of yet another invasion from beyond the Great Wall.

Eventually Hui Tsung was captured by the Jurchen Tartars, and forced to live out the last nine years of his life in what must have been a living hell—drinking coarse black tea mixed with salt and camel's butter, the daily beverage of the invading nomads.

Amidst the shames and glories of these empires, however, one period has been elevated to the level of legend in China's national consciousness—the so-called Three Kingdoms period of 220 to 265 A.D., immortalized in a work of historical fiction called *Romance of the Three Kingdoms* by Lo Kuan-chung.

Although *Romance of the Three Kingdoms* (or *San-kuo Chih Yen-i*) was written over a thousand years after the period it describes, its melding of official records and oral traditions into a single epic narrative ranks it with Homer's achievement in Western literature, or with the Camelot of English folklore. Lo Kuan-chung wrote about the claim of the Han prince Liu Pei to the Dragon Throne. Liu Pei's claim was doubly contested, first by Sun Ch'uan, the founder of the Wu Kingdom that controlled China from the lower Yangtze Basin down to the Gulf of Tonkin; and by Ts'ao Ts'ao, an unscrupulous warrior and founder of the Wei Kingdom of northern China, with its capital at Louyang on the Yellow River. The kingdom of Shu, ruled by Liu Pei, claimed the upper Yangtze drainage and western China (roughly, today's Sichuan), with its capital at Chengdu.

The hero of the *Romance* is not the ruler Liu Pei, however, but rather his advisor Chu-ko Liang, a poet-recluse who had to be repeatedly entreated by Liu Pei before consenting to enter the political arena. Blessed with the insight that only a serene and simple personality can attain, Chu-ko Liang was able to engineer the defeat of Ts'ao Ts'ao at the famous Battle of the Red Cliff, on the banks of the Yangtze between Hankou (Wuhan) and the enormous lake Dongting Hu—a victory celebrated in poem and song for centuries to come. The result was a power balance between the Three Kingdoms and the imposition of a miraculous if short-lived period of peace.

The literature of China is rich with poetry of the Three Kingdoms period, a veritable Golden Age of heroes. Later rulers, including the last Manchu emperors, forbade the reading of *The Romance of the Three Kingdoms* as a bad influence on the stability of the state. Not untellingly, it was one of Mao Zedong's favorite books as a child, and the landscape of the Yangtze was already familiar to him from its pages when he led the First Front Army on its own epic, the Long March of 1935–36.

The Long March took the Communists from their stronghold in Jiangxi Province in the south of China more than six thousand miles (or 25,000 *li*, in Chinese measurement, a *li* being roughly a third of a mile) to Shaanxi Province in the northwest. The march became necessary when the Nationalist forces under Chiang Kai-shek surrounded the Jiangxi stronghold (a region which Edgar Snow popularized as "Red China") and promised to exterminate the Communists. For most of the march, Mao Zedong was its leader; his subsequent position at the forefront of China's politics following independence until his death in 1976 was largely due to his success in the Long March. His first great coup on the Long March was eluding capture by Chiang when he led his forces across the Yangtze River, the traditional dividing line between north and south China. The crossing took place at Jiaopingdu, about a hundred miles north of Kunming, on May 1, 1936—more than halfway into the yearlong march.

To the Yangtze did Mao himself return, when all the world wondered if the aging leader of the People's Republic were still at the helm. He had barely been seen in public for years; rumors of his death or debility flourished. But in the summer of 1966, at the age of seventy-two, Mao went for a very public swim in the Yangtze River. He was to live for another decade, during which, in Harrison Salisbury's words, the brotherhood of the Long March "disintegrated in the madness of Mao's final years."

Thus we return to the present day, after having ridden the river's course through the centuries. But despite all the sound and fury of humanity's history, it is the river that remains constant—the river, itself the very image of the Taoist concept of life: ever changing, always the same. In summarizing his survey of Yangtze river craft, G. R. G. Worcester offered up this overview of Chinese history itself, one which we see no reason to resist repeating here:

Dynasty after dynasty has risen and flourished and passed away within sight of its waters. It has not always been a kind and beneficial force. Wild fits of madness come over it at times, and then it is a fury and a demon that spares neither man nor woman nor child. When the great mountains beyond send down their floods, and the rains in springtime descend in sheets, then the river, filled to the brim, breaks its banks and races wildly for the plains.

Nevertheless, despite all fleeting human tragedies, the life of the river pursues its course with little apparent change. Revolutions, wars and lesser strifes, floods and droughts, famines and bumper harvests, recur and pass; but the Yangtze, with its changing face, beautiful and wild in its upper reaches, majestic and sullen as it sweeps across the great alluvial plain, basically the same as it was five thousand years ago, yet superficially utterly unpredictable, like its people, still rolls on.

CHAPTER TWO

Explorations Beyond
the Upper Yangtze

> Wind batters me, waves hit me—I don't care
> Better than walking lazily in the patio.
> —MAO ZEDONG
> *Swimming,* 1956

For nearly a thousand years the Yangtze has been defined in three main sections—the Lower, Middle, and Upper River. The Lower is the relatively placid, slow-moving, mature river that rolls mightily toward the East China Sea, from Hankou to Shanghai, through the vast, fertile East China Plain. In contrast to the wild tumult of the river's exit from the Tibetan Plateau over three thousand miles away, the Long River here drops only an inch and a half per mile. The Middle River, between Hankou and Yichang, boasts a number of large lakes and tributaries, and is one of China's most quickly developing agricultural areas, in large part because of diking and other flood-control measures, which have led to the reclamation of over a million acres of farmland from Lake Dongting Hu alone.

Above Yichang, the Upper Yangtze begins—the Three Gorges, the Red Basin of Szechwan, and the navigable waters up beyond Chongqing to Yibin. Here, at Yibin, is the uppermost limit of navigability— in the words of Lyman Van Slyke, "I-pin [Yibin] marks the beginning of the Long River's true entry into central arenas of human history." For the most part, this is a self-fulfilling judgment: history is made by those who write it, and for many historians it is as if the 1,900 miles of the Yangtze above Yibin—the farther half of the Long River—simply does not exist.

We take the opposite tack: for us, the well-traveled waters downstream of Yibin are for the most part of little interest. It is the region of mystery and legend, the secret canyons and snow-braced currents of the Jinsha Jiang, the Tongtian Ho, and the Tuotuohe, that intrigues us. If the Yangtze is a dragon, we pass lightly over its boasting jaws and bloated belly, and follow the tail of the monster into its true lair, treading the path that snakes beyond the Upper Yangtze to the origin of the water's serpentine course.

In this, we find surprisingly few predecessors. Most of the explorers who have found their journeys immortalized in encyclopedias and overviews failed to penetrate these caverns of mystery. Which is not to deprive them of their place in the annals of exploration: Isabella Bird, for instance, surely deserves a seat at the table of the Explorers Club, for her nervy and eye-opening 1896–1897 overland treks up *The Yangtze Valley and Beyond*, as her reminiscence is titled. So too does Thomas Blakiston, even though his *Five Months on the Yangtze* took him but a few miles beyond Yibin, for he undertook his journey at the very outset of foreign travel up the Great River, in 1861. Still, the less well known individuals who penetrated beyond the great wall of the unknown, driven perhaps by any number of motivations—monetary greed, geographical hunger, intellectual curiosity, or even the spiritual salvation of non-Christian peasants—may be more deserving of a closer look.

"Salvation" may seem like an aberrant motivation, but religious missionaries have often played a significant role in the exploration of unknown regions. Perhaps the best-known example is David Livingstone, the Scots Protestant whose unswerving commitment to a trinity of "Christianity, commerce, and civilization" led him to spend over thirty years in what was then known as "darkest Africa." No single name stands out in equivalent boldness for China, but a single agency does—the Société des Missions Etrangères. The French Roman Catholic missionary society managed to Catholicize perhaps 70,000 people in Yunnan, Sichuan, and Guizhou by the outset of the nineteenth century, well over fifty years before the more publicized English explorers made their way into China's southwest. Though Catholicism had been outlawed in 1724 by the Qing emperor, the French missionaries continued their soul salvage operation out of the French colonies in Indochina, more than once disguising themselves as local Chinese or tribesmen to continue their contact. By the time the British explorers penetrated the most remote provinces of the Celestial Kingdom, they invariably found French priests calmly yet firmly ensconced.

Several of these clerics deserve special mention. When T. T. Cooper endeavored to reach Tibet from Chengdu in 1868, for instance, in remote Ta-Chien-Lu (present-day Kangding, Sichuan) at the very border of imperial China with cultural Tibet, he found, much to his surprise, "a venerable old man, dressed in Chinese costume, with a long snow-white beard"—Bishop Chauveau of the French mission. "I shall never forget him as long as I live," wrote Cooper. "He was sixty years of age, forty of which he had spent in China as a missionary—his long illness made him look older; his countenance was very beautiful in its benignity; his eye, undimmed by age and suffering, lighted on me with a kindly expression, and he bade me welcome in English, which he had learned from his mother, an English lady, with a tremulous but musical voice."

From this and other evidence, we may suppose that Bishop Chauveau reached China in about 1830; by 1865 he was in charge not only of the mission at Ta-Chien-Lu but of outstations on the Mekong River even farther to the west, with the official title "Vicaire Apostolique du Lassa," the center of Tibetan culture. "But," he told William Gill in 1877, "I call myself by the less pretentious one of Vicaire of Tibet, for I feel that my eye can never look over the border into the promised land." It was his life's dream, again according to Gill, to be able to follow the English into Lhasa, and, "sweeping at last across those wild wastes of superstition, carry the Christian faith to the very home of the Dalai Lama, shake the throne of that arch impostor, and strike with mighty strokes at the very root of the Upas-tree of Buddhism." History was to give that pleasure to another faith entirely.

Needless to add, his attitude was unpopular in Lhasa. As a direct result of this mutual antipathy, two other French missionaries who did manage to penetrate to the capital of Lamaism may have been among the first non-Tibetans to cross over the Tongtian Ho, the River to Heaven, that is the uppermost quadrant of the Yangtze. In 1845, Abbé Huc and his clerical companion Gabet (first names seem expendable in the service of the Church) crossed the icy waters of the Tongtian Ho, but their powers of observation were somewhat obscured by the conditions of their travel: they were under arrest by Tibetan guards at the time, being returned to the Catholic mission at Chengdu. Huc's account of their journey came under almost immediate suspicion, and indeed he seemed guilty of considerable embellishment—unnecessarily, for theirs was an exceptional adventure. Although Huc and Gabet may have been preceded in this region over one hundred years earlier, in 1730, by a Dutchman named Samuel Van de Putte, about whose doubtless fascinating travels very little is known, their crossing from Lhasa to Chengdu was otherwise the first by Westerners.

Beginning with the four treaties negotiated at Tientsin in 1858, at the conclusion of the Opium Wars, explorations by nonclerical adventurers became more common. The treaty allowed free travel by British subjects, and almost at once the long-frustrated goal of reaching India from China, and vice versa, began to be pursued. It became a race in its own right, a challenge to penetrate a long-impossible barrier. So difficult is the obstacle of the Himalayas and the great river trenches of the Mekong, Salween, and Yangtze that there is a virtual "iron wall" between the two countries (a term of nineteenth-century geographers), whereby only Tibet stands as a curious intermediary between them—itself practically inaccessible to both, rather than accessible to either. There were, however, two main trade routes out of China in this general direction: from Chengdu to Lhasa, via Batang on the Jinsha Jiang; and southward to Bhamo in Burma, through Kunming and Dali, the course of the present-day Burma Road. The well-known Silk Road followed by Marco Polo and his successors is a far more northerly route, over the Karakorams from Afghanistan into the Xinjiang region to the trading capital of Urumqi.

The aforementioned Captain Thomas Blakiston, with three companions, set out from Shanghai early in 1861, with a goal of being the first to reach India overland. The route they chose was up the Yangtze to Yibin, thence northward to Chengdu, overland via Batang to Lhasa, and from there on to India, somehow crossing that iron wall. In fact, Blakiston fell far short of his goal, achieving only the first part of the endeavor by ascending up the Yangtze as far as a village forty miles from Yibin. But their limited success was in a way sufficient, for the survey of the Long River—with its certain potential as an avenue for trade—was the primary purpose of their journey.

Seven years later, a French party under Navy Captain Doudart de la Gree managed to extend their survey of the Mekong River up from Indochina to cross overland east to Yunnanfu (Kunming), thus becoming the first Westerners to reach the provincial capital since Marco Polo visited the town (which he called Yachi) around 1283. But their continued explorations, and those of others in western Yunnan, were continually frustrated by the ongoing Islamic revolt in Dali, which continued until the 1873 execution of its leaders and thousands of its followers.

Doudart and, following his illness and subsequent death, his subordinate officer Lieutenant Francis Garnier pursued another mystery in their travels, one which had puzzled generations of geographers: the course of the other great rivers of Asia, the Mekong, Salween, and Irrawaddy, and most especially the Brahmaputra. It had long been suspected that the Tsangpo River that ran west-to-east through Tibet found its outlet to the south, on the other side of the Himalayas; but which of the large rivers that exited there was the continuation of the Tsangpo? The controversy raged, with the Irrawaddy and the Brahmaputra being the most likely candidates; all sorts of theories were offered, including the bifurcation of the Tsangpo somewhere in the wilderness of the Himalayas and its subsequent emergence as two enormous rivers. The solution was first posed as far back as 1765, when geographer James Rennell wrote, "I could no longer doubt that the Burrampooter [Brahmaputra] and the Sanpoo [Tsangpo] were one and the same river." Only toward the end of the nineteenth century was Rennell's thesis proven, and the full course of the river's 1,800 miles chartered.

The first noncleric to come within striking distance of Lhasa from Chengdu was T. T. Cooper, an independent traveler interested in developing trade contacts. The young Englishman traveled from Hankou to Chengdu to Ta-Chien-Lu early in 1868, and continued on to Batang on the banks of the Jinsha Jiang. From there he ventured south, down the Mekong River to Dali, where he was imprisoned for five weeks by the Islamic sultan. Upon his release he made his way back to the Great River and returned to Hankou in November, after an epic journey of some two thousand miles over ten months. Amazingly, a year later Cooper tried to reach Batang from the other direction, following the Brahmaputra through the Himalayas to the Tibetan border, where he was turned back.

In 1872, Baron Ferdinand von Richthofen—by then an old China hand—made his attempt to break through the "iron wall" from China, with an expedition from Chengdu to Bhamo on the Irrawaddy. Despite his years of experience in China, he only made it halfway to Dali, where a band of Chinese troops attacked his party and compelled him to retrace his steps. It seemed as if the "iron wall" would stand forever when, in 1874, a young consular officer named Augustus Margary was dispatched from Hankou across Hunan and Guizhou provinces to Yunnan, reaching Dali by mid-December. His arrival in Dali was certainly facilitated by the crushing, the year before, of the Islamic rebellion; Margary found the mandarins well in control of Dali.

Following a surprisingly brief and uneventful journey, Margary reached Bhamo in Burma a month later, after crossing over the gorges of the Mekong and Salween, thus becoming the first Westerner to break through the iron wall. His pride was to be short-lived, however: a few weeks later, on February 21, 1875, as he began his return journey, his party was attacked and slaughtered by a Chinese brigand, possibly operating under orders. Diplomatic outrage resulted, and the murder became a cause célèbre back in England and throughout the diplomatic world. As a result of Margary's murder, the British and Chinese hammered out another series of agreements further protecting British travelers, indemnifying the victims, and allowing the stationing of British officers in Yunnan.

Such were the conditions, then—the revolt in Dali ended, diplomatic security virtually guaranteed for all British travelers—when William John Gill embarked on his ambitious travels in Western China early in 1877. Born in India as the son of a career officer, Gill inherited a substantial sum of money from a distant relative at the outset of his own military career, and by the time he arrived in China at the age of thirty-three he was already well traveled. His arrival coincided with Margary's murder and its aftermath, and several commentators have pointed out the effect this news may have had on Gill, for he and Margary were contemporaries and schoolmates at Brighton. But whether or not Gill intended to duplicate Margary's itinerary when he and E. C. Baber left Shanghai in January is doubtful: "I eagerly availed myself of [Baber's] invitation, but as yet formed no definite plans as to my future movements, only making up my mind that I would be ready for anything that might turn up." Ready he was, and his curiosity led him deep into the great unknown regions of the Celestial Kingdom.

From Shanghai to Hankou, Gill traveled by steamer; through the Three Gorges to Chongqing, he journeyed by junk, making the entire ascent of the Yangtze in the company of Baber, the consular officer who later edited Gill's writings. Taking leave of Baber, Gill headed north to Chengdu, at the time the westernmost outpost of civilization as Europeans, and most Chinese, knew it. Up until this point, Gill's travels were unusual, but by no means unique; but now Gill set out to the north, following the Min Jiang to the mountains at its origin, the Min Shan range, which had long been believed to be the primary source of the Yangtze—at the confluence of the Min Jiang and Jinsha Jiang at Yibin it is the former that appears to be the dominant stream. Thus, Gill became one of the first adventurers to actively seek the origin of the Great River, or at least the headwaters of its most celebrated tributary. Almost incidentally, he also became a precursor of the river runners who would follow him to China over a century later.

With typical modesty, Gill termed his six-week journey into the Min Shan region a "loop-cast towards the northern alps," as if it were no more than a walking holiday. It was far from that, being in one of the most dangerous mountain regions of China, where sixty years later the Red Army's Long March suffered its greatest losses due to the merciless elements—cold wind, deep snow, and treacherous terrain. But Gill's description, in his *River of Golden Sand* (1880), is filled with wit and generosity as well as insight, rendering the certain trials of his travels all but invisible.

Although he traveled in the elevated style of Westerners at the time, either atop a mount or seated in a chaise carried by "chair coolies," he lets neither experience swell his head. "Whenever I got on and off my pony," he says of riding, "as much fuss was made about me as about a jockey mounting for the Derby: one man to each stirrup, another to the pony's head, a fourth to his tail, and the Ma Fu [horse servant] to give me a lift, as if the animal was about eighteen instead of eleven hands high."

Unlike his predecessors Huc and Gabet, Gill made exacting scientific measurements and cartographic observations, and his descriptions of the Min Shan rank among the best yet committed to paper (or processor). His descriptions also took note of the human component of the landscape, for here lived the so-called Man-Tzu, a Tibeto-Burman tribal group now known as the Qiang minority. "These mountains, whose heads are crowned with dazzling snow, into whose inmost recesses man has never penetrated, and whose rugged sides and mighty precipices must inspire awe in the most unpoetic soul, have not been without their influence on the minds of the inhabitants. Not only the shout of battle, but the miracle wrought by some Buddhist saint, the mystery attendant on some freak of nature, and even the gentle song of love, finds its place in the legends that cling to the sides of these romantic valleys."

Gill was savvy enough to recognize that it was the Han Chinese who were impinging on Qiang territory, and that tales of savage barbarians had another side. "The story as told me was always the same. How the Chinese came peaceably up the valleys, and were received by the inhabitants with every show of welcome; how unprovoked and unex-pected attack was made on the newcomers, who, at first fighting only for existence, ultimately secured the victory, and established themselves in the place of their treacherous foes. The Chinese . . . dwelt with delight on the valour of their race and the cowardly conduct of the barbarians, and never thought it possible that I should wonder what account these same barbarians would render, should they have the opportunity of telling their tale."

Later he relates a tale of how the Si-Fan (Tibetans) "descended from their fastnesses, butchered five hundred soldiers in cold blood, and burnt all the houses without any provocation on the part of the Chinese." "But what were five hundred soldiers doing here in the country of the Si-Fan?" he asked his informant, to which no answer was forthcoming. One might recognize the national outrage attendant on the "massacre" of 206 soldiers at Little Big Horn only the year previous and pose a similar question.

Aside from his refreshing perspective, Gill's undoubted tact and perseverance rendered his "loop-cast" an example of exemplary exploration, rare in these early years of Western adventuring. His course took him to the distant township of Sung-p'an, where even French missionaries had not yet penetrated, and up to the summit of the Great Snowy Mountain, Hsueh Shan, which he measured at 13,148 feet. From there, Gill and his coolies continued their loop through magnificent gorges on the upper Min Jiang, leaving us a description of one that bears reconnaissance by later SOBEK crews:

> The river . . . dashed in a succession of waterfalls over its uneven bed, now blocked by some gigantic rock, or almost stopped by the perpendicular cliffs, that hem it in on either side so closely that it sometimes seems an easy jump across the top. It is quite impossible to give any idea of this extraordinary gorge: I could hardly have believed in the existence of a rift so narrow and so deep, and yet so wonderfully clothed with trees, ferns, and shrubs. On emerging from it and looking back, there was nothing to be seen but a giant wall of rock; the chasm through which the torrent finds its way was nowhere visible, and it seemed almost impossible that there could be a road through that apparently impenetrable barrier.

Gill concluded his journey with what may be the first "first descent" in the annals of Chinese exploration, a downstream run on the upper Min Jiang for forty-five miles over two days, on a boat large enough for his entire entourage of sixteen. "There were rapids at about every half-mile, and the current was everywhere very strong. . . . We seemed to fly past the shore, and several times in the shallows there was a scraping and bumping and a taking in of water over the bow that would have been alarming to weak nerves."

On June 20, 1877, Gill returned to Chengdu, having completed a remarkable journey that would be only a prelude to his later accomplishments. The next day William Mesny, a British consular officer possessed of a similar spirit of adventure, appeared in Chengdu. Committed to travel, the two men found that their initial objective of crossing to Kashgar via the famed Silk Road was virtually impossible because of the ongoing Russo-Turkish War, in which England was at that time a participant. Anxious to return to England to serve their country, but eager to return by the most rewarding route, the pair plotted a course across northern Sichuan to Batang, at that time the gateway to the unknown land of "Lassa," or Tibet; from there, they would head south to Dali and thence to Burma, retracing Margary's route of eighteen months earlier. They left Chengdu on July 10, less than three weeks after Gill's return from the Min Shan.

Their first destination was Ta-Chien-Lu, the Chinese outpost where Bishop Chaveau had lived for three decades. To get there, they had to cross over the passes and rivers of the rugged western Sichuan terrain which, geologically and culturally, is the frontier of Tibet. Among the rivers they crossed was the Tatu (Dadu), by means of a hundred-yard-long suspension bridge of iron chains, a bridge which—still standing strong in 1935—became the scene of one of the most critical battles of the Long March. Gill took time to examine the bridge, then retired to an inn across the river.

Airing ourselves at the inn door, we entered into conversation with a man, who told us that the bridge was three hundred Chinese feet long, and had thirteen chains. On inquiring the reason of this gratuitous information, we were told that our reputation for asking questions had preceded us, and that the bridge had been measured for the first time within the memory of man expressly for our gratification.

At Ta-Chien-Lu, whatever fantasies Gill and Mesny had entertained about venturing into the Land of Snows were put to rest by daunting rumors of orders sent out by the lamas for their capture, should they make a run for the capital. But they still had to persist across the plains to Batang. Almost at once they met numerous nomadic groups herding their yaks and sheep in the increasingly folded terrain, sure signposts that they had entered Tibet culturally if not in fact.

Gill, Mesny, and their entourage made their way over a series of passes of increasing altitude, including several above 15,000 feet. Mountains of this scale naturally caused symptoms of altitude sickness among the Chinese, and Gill suggests that "being quite unable to comprehend the sensations they experience, they attribute them to noxious vapours, or other causes, and call the mountain a medicine mountain." One pass, at 15,753 feet, was so high and the trail so "dreadful" that the way was littered with the skulls of pack animals.

The high point of the trail seems to have come just east of Batang, on a mountain pass towering above the Jinsha Jiang.

> When we halted to use the hypsometer a little below the summit of the pass of Ta-So, the scene would have made a splendid picture—the wild surroundings of bare rocks, and the still more wild-looking fellows grouped about, with their tall felt hats, their sword scabbards set with coral and turquoise, and long matchlocks, with prongs at the end of the barrel; Mesny with a long scarlet cloak reaching almost to the ground, the ponies with their queer saddles covered with felts and sheepskins, and the transparent water of the little pond reflecting the proceedings. We were 16,129 feet above the sea, and the summit of the pass was 540 feet above us.

They reached Batang on August 25, 1877, three weeks after leaving Ta-Chien-Lu. The town, which marked the gateway to Tibet proper, and which 110 years later marked the cruel terminus of the Warren expedition, was home to only three hundred families; but the huge lamasery housed 1,300 lamas, proof of the power of the Tibetan Buddhists. Gill, like most other observers of Lamaism at its height, found much to criticize in the feudal nature of the faith, which exerted considerable economic control over Tibet. He called the lamas usurers, slave owners, profligates, and worse, concluding that they represented "a curse to the country and the people." Perhaps most telling is his observation of empty and deserted villages, abandoned as their inhabitants fled to the relative security of life in China to the east.

Here, the rumors of Tibetan opposition to their continued westward progress were confirmed. "We were . . . told that the Lamas had ordered out six thousand men to guard the frontier. . . . Numbers are of course always enormously exaggerated, and the six thousand was not, in all probability, as many hundreds; but there can be little doubt that the Lamas, whose power is almost absolute, had made up their minds to resist any attempted advance upon our part; and even if open hostility and violence had not been attempted, they would have simply starved us out." Not surprisingly, being but two Englishmen stouthearted and true, Gill and Mesny quickly reaffirmed their intention to pass southward to Dali rather than risk the ire of the lamas.

Their route took them along the Jinsha Jiang, the River of Golden Sands, from Batang to Shigu. Although they followed the river for a few miles, they soon crossed over it and followed the trail to Yunnan into the ridge of mountains on the west side of the Jinsha, to the mountain trading town of Atun-Tzu. "It might be expected," remarked Gill, "that as the road to Yun-Nan again returns to the Chin-Sha valley, south of Atun-Tzu, there would be another and easier road, by following the valley of the great river instead of leaving and returning to it. But in all probability there is no road down the valley of the Chin-Sha; the river appears to run through a succession of deep gorges, much as it does between Ch'ung-Ch'ing and I-Ch'ang. . . ." Gill continues:

> Moreover . . . near Deung-do-lin one glimpse is all that is gained of the river, a few miles distant, evidently tearing through an exceedingly deep gorge. The road then leaves the river to the east and, by two exceedingly difficult passes, crosses two very elevated spurs. . . . In crossing these spurs, the road passes no town whatever, and there is clearly no reason why it should not follow the river, if there was a practicable route. The probable conclusion is that the river, at all events between Deung-do-lin and La-pu flows through narrow gorges, where there is neither a road nor a possibility of navigation. . . .

Once the men headed south out of Batang, they entered the wettest monsoon that western Yunnan had experienced in decades. Their progress was rendered slow and miserable, even according to the usually good-natured Gill, by pouring rains and slippery trails. The mood was not improved upon by the presence of several encampments of armed and dangerous-looking Tibetan soldiers, apparently making good on the lamas' promise to forbid them entry to the Land of Snows. Finally, upon entering Yunnan at the border town of Atun-Tzu, they had to contend with the abundance of opium, which considerably slowed their progress through the impaired performance of their porters. It was not until September 27 that they reached Dali, making the three-hundred-mile journey from Batang by far the longest and most difficult single leg of their travels.

The depression that seemed to settle on Gill and Mesny on the road from Batang did not lift with their arrival in Dali. In addition to the persistent rain, they found all about them the destruction left by the recently concluded Islamic revolt. "It was sad, indeed, in this frightfully poverty-stricken land, to think that so large a population would lose nearly all they had to depend upon until the next crop [due to the floods].

The poverty was awful, the result of the terrible ravages during the Mahometan rebellion. At almost every step the ruins of some cottage were passed, where, in the place of a peaceful family happily living under a comfortable roof, wild thorns, briars, and huge rank weeds flourished between the remains of the walls, on the tops of which great prickly pears flung up their spiny foliage." And, upon entering through the east gate, "the interior of the city presented a sadder scene of desolation than the country round. The streets were wide, but half in ruins, and bore the same aspect of poverty that was everywhere apparent."

A week in the rainy, depressing town was long enough for them to recover their strength and gather what supplies they could for the next leg, the final pitch on the road to Burma. They left Dali on October 4, and as they continued westward still saw the sad results of the Islamic revolt's effect on the stability of the countryside. Deforestation, depopulation, and poverty combined to give a bleak picture of life in western Yunnan a century ago, but Gill's description of just one day on the road itself is painful as well.

> Now commenced our day's work, and a hard one it was. The road at first led along the side of the hill; it had once been paved with great round stones, which now, half misplaced, lay about, leaving great muddy chasms. At the end of this was a village; and here the path left the river and went straight up a gorge, which, with a little poetic licence, might be said to be like the wall of a house. The muleteers had told us that we could never conceive the badness of the road, and they can hardly be accused of exaggeration. It was enough to break the heart of a millstone, not to speak of the unfortunate little ponies that carried our baggage or ourselves. We had to face it somehow, zigzag after zigzag, mile after mile of steps, sometimes a foot high, of round and slippery stones, and muddy bogs, into which the feet of the unfortunate animals would slip with a bang and splash mire in all directions. But still, right overhead, the interminable track appeared; and when at length an ascent of 2,300 feet brought us to the end of this desperate gorge, men and animals "knocked their heads" [to the ground in gratitude] each after his own fashion.

For the last week of the journey, almost within sight of safety at Bhamo, Gill accepted an armed escort from regional authorities to assure his safety from the bandits who inhabited the frontier hills between Yunnan and Burma. His caution was certainly motivated by his awareness of the fate that had befallen his countryman Augustus Margary less than two years earlier. Ironically, almost chillingly, Gill was greeted in Burma by the very man accused of Margary's murder, the bandit chief Li Sieh Tai.

Shortly after this meeting, Gill paused at the scene of Margary's death, a hot spring near the town of Man-Yun, and considered making a sketch of the spot in tribute "[B]ut it might have raised suspicions in the superstitious minds of our companions, and long after such a paltry record would have perished his name will stand bright and clear in the recollection of his regretful countrymen. I uncovered my head as the only tribute of respect that I could pay to the memory of one who will ever be dear to our hearts, not only of those who knew him, but of all who value the noble qualities of uprightness, courage, and determination."

At last, after several armed confrontations with the area's bandits, Gill and Mesny reached the relative security of Bhamo, on November 1, 1877, where they were greeted by the same T. T. Cooper whose journey to Dali via Chengdu and Batang had preceded Gill's by nine years. It marked the conclusion of a trip that would be difficult today, and was nothing short of epic in its time; sadly, the fate that befell these pioneers into the unknown lands beyond the Upper Yangtze was anything but grand.

Within a matter of weeks after Gill and Mesny enjoyed Bishop Chauveau's hospitality in Ta-Chien-Lu, Chauveau died suddenly of his years. Five months after Cooper greeted his fellow Englishmen in Bhamo, he was assassinated by a soldier in his own guard. In the middle of the night of August 9, 1882, William John Gill and two other Englishmen, on a reconnaissance of the Sinai Desert for the British Army, were captured by Bedouins. They were killed two days later, and their bodies not recovered until October. The elegy Gill delivered for his compatriot Augustus Margary could well have been his own.

CHAPTER THREE

The Source
of the Great River

Frankly speaking, it is difficult
to trust the Chinese. Once bitten by a snake
you feel suspicious even when
you see a piece of rope.
—THE DALAI LAMA

One of the classic goals for explorers of past centuries has been to find the
source of the great rivers. Sir Richard Burton and John H. Speke raced to
the source of the Nile; Alexander von Humboldt tried to determine the
source of the Amazon; Lewis and Clarke made the discovery of the source
of the Mississippi a subtheme of their epic transcontinental journey. For
centuries, the source of the Yangtze had been thought to be up the Min
Jiang, and that may have been one consideration that led William Gill on
his 1877 "loop-cast to the northern alps." During the better part of this
century, however, the source of the Yangtze has been considered the
Garqu River in the Tanggula Mountains of Qinghai, which gave the
Yangtze a length of 3,400 miles. In the 1970s, it was determined by
Chinese geographers that the Tongtian Ho's tributary the Tuotuohe was
the longer source stream, adding some 500 miles to the river's length. But
rumors persisted of an even more distant tributary, the Dam Qu, which
might add another couple of hundred miles to the Yangtze's length—an
inconsequential amount for a river nearly 4,000 miles long, but perhaps
just enough to lift the Yangtze beyond the Amazon's length, and put it
behind the Nile as the world's second longest river.

In 1985, the National Geographic Society sponsored a small but ultimately important expedition to trace the Yangtze to its source. The expedition's goal was to trace the course of the Yangtze to its headwaters, and in so doing to confirm the actual stream that is the farthermost source of the Long River. The expedition leader was How Man Wong, who had the previous March written an article for *National Geographic* entitled "Peoples of China's Far Provinces." Wong—who for a time styled himself Herman Wong, the better to swim in the American melting pot—was born in Hong Kong, but he was educated in Wisconsin and now lives in the Los Angeles area. Jeffrey Chop served as expedition equipment manager and photographer. The third member of the team was medical expert Warren Gee who, like Chop, lives in Los Angeles. For eight months in 1985, they found themselves as far from their usual life as they could imagine, both physically and psychologically.

Any attempt to follow the Yangtze beyond the reaches of the Upper River, into both the landscape and the history of China, brings us ultimately to the mysteries of Tibet. Not just the old Kingdom of Tibet, known today in the People's Republic of China as the Xizang Autonomous Region, but the wider geographic and cultural area that includes the western borders of Sichuan and Yunnan, and the large and virtually unknown region to the north of Xizang, Qinghai Province. This area is a geographic as well as a cultural reality: the Tibetan Plateau is one of the great physical features of the planet, a giant whale-shaped plateau, incomparably large, impossibly high, dammed behind the Himalayas. Tibet is the closest land to heaven.

The Tibetans are perhaps the most well known of fifty-five distinct cultural minorities within the borders of the People's Republic. Of its billion-plus citizens, China recognizes fifty-five "national minorities," some 67 million people, many of whom live in over a hundred autonomous areas that cover over half—60 percent—of China's territory. The foremost ethnic group in China are the Han, who have dominated Chinese history for over two thousand years. But the contributions of the fifty-five minorities are considerable, and to visit the outlying regions of China— the forested mountains of Guizhou, the barren steppes of Qinghai, or the majestic landscapes of western Yunnan—is to dive into a rich mix of cultures. Here are ethnic traditions, cultural values, and even genetic strains that rival, and in many ways exceed, the renowned treasures of such anthropological paradises as New Guinea and Amazonia.

There are, for instance, over five million Miao, one of the most ancient of China's cultures. Their traditions tell of their former lives in the farthest north of the country, and their subsequent migration across the Yellow and the Yangtze to their current homeland in China's southernmost reaches, including the offshore island of Hainan in the South China Sea. The most numerous ethnic group is the Zhuang, a polytheistic agricultural people of the southern provinces of Guangxi, Guangdong, Guizhou, and Yunnan. Other minorities include such surprises as the Manchus, formerly the royal class of the "last emperors" of the Qing Dynasty. Today, almost 250 years after they overthrew the Ming Dynasty, and three-quarters of a century after they themselves abdicated in favor of the republic, they are just another minority, numbering about four and a half million, based mainly in the northern provinces. Among the more exotic cultures are the Kirghiz, nomadic tribesmen of the Xinjiang steppes and Pamir Mountains, whose domain stretches into the Soviet Union and Afghanistan. There are also many Islamic minorities, several shamanistic groups, a few whose variety of Buddhism is the simple Hinayana, or Lesser Wheel. There is one, the ten-thousand-strong Jino, who worship Kong Ming, a historical hero.

But it is the Tibetans who are most notable on the world stage. This four-million-strong minority is largely based in what is now called Xizang, a name meaning "Western Treasure House" in Chinese. Along with such little known minorities as the Lhoba, Moinba, Pumi, and Daur, stretching from Inner Mongolia and Xinjiang in the north to Yunnan in the south, these people share a belief in Lamaism. Known also as Tibetan Buddhism, this religion is a distinctive blend of the shamanistic Bon religion with the Buddhist and yogic teachings brought into Tibet by Padmasambhava in the eighth century. The Buddhist saint's influence on the nomadic Tibetans was considerable, elevating a local animistic cult to the rarefied atmosphere of universal truth; but it did not altogether eliminate the cruder aspects of shamanism.

Shamanism is thought to be one of the links between humanity's present and its remotest past. Some scholars trace nearly all religious traditions to a common origin among the Aryan cultures that emerged in the interior of Asia some eight thousand years ago, a region known in Tibetan Buddhism as Shambala, or the Center. Along with its implicit belief in the reality of the spirit world and its influence on daily life, it includes rituals of possession and exorcism, all features shared by many primitive religions of North America, Africa, Oceania, and even Europe, as well as Asia. Peter Matthiessen, who seems to have consistently preceded most of the rest of us to regions of interest to the modern traveler, wrote about the universality of shamanism in his classic of Himalayan travel, *The Snow Leopard:*

Tibetan oracle-priests and Siberian shamans practice dream-travel, telepathy, mystical heat, speed-running, death prediction, and metempsychosis, all of which are known to New World shamans; the Algonkian medicine man who travels as a bird to the spirit world, the jaguar-shamans of the Amazon would be impressed but not surprised by the powers attributed to yogis and *naljorpas* [Tibetan yogis]. The energy or essence or breath of being that is called *prana* by Hindu yogis and *chi* by the Chinese is known as *orenda* to the Cree. Such concepts as karma and circular time are taken for granted by almost all American Indian traditions; time as space and death as becoming are implicit in the earth view of the Hopi, who avoid all linear constructions, knowing as well as any Buddhist that Everything is Right Here Now.

Not everyone has such a sympathetic view of shamanism. The Chinese Communists, for example, see in its beliefs the blindness of superstition, and in that the roots of oppression. Others, such as Peter Goullart, who lived among the Lamaist Naxi in the Great Bend region during the 1940s, are quick to note its more savage elements.

It is founded entirely on the practice of Black magic and communion with evil spirits through necromancy and other morbid and macabre rites. The cups, made of human skulls, and flutes of human bone are used freely in certain religious services. . . . [It] was occurrences such as these [services] that helped make Tibet known as a land of horrible occult rites and other unspeakable practices.

One of the cardinal features of Tibetan Buddhism is the mantra *om mani padme hum*, a resonant phrase that can be translated as "The Jewel in the Lotus." Devotees chant the prayer before altars illuminated by yak-butter candles, murmur it to themselves throughout the day, and spin carved wooden tops on which the phrase is inscribed to generate the prayer for every revolution of the wheel. Tibetan villages are often decorated with colorful prayer flags fluttering in the breeze, broadcasting the holy phrase into the atmosphere on the winds. Explorer Joseph Rock, on one of his Sichuan expeditions for the National Geographic Society in the 1920s, found one lama squatting beside a tributary of the upper Yangtze with a stack of blocks carved with the prayer; the man would reach out into the water, imprint the prayer on the surface of the river, and thus send it downstream with the currents.

With its colorful pantheon of wide-eyed demons and fire-breathing dragons, and its mysterious Tantric sexual practices, Tibetan Buddhism became popular in the American counterculture during the sixties and seventies. The presence in the Western world of the Dalai Lama, highest religious authority in Lamaism, as well as other "living Buddhas" who have come to the United States following flight from Tibet in 1959, has kept attention focused on the Tibetan minority in China. Recurring efforts of Tibetan lamas to lead a secession from China, or at least to have a securely independent regional authority free from Han domination and influence, continue to provoke reaction from Beijing, which outlawed secession in the 1954 Chinese constitution.

The argument over independence is an ancient one, with each side claiming historical precedent for its point of view. While the Tibetans cite their ancient philosophical distinction from China, the Chinese point to such historical alliances as royal marriages between the Tufan rulers in Tibet and the Tang Dynasty in Nanjing over 1,200 years ago. The cultural differences are profound and part and parcel of the political division: one of the proofs cited for Chinese rule by Beijing is a painting in the Potala (the historic seat of the Dalai Lama in Lhasa) which they interpret as the fifth Dalai Lama making obeisance to the Qing emperor Shun Chih, circa 1660. In fact, Tibet's lamas point out, the Dalai Lama is using a *mudra*, or sacred hand gesture, of teaching, not obedience.

Recently the Chinese have backed off from their longstanding insistence that if the Dalai Lama returns to his homeland he must live in Beijing, and now say he can live in Lhasa, as long as he accepts Chinese sovereignty. The Dalai Lama, for his part, seems to be asking that cultural Tibet—an area far larger than the present Chinese province of Xizang—be allowed a semi-independent government. If this broader definition of Tibet is to include the Lamaist people of neighboring areas, much of Qinghai to the north, as well as the western frontiers of both Sichuan and Yunnan, would become part of Tibet. These regions are essentially congruent with the uppermost course of the Yangtze, from its headwaters in the Tanggula Mountains to the Great Bend section. But any solution in this conflict is bound to be a temporary one; China's, and Tibet's, histories are too lengthy for us to think otherwise.

The 1985 National Geographic expedition focused on the Yangtze's headwaters in the Qinghai Plateau, among the least inhabited regions of China, a vastness populated for the most part by a scattering of nomadic herdsmen. The Tibetan nomads that How Man Wong, Warren Gee, and Jeff Chop met on their journey of discovery had a well-established and doubtless ancient routine. From their temporary camp, different members of the group took livestock out to pasture in the morning, while the children and one or more of the women gathered yak dung for fuel, churned butter or ground barley into flour, made yak cheese or yogurt, or spun yarn from the livestock's hair. With evening, the herd was brought back to camp and tied down for the night; all members of the community then helped to milk the cows.

It is this yak milk that is the most crucial part of their simple economy: not only are cheese and yogurt made from it, but so is butter—and butter is a staple in their diet to a degree unheard-of in Western kitchens. Nearly all travelers to Tibet have had occasion to mention the rancid, hair-flecked yak butter they are offered, most commonly in the celebrated main beverage of Tibet, *cha*. Tibetan tea is a drink that goes "instant breakfast" a giant step better, or at least further: it consists largely of rancid yak butter and brick tea, usually with extra salt. The drink supplies a superabundance of protein, calories, and minerals, and is by all accounts one of the most revolting beverages in the world; yet the average Tibetan nomad may swill down fifty cups of the stuff each and every day of his life.

For Jeffrey Chop, whose report for the UCLA communications program adds a personal dimension to the expedition's journey, their encounters with the nomadic Tibetan herdsmen were memorable and touching, for they seemed to live an existence out of the wheel of time.

> When in these lands, I wanted to own the stars, clouds, and even the grass, but the nomad moved on. This was a subtle land. When the nomad traveled, he took everything he brought, leaving nothing except piles of yak dung which, when left in the fields, will fertilize the grass for the next year or if remaining in a pile, will provide another person passing through with some fuel. Either way it will be well used. The concept of waste was simply unimagined in this place. . . . Man was meant to tread quietly with light steps. It was a fragile world, where life clings to the edge, the sky almost touching the earth. The land was hardly a solitary place, with nomads within walking distance of each other. But they travel like the wind, moving with the season.

The Yangtze was thought to originate from the glaciers at the foot of Mt. Geladandong, and the team followed an old and rutted road for much of the way to an abandoned quartz mine on the mountain's flanks. Finally, cresting a high pass, they looked down on the alpine valley of the Tuotuohe, final root stream of the Long River. As Chop reported:

The two main glaciers were on two sides of the valley, feeding the Tuotuohe running down the middle. As I surveyed the landscape from the nomad camp, the two glaciers were set aglow by a bright August moon. To the right of the closer glacier, a broad slow-rising cone was the most prominent feature of a small range of mountains spreading off to the horizon. Venus shined like a diamond between the moon and the mountains.

In the morning, I explored my first glacier. We were walking from our camp, and I kept walking faster as we got closer. At 16,500 feet, it was quite an effort, but I beat the rest of the party by 20 minutes. I knew that I was not the first person to set foot here, since this valley had long been inhabited by Tibetans; but I was certain beyond a doubt, that I was the first person from Oakland, California.

Several more days of hard driving over crusty surfaces that broke through to mud brought the team to a Tibetan yak herders' camp, from where they launched their final assault on the Yangtze's origin. On August 3, the three adventurers set out with a guide, an interpreter, and four yaks to trek the final few miles. They found that the shallow braided channel was flushing with milky gray water, typical of glacier flows, which carry a full load of "flour"—actually fine-ground stone—in suspension. Wildlife was scarce, just an occasional marmot and tiny insects; the antelope they had seen a few days earlier were not in evidence here, so close to the glacier; a scattering of tiny wildflowers bloomed in the tundra grass. The next afternoon they at last reached the smallest trickling of water from the glacier of Geladandong, seven months after their trip began. Chop recalled:

> Even here, the water flowed strong, as if already running in a race to the ocean thousands of miles away. Here at 17,200 feet, the water ran on a long downhill course picking up more speed rapidly. The spirit of the stream here was one of youth, fresh and vibrant, unlike the slow dark river meandering through China's heartland on which we had spent so much time.
>
> I marveled at the silence of the mountains. This corner of the earth seemed to be the ultimate meeting of sky, land, and water. The landscape seemed a miraculous paradox. The mountains were barren, empty, and cold as the surface of the moon. Yet there was sublime beauty in the scene. The land seemed too still, the sky too close, but there was motion in this valley, the river flowed, nurtured by the thousand drops of melting ice. The Tibetans said that the glacier grows out of the ground, like a flower

reaching for the sun. The waters that flowed from the glacier were its fragrance.

Despite finally reaching the headwaters of the Tuotuohe, the possibility that they had reached the "wrong" source still rankled the team members. Within a week they found themselves in another part of Qinghai, headed for the headwaters of the Dam Qu. That there would be some confusion over the actual source of the Yangtze is not surprising; rivers are notoriously difficult to measure, with their meanders and alternate channels, and it is said that the Nile is only longer than the Amazon depending on which channel the latter takes to the sea. In the remoteness of an area as uninhabited and unknown as Qinghai, finding the "true" source is a matter of guesswork and luck, until sophisticated orbiting satellites put their technology to work on the question. Ironically, though the Chinese told How Man Wong and his crew they now thought that the Dam Qu was the source river, they had identified the wrong fork of the Dam Qu—the Tibetan nomads who lived in the area seemed to be certain it was a stream at the southeast, rather than at the northern part of the valley, that must be the farther source.

With two college-educated Tibetans as their guides, the team set out on horseback from Yushu to find the "ultimate farthestmost source," and in so doing became the first expedition to explore the Dam Qu for its geographical significance. Once again they were in a land of mystery where, as Chop phrased it, "almost everywhere in these hills and valleys, the water can be heard like celestial wind chimes."

One month after they reached the headwaters of the Tuotuohe, the National Geographic team reached the headwaters of the Dam Qu, on the marshy northeast side of the valley beneath Mt. Torla. "Finally, less than 100 yards from the crest of the hill, we found the last and first pool of the actual longest tributary of the Yangtze. We got off our horses and broke open a bottle of Moët Chandon champagne. It had been a long, wonderful ride to the new source. . . . Tomorrow we would begin the descent back to the world where facts and figures were more important than pure experience. What new extensions of facts we might have contributed to were not as important as having been there."

Upon their return to the States, How Man Wong began working with scientists from the Jet Propulsion Laboratory in Pasadena, using imaging radar to confirm his discovery that the Dam Qu was the longest source of the Yangtze. Confirmation of a less sophisticated sort came a year after Wong, Chop, and Gee returned to the States. The *People's Daily* from

Beijing reported that a 1986 expedition of eleven scientists from China's Geographic Research Institute had made an extensive survey of the Yangtze valley—presumably during the river expedition sponsored by the Chengdu offices of the institute—and concluded that the Dam Qu was indeed longer than the Tuotuohe, by all of two kilometers, but with a flow three times as great. How Man Wong, Warren Gee, and Jeff Chop had been right, and they were there first.

CHAPTER FOUR

Here Come the Round=Eyes

> Ah, but a man's reach
> should exceed his grasp.
> —ROBERT BROWNING

For Ken Warren, fifty-nine, father of six, grandfather of eight, former vitamin salesman and packhorse guide, it had been a seven-year odyssey to reach the Yangtze. Warren had been a boatman for Lute Jerstad Adventures, a Portland-based adventure company owned by Everest climber Jerstad, when, in 1976, the outfitter made the first descent of the Ganges River's western source stream, the Bhagirathi, in northern India. The Indian and American press gave the trip some good ink, and one of the boatmen convinced ABC to film an attempt to raft the eastern fork, the Alakananda, in October 1977.

ABC's "The American Sportsman" agreed, and signed up actor Robert Duvall as the showcased talent for the episode. Mark Lucas, the field producer, put him in Ken Warren's raft. Warren is a big, barrel-chested man with big arms and big ambitions, and his rugged good looks made him a natural to host Duvall down the river. Warren's performance in the finished program turned him into a Warholian fifteen-minute star, a larger-than-life figure; Robert Duvall called him a "hero." Some people suggest that from that point on, Ken Warren was a changed man.

At the end of the Alakananda expedition, Ken said to the camera, "That had some of the biggest stuff that a boat has ever been dropped into of that size, bar none." Mark Lucas then turned to Ken and, echoing the name *What's Next?* painted on Warren's raft, asked, "What's next, big fella?" In reply, Ken looked over his shoulder, up at the soaring Himalayas, and said there was only one great unrun river left in the world—the Yangtze, on the other side of those mountains.

For the native Hindus of India, the Ganges and its tributaries are holy waters, and millions of spiritual aspirants, called *dharmashalas*, make pilgrimages to the river to cleanse and purify themselves. Perhaps Ken Warren was an American *dharmashala* who, repeatedly washed by the sacred waters of the Ganges in his runs through its rapids, achieved revelation through his pilgrimage to India. Certainly it was a turning point. Shortly after returning to Oregon, he left Lute Jerstad Adventures and started his own outfitting operation, Ken Warren Outdoors. From then on, he would be the star of his own show.

Ken Warren was always an independent man. In 1948, he bought a small Navy survival raft to use duck hunting; his first ride was on Oregon's Clackamas River, a small tributary of the Willamette south of Portland. Later, as a vitamin salesman, he would take his clients down rivers, favoring the outdoors as a way to make friends and influence people. But his professional career in the outdoors did not begin until 1975, when he joined Lute Jerstad Adventures. For Jerstad, he worked the commercial stretches of the Snake through Hells Canyon, the Deschutes, the Rogue, and the Owyhee, rivers which would become the cornerstones of Ken Warren Outdoors when he returned from the Ganges in 1977.

At some point after his return from India, Warren began to commit much of his time to organizing an expedition to the Yangtze. His researches indicated a German team had attempted to run part of the upper river in the early 1940s, but they disappeared and were presumed drowned. In 1980, he married his second wife, Jan Warren, a former health education teacher who came to share his vision of the first-ever descent of the Yangtze. In 1981, they teamed up with professional adventurer Jack Wheeler, and advertised for "a physician with whitewater experience and an additional oarsman with photographic or other skills" to join their team in an attempt to run the upper Yangtze after the monsoon season. The Chinese, however, ignored the scheme, and never issued a permit for the enterprise. Wheeler went off on his own to organize tours for those adventurers eager to visit the political hot spots of the world, such as Angola and Central America.

In September 1983, with his own camera crew and, according to Jan Warren, $400,000 in privately raised funds, Ken Warren made his way to Chengdu, the 2,500-year-old capital of Sichuan Province on the Yangtze's major tributary, the Min Jiang. There he and his fourteen-member team spent twenty-eight days waiting for final permission from provincial authorities to raft the Yangtze. It was never granted. So close to his goal, Warren must have felt like Tantalus, the ancient Greek king condemned to a special place in Hades. The gods made Tantalus stand in water that receded when he bent to drink, while the fruit hanging overhead would rise beyond his grasp.

While his crew flew back to the United States, Ken and Jan flew to Beijing to discuss the matter with China's sports authorities. They met with a brick wall and never received any of their fee money back. The price, in fact, went up. The Chinese now wanted a cool million dollars for Ken Warren, or anyone, to raft their river.

Following the 1983 debacle Warren hit upon a new scheme, one he felt would gain the allegiance of the Chinese instead of their resistance. He agreed to house, at his own expense, three young Chinese and train them in whitewater skills so they could join his American team on the first descent of the Yangtze. The word went out to the China Sports Service, who came up with three volunteers and a fourth to act as interpreter. Thus was born the Sino–USA Upper Yangtze River Expedition, the name under which Ken Warren would finally get to the river.

In April 1985, Ken and Jan Warren sat down in their Oregon home with four young Chinese men for an Easter turkey dinner. For whatever reasons, after only three days of whitewater training, one of the athletes decided this was not his cup of tea, and he quit. At once translator Chu Siming, a twenty-eight-year-old from Beijing, eagerly stepped in, even though his previous outdoor experience was limited. The most capable team member was Xu Jusheng, twenty-six, who had grown up in Wuhan, the capital of Hubei Province on the banks of the Middle Yangtze. Xu was a canoeing instructor at the Wuhan Physical Culture Institute, as well as a coach for the Chinese Olympic rowing team, and he had been to Los Angeles for the Games in 1984. Zhang Jiyue, twenty-five, from Chengdu, was a mountain climber, apparently picked in part because much of the trip was to be in Sichuan Province, where he lived.

The three remaining Chinese spent three months in the United States under Ken Warren's tutelage, taking a total of thirteen raft trips on seven different Northwestern rivers, including the Snake through Hell's Canyon, the Rogue, the lower Owyhee, the upper Clackamas, and the middle and south forks of the Salmon. Chu Siming later acknowledged it was the best possible experience for their coming adventure—"You learn to move with the water, how to read the river. It was a very valuable experience for the Yangtze trip." It was a lesson that Chu learned best of all—he would become the best Chinese boatman of the expedition.

Warren's strategy worked. Once the three Chinese returned to their home country, CSS dropped their price—to a mere $750,000. The Warrens went on a money-raising campaign, but Ken alone could not raise that kind of money, and he had to borrow $5,000 to fly to Beijing to inform the Chinese that 1985 would not be his year on the Yangtze. But disappointments notwithstanding, he refused to give up.

Ken Warren liked to call the Yangtze "the last great exploration on this planet," comparing it to the first ascent of Mt. Everest. He felt his years of dreaming gave him priority to make that first descent, and his naturally competitive spirit was goaded by the fact that others were trying to get there as well. He heard groups from West Germany, France, Australia, New Zealand, Canada, and Japan were vying for permits, and he heard the Japanese, who had reportedly paid a million dollars to navigate and film the Yellow, were offering the same for the Yangtze but had yet to be issued a permit. He also knew SOBEK Expeditions had been doggedly pursuing the permit for at least as long as he had.

Early in 1986, Warren went back and negotiated once more with the China Sports Service. He laid his cards on the table, playing his trump—the three Chinese boatmen would make the trip a model of international relations, deserving of the diplomatic title the Sino–USA Upper Yangtze Expedition. Pressing hard, Warren said that if the Chinese would lower their fee to $300,000, he could make it happen. They countered with $325,000 calling the additional $25,000 compensation for expenses accrued in the cancelled 1985 expedition. Warren agreed, signing a contract with Zheng Fengrong, vice president of CSS, on March 28.

That didn't leave much time before the early summer departure their ambitious project called for, and the Warrens had to scramble. Though Warren set to work gathering his crew and equipment, financially things were looking bleak. He had managed to get $25,000 from *National Geographic* for first rights to the story, but he was still over $100,000 short of his goal.

Then came a miracle: John Wilcox, the former executive producer of "The American Sportsman," who knew of Warren from the Ganges film five years earlier, stepped in. Though ABC had canceled "American Sportsman," the Aspen-based independent producer had found a new sponsor, Mutual of Omaha, who was interested in the kind of programming Wilcox had made a specialty. For twenty years Mutual of Omaha had produced the Marlin Perkins-hosted "Wild Kingdom," the longest-running syndicated program in television history. But in 1984 the ailing

Perkins had retired, and the giant insurance firm had decided to jettison the old format. They wanted something snappier, something jazzier to put them in touch with the eighties—they wanted something adventurous. Wilcox convinced them to produce an entirely new series, "Spirit of Adventure," and landed an agreement for six hour-long programs. Ken Warren's Yangtze River expedition was a natural for a special two-hour, two-part series premiere.

Wilcox and Mutual of Omaha agreed to pick up the remaining tab for the expedition, plus the expense of filming, an additional $115,000. The total cost eventually came to a reported $750,000. Ken Warren received the first of Mutual's monies on June 6; just three weeks later he left for China. There seemed to be no further obstacles to Warren's claiming his place in the history of exploration as leader of the Sino–USA Upper Yangtze Expedition.

As Warren refined his plans for the Yangtze expedition, it had turned into a truly ambitious epic. He vowed to run nearly half of the world's third longest river—the upper half, the half that had been considered "unnavigable" for centuries of exploration—from its headwaters in the glaciers of the Tanggula Mountains of Qinghai Province to the town of Yibin, the traditional end point of river traffic. The river would drop from 17,660 feet at Mt. Geladandong to 797 feet at Yibin, nearly 17,000 feet in 1,973 miles, an average drop of 8½ feet per mile—the drop of the Colorado through the 223 miles of the Grand Canyon. Centerpiece of the run would be the infamous Tiger's Leap Gorge, that two-mile deep, knife-sharp cleft in the mountains of Yunnan. Here, the maps showed the river dropping over 50 feet per mile. For a river that might well flow over 100,000 cubic feet per second during the summer months, when Warren was planning to run the Yangtze, that is a prodigious drop indeed.

But to accomplish this ambitious goal, Warren had to make some bold promises. There was, for instance, the matter of his itinerary. In order to cover nearly two thousand miles in the sixty days he allowed his expedition, he would have to cover a minimum of thirty-three miles a day, every day, for over two months. Allowing time for resupply stops, this had to mean days of up to fifty miles, unprecedented in exploratory rafting on a major river. Most rivers flow at far below five miles an hour, but even if the mighty Yangtze kept up that rate for its length, Warren's plan called for ten hours on the water, day after day, with virtually no time off for scouting difficult passages, recouping after unforeseen events, or portaging.

Having given so much of his time to planning his expedition, Warren continued to maintain that his proposal was reasonable and safe. "I am confident of our success in completing the Yangtze Expedition in complete safety," he declared in his final letter to team members for the 1986 trip. He went on to outline the "custom design" of his rafts, manufactured with the "new synthetic rubber made by DuPont" called Hypalon, a material that actually has been the standard of riverboats for nearly twenty years. The rafts he eventually used—including three PVC Maravias built in Oregon and four eighteen-foot Havasus from Campways—were all off-the-shelf models, good riverboats but hardly the superboats he described.

Continuing in this same vein, he insisted that "only myself and the other boatmen will attempt to navigate an extremely treacherous section of the river. Other team members will go overland and be picked up down river. . . . The most important factor in safely navigating a magnificent river such as the Upper Yangtze is the experience of the Expedition Leader and his boatmen. . . . The other boatmen have been carefully chosen and are all rated at the top of their professions. No one's life will be risked at any time.

"We will never commit more than two boats at a time to a dangerous run. We will never try a run with only one raft. The lead raft will be pushing ahead at certain times to locate the dangerous sections of whitewater. This will give the others time to get pulled over safely for scouting or possible lining." (Lining is a procedure wherein a tethered empty raft is negotiated down the side of a dangerous rapid by the guides working ropes from shore.) These and other precautions—sensible and well-intentioned as they are, the results of years of whitewater experience by hundreds of river runners—were, as it turned out, eventually compromised by Warren in his determination to complete his run of the Yangtze.

Warren based his justification in planning such a monumental expedition on his experience: "With 35 years of experience and over 70,000 miles of running rivers and leading expeditions all over the world, we have been able to build an enviable reputation for safety." We have no reason to question Warren's safety record, but between the formation of Ken Warren Outdoors in 1978 and the 1986 Yangtze expedition, and even counting his occasional trips with vitamin clients down Oregon's recreational rivers before that, his tally of river miles is unlikely at best. One boatman who later joined Warren on the Yangtze told of filling out the application the China Sports Service requested and hesitating over the "previous experience" section. "Just make something up," Warren advised; "make it sound good."

Heroes are often felled by their own pride, and Ken Warren is a very proud man. In anticipation of his epic adventure, he had released several notices, saying in one that he was "widely recognized as the world's leading whitewater oarsman"—a claim most boaters recognize as pointless. In what kind of whitewater—big water? Technical whitewater? On what river, with what kind of boat? What kind of trip—a commercial run down a well-charted river, or a first-ever descent of a rapid first seen just a few seconds before? There are "good" boatmen, and there are "real good" boatmen; but there is no best.

Warren continued to make bold claims for his own experience and that of the others on the trip, at one point noting that "Three of our Expedition members are expert mountain climbers and they will be fully equipped with climbing gear," at a time when only Ancil Nance came close to fitting such a description. Of Toby Sprinkle, who was twenty-four, Warren told John Wilcox, "We have researched the subject and I think he could be the youngest person ever involved in a major expedition," ignoring the many younger climbers who had joined assaults on Everest (not to mention my own still-wet-behind-the-ears expedition through Ethiopia on the first descent of the Omo at the age of twenty-three).

Two other statements were to prove more troublesome yet. One press release stated, "Sophisticated satellite radio communications will insure the safety factor and provide valuable up-to-date progress reports to the outside world." Had this been true, it would have been analogous to David Breashears's relayed broadcast from the summit of Mt. Everest in 1983, as part of another Wilcox production. But initially, John Wilcox didn't supply any communications equipment of that sophistication; when he finally attempted to do so—in September, after the expedition had been on the river for six weeks—he tried to send in a TelSystems TCS 9000, indeed one of the most advanced satellite communications systems in the world. "You could bounce a signal off anything with that," said Dewey Pendergrass, the US consul in Beijing. But its sophistication became its liability. There was no way customs officials of the People's Republic of China would allow such advanced intelligence equipment into a remote region of their politically sensitive western provinces—within calling distance of Afghanistan, India, and the Soviet Union.

Finally, Warren's "Safety Program" statement concluded with a flat assurance of helicopter support. "The Chinese Government is supplying the Expedition with the support of a Sikorsky BLACK HAWK helicopter capable of flying at high elevations. In the event of a serious injury or trauma, we can immediately radio out to the Road Support Team, and they will call in the helicopter."

Warren was only telling others what the Chinese had told him, and for once he may have been the one misled. The only helicopters available in western China, according to Dewey Pendergrass, though they are indeed BLACK HAWKS, are stationed in Chengdu, 300 miles from the Jinsha Jiang at Batang and even farther from the two uppermost tributaries of the river, the Tuotuohe and Tongtian Ho. Standard BLACK HAWKS have a flying range of only about 375 miles—which meant a 160-mile flying radius, since there was no established fuel supply stop in Sichuan anywhere other than Chengdu. According to a spokesman at Sikorsky Aircraft, the BLACK HAWKS in China were outfitted with up to four auxiliary tanks, which could contain 230 gallons of extra fuel. Just how far that extra fuel could extend the flying range of the helicopters, however, depends upon several factors, not least of which is altitude.

In any case, there was grave doubt that any private endeavor such as Warren's could finagle the use of the aircraft, even in an emergency. For the upper reaches of the river, at least, Pendergrass stated flatly, "Helicopter support was never in the cards."

None of these embellishments on the truth were of themselves cause for alarm, nor are they unusual in the annals of adventure. The recent revelation that Commander Robert E. Peary may not have reached the North Pole in 1909 shows but one example of burnishing the facts. In fifteen years of running SOBEK, and writing about our trips for magazines and books, I've made a few grandiose statements myself, and stretched the truth a time or two to fit a finer cut of cloth. The problem is that Warren was able to convince a number of inexperienced Americans and Chinese that he was the big man for the big job. Among the neophytes Warren comforted with his soothing assurances was a young photographer from Minnesota named David Shippee.

In some ways, Warren's approach to the entire endeavor was idealistic: a powerful dream led the man to the river. Had the big hunter-turned-boatman been so inclined, he might have consulted the Chinese Book of Changes, the *I Ching*, the oldest oracular text in the world, and foreseen his fate. The Book of Changes is based on the linking of pairs of trigrams, each of which is representative of a feature of the natural world. The resulting pattern of six lines, or the hexagram, is read for its inner structure and meaning. Warren's inspired dream (*Ch'ien*, the Creative, Heaven) was to ride the Long River (*K'an*, Water, the Abysmal) through its most remove reaches, especially that stretch known as the Tongtian Ho, the River to Heaven. The hexagram that places Heaven above Water is known as *Sung*—Conflict. In Richard Wilhelm's respected translation of the Book of Changes, the Judgment for the hexagram reads as follows:

> *Conflict. You are sincere*
> *And are being obstructed.*
> *A cautious halt halfway brings good fortune,*
> *Going through to the end brings misfortune.*
> *It furthers one to see the great man.*
> *It does not further one to cross the great water.*

When the word went out, early in 1985, that an American was drawing close to an agreement to run the Yangtze, Yao Maoshu was goaded into action. While a twenty-six-year-old at the Southwest Jiaotong University in Sichuan in 1979, Yao had hit upon the idea of running the Yangtze in a raft. His plan was to float the river's entire length, from Mt. Geladandong to Shanghai, a 3,900-mile run that would put his name in the record books. As a photographer, he also saw the opportunity to record an unusual expedition, to gather shots of places rarely if ever seen by his countrymen. A book would naturally follow his success; his life's course lay ahead of him.

At first, Yao believed his best chance to run the Yangtze was to join up with the American expedition, and he applied to go to Oregon for whitewater training. When he was passed over for the appointment, a part of him was relieved: Why should he need an American's help? He was Chinese, and it was China's river. He had been researching the Great River for years, had visited various parts of it, practiced rafting with the used equipment he bought at a discount from the university's athletes— he had even convinced his wife and parents that his projected journey down the Yangtze was not only possible, but a good thing for his future. Yao realized that if the Americans were to get on the river later in 1985, or even in 1986, there was no time to waste. He must begin at once.

Quickly, he scoured his contacts for contributions and donations—and built up his equipment to include the necessary cameras, film, raft, and waterproof clothes. At the end of May, while his compatriots were still learning the ropes on the rivers of Oregon and Idaho, Yao kissed his wife goodbye and left Chengdu. By train, bus, and finally a yak caravan, he reached the glacier at the foot of Mt. Geladandong. He arrived nine years after the Chinese Geographic Research Institute had determined the headwaters of the Yangtze, and there was little evidence that anyone had been there in between. In mid-June, he set off down the Yangtze.

A month later he arrived in Yushu, after floating six hundred miles down the Tuotuohe and Tongtian rivers. According to Zheng Guoqing, a reporter and photographer for the *Guangming Daily*, Yao burst into the district government offices and announced, "I have floated here on a rubber raft all the way from the source of the Yangtze." No one believed him. Unlike the expeditions to follow, Yao had not enlisted reporters and press agents to publicize his trip, and it was not until he reached Yushu that his bold attempt became known.

Zheng befriended the young adventurer—they were about the same age, thirty-two, and shared an interest in photography—and for the next four days the two gathered supplies for the next leg in Yao's journey, down the river to Dege. Yao was voluble about his experiences and related many of them to his new friend. Just a few miles after he set out down the Tuotuohe, he told Zheng, he had found an island full of swan eggs scattered by the thousands of birds that nested on the isolated tundra. The river's water was icy cold and so crystal clear that Yao recalled seeing dead birds and animals lying on the bottom of the streambed. He had caught a small lynx and tried to tame it so he would have a companion on the trip, but, fearing the cat's claws would puncture his inflatable raft, he let it go.

It was not his only encounter with animals—downstream on the Tongtian Ho, his camp had twice been threatened, once by a large bear and once when he was surrounded by wolves. He had responded by leaping into his raft and rowing into the river, but the animals had eaten his food. On these occasions, he went hungry until he came to the next encampment of Tibetan nomads, as long as three days away in one instance.

And of course there was whitewater—nothing too big, as the Tongtian is but a whisper of the river the Yangtze becomes downstream. But the icy water had washed easily over his small twelve-foot boat, and despite his waterproof clothing the cold had chilled his bones.

But it was not cold or hunger that bothered the young rafter most. "The most unbearable thing is loneliness," he confided to Zheng. "I had nobody to talk with and many times I thought I would go mad. To kill the loneliness I thought about my past and sang to myself. I am so happy to find somebody to talk with."

On July 22, Zheng helped Yao repaint the name on his small inflatable, *Dragon's Descendent*. Yao left Zheng the film and notes on his first six hundred miles, the top sixth of his projected journey, as well as letters to his parents, his in-laws, and his wife. They gathered up food from the Zhimenda Hydrologic Station near Yushu—plenty of food this time, so Yao would not go hungry in the coming miles. The government officials in Yushu, by now caught up in the ambition of the young adventurer, donated a shotgun, so if he met up with any more bears, Yao would be prepared.

Just after ten o'clock the next morning, to a chorus of blessings from the Tibetan inhabitants of Yushu, Yao pulled away from shore, rowed into the current, and waved goodbye. The heavily laden *Dragon's Descendent* was swept away downstream.

Perhaps later that day, perhaps the next, Yao Maoshu entered the short, narrow Tongtian Gorge. There are seven visible drops in the short canyon, and somewhere among them his raft flipped, perhaps too heavy to control with the extra equipment and supplies. His lifeless body was sighted by herdsmen eighteen miles downstream from Yushu, swirling in an eddy on the far side of the river. They gathered up those of his belongings that had washed to their side of the river and took them with the bad news back to Yushu. The Yangtze had claimed its first martyr.

CHAPTER FIVE

Reaching for
the Brass Ring

I thank the spirit of the river,
But what good has it done?
Just as its waters cannot
Return to their source, so I can
Never return to my native land.
—SU TUNG P'O

Yao Maoshu's noble and solitary effort, and his lonely death in July 1985, became headline news in the People's Republic of China. Suddenly the idea of rafting the Yangtze swept over the idealistic young of China. A survey of Chinese college students asked, "Whom do you most admire today?" and Yao Maoshu's name ranked high on the list. Embedded in the story was Yao's motivation—that an American, a certain Ken Warren, had contracted to run the Yangtze, to be the first down the Great River. Down China's river. The Chang Jiang, with its sister stream the Huang Ho, virtually defined twenty-three centuries of Chinese civilization. Such an outrage should not be permitted, young athletes and students told each other. Chinese climbers had been the first to climb the highest mountains in their country, the Chinese Mountaineering Association had seen to that. Why should this round-eye, this barbarian, appropriate the glory that rightfully belonged to a Chinese?

One of the young men moved by the story of Yao Maoshu was a thirty-year-old shoemaker from Luoyang, Lang Baoluo. Inspired, he found seven friends to join him in following Yao's example, and together they formed the Luoyang Expedition for Sailing and Exploring the

Yangtze. They pooled personal resources—about 20,000 yuan, or $6,000—bought boats and equipment, and accepted further donations from friends in Luoyang. Finally they had enough money to travel to Mt. Geladandong and the source of the Yangtze. Lang Baoluo and his comrades would not let any American be the first on the river.

Meanwhile, in April 1986, the Institute of Geographic Research, a branch of the Chinese Academy of Sciences located in Chengdu, capital of Sichuan, allocated 200,000 yuan (about $60,000) to form their own team, the China Yangtze River Scientific Observation Drifting Expedition. Some forty-eight people were initially included, though as the expedition progressed the number would swell to seventy, including newspaper writers and photographers, film teams, and "security guards." Included were citizens from ten provinces and five ethnic minorities, making it a far more "national" team than that of the young renegades from Luoyang.

While this Sichuan group, with its Academy of Sciences backing and pan-national makeup, had the appearance of an "official" Chinese team, China Sports Service in Beijing was not happy with its formation. The sports agency, a branch of the official China State Council, which governed the country, had contracted with Ken Warren for first-descent rights; CSS regarded Warren as something of a world figure in river rafting. Besides, Warren had come up with the money. Though CSS was uneasy with this popular uprising against government contracts, nobody in Beijing was about to tell China's ambitious youth that they should shelve their dreams and let the Americans go first.

Hoping perhaps to talk the Sichuan team out of its plans, or at least to avoid antagonism, CSS sent one of China's sports heroes, the 1957 women's high-jump record holder Zheng Fengrong, to Chengdu to meet with the Academy team. There she hammered out an agreement with the Sichuan rafters that would allow four of them to join Warren's trip if the China team ran into trouble. The arrangement did not sit well with all the members of the Sichuan team—some thought it implied not "if" they ran into trouble, but "when," a clear signal that CSS put little faith in its own nation's athletes.

A little over a month later, on May 30, as the roads in Qinghai and Xizang provinces were cleared of the winter's ice, three members of the Sichuan team left on their own for the river's source. Calling themselves the China Youth Team, the three left a letter with their former teammates stating their purpose boldly and unambiguously—"The Yangtze will be conquered successfully for the first time in the history of mankind by Chinese." The message was clearly that for some Chinese, at least, there would be no under-the-table deal struck with the Americans.

As June 1986 began—the Month of the Tiger in the Year of the Tiger—the several teams of Chinese began to converge on the source of the Yangtze. Just as the dragon rules the waters, the tiger rules the land; the Chinese king of beasts is a model for soldiers because of its courage and dignity, and a harbinger too of danger and fear. Courage and danger, dignity and fear would alternately plague and elate the Chinese and American teams that rode the waters of the Yangtze through the coming months.

For the Chinese, whose experience in whitewater rafting was virtually nonexistent, courage and dignity also took precedence over common sense. In general, the equipment they had to draw upon was a far cry from the Hypalon or PVC whitewater inflatables Ken Warren, and later SOBEK, would bring into the country. The Luoyang team had two fourteen-foot paddle rafts, not much better in quality than the much-maligned commercial "rubber duckies" popular in the United States (also called, somewhat ironically, "yellow perils"). The Sichuan team, with its institutional backing, fared better with a dozen heavy but well-built rubber and leather inflatables. Life jackets were mostly older models made of kapok, the product of a tropical tree that fruits a white corklike fiber which, once it becomes waterlogged, slowly loses its flotation. Paddles were plastic, easily broken, or handmade of wood; oars were lightweight and not up to the demands of the river.

Both teams eventually began to experiment with capsule rafts—the Luoyang team first, and later the Sichuan rafters. These were pillbox-shaped cells of rubber with inner-tubes lashed on the outside for extra flotation, in which they planned to run the biggest rapids. Many American rafters later scoffed at the craft—they were not "running" the river in any real sense, since they had no navigational control over the capsules. Chinese as well as Americans who looked at pictures and films of the capsules would subsequently compare them to the barrels that ran Niagara Falls. They might float, they might have human occupants, but were they really boats? And, more importantly, were they safe?

As the days of early summer lengthened, the Chinese teams began to converge on Tuotuoheyan, the uppermost bridge across the headwaters of the Yangtze. The first wave began its assault on the river from Mt. Geladandong on June 13, when the China Yangtze River Scientific Observation Drifting Expedition from Sichuan reached the putative source of the Yangtze. A wooden stela, with the name and purpose of the

Sichuan team's expedition, was erected at the site as team members cheered and fired off pistols and rifles in celebration. And then, so says the official story, the Sichuan team began its descent of the Yangtze.

However, working from the press reports published in China's English-language press, and the translation of Chinese sources, there is reason to doubt some of these claims. Both the Luoyang team and the Sichuan team assert they ran this section of the river, from Lake Qemo to Tuotuoheyan. Possibly a small crew of river runners from the Sichuan team did paddle down the tiny river 197 miles to Tuotuoheyan; but it was only three days after they set out—on June 16—that the Sichuan rafters officially left Tuotuoheyan for their float downstream, while the Warren team took eight days to kayak from Qemo to Tuotuoheyan. Likewise, the Luoyang team asserted that they had started down this section five days later, on June 18, and paddled the next 735 miles in twenty-five days, a very impressive rate of 30 miles a day. Perhaps both groups looked at the shallow, braided channel and decided that it just wasn't worth the trouble, not believing that the Sino–USA team would bother running the stretch when they arrived a month later. Of course, if it's firsts that concern us here, Yao Maoshu beat all three teams down the source stream by over a year.

In any case, the official beginning of the expedition took place on July 16, when the Sichuan team left Tuotuoheyan just as a hailstorm broke loose. The Chinese of today are far less superstitious than their forefathers, or they never would have launched. In Tibetan culture especially, hailstorms are a sign that the spirits are displeased with an endeavor. The rafters took other signs more seriously, however, as when their lead freight boat developed a bad leak shortly after the four P.M. launch. This prompted an early camp, where it was discovered the solid fuel for their fire had been left at the Chengdu airport. The rafters scoured the barren countryside for yak dung to fuel their fire, but finding none, they decided instead to burn their spare oarlocks. It was a rough beginning indeed.

The Sichuan team was lead by a fifty-year-old army officer named Zhu Jianzhang, who established his authority quickly at the team's rendezvous at Lhasa during the first week of June. Wearing his military uniform, he barked orders and berated team members for pleading sickness when the freight had to be loaded onto trucks. A few days later, before they left for Tuotuoheyan, Zhu laid out the rules for avoiding high-altitude sickness, and threatened to send anyone who got sick back to Chengdu. But even before the expedition got onto the water, Zhu's own health deteriorated badly. His stamina collapsed, his appearance became frightful. Expedition members recalled that he would make at least three mistakes a day because of lack of oxygen, which in Chinese can be translated as "plateau stupid disease." His authority quickly eroded, and the team became democratic by default.

A number of newspapers were covering the team's descent, and one of the reporters who traveled with the Sichuan team was Dai Shan Kui, who later wrote a book about his Yangtze adventures (*Drift*, published by the China Scientific Technical Press and available only in Chinese). His reporter's need to find "an angle" began to focus on Jiehu Arsha, one of four women on the Sichuan team. As a member of the Yi minority, a notoriously independent ethnic group of Yunnan and Sichuan provinces (*see* chapter 14), Arsha had a cultural propensity toward independence that stood out among her well-socialized Han teammates. She was a dancer and a singer, who wore the heavy makeup of an actress even in isolated Qinghai. On the other hand, she was a public security officer, a policewoman by another name, the very figure of authority. Moreover, she was divorced—still not a common situation for a woman in China; and her involvement with a married man she met at a dance party had caused a furor shortly before the trip began, when the man's wife came to the team to demand that Arsha return a gift worth 3,200 yuan (about $100).

Most significantly, she wanted to go on this historic trip, and would stop at nothing to be a part of the team. During the training at Luding on the Dadu River in Sichuan, her performance was better than many men's, but she—and three other women who became part of the team—was initially left off the roster. Her determination then took a strange and compelling twist: she killed her favorite pet, a lovely Tibetan dog, barricaded herself with the other women in a car, and then physically attacked team leader Zhu Jianzhang. She got her wish, and the four women were appointed to the forty-eight-member team, but she failed to win the affection of her teammates.

On the second day, the team drifted into a large shallow lake, which Yao Maoshu had called "Dead Lake," and had to work all day dragging their heavy boats across muddy channels, not finding a suitable campsite until eight P.M. Arsha worked as hard as many of the men, and despite her affectations earned the grudging respect of her teammates. But the contradictions of her character did not evaporate in the high altitudes; if anything, they were to become more marked.

Although at the outset of the trip the four women tented together in pairs, and the men left them their privacy, the walls soon began to come down, and Arsha played the part of Joshua. A couple of the men refused to sleep with Zhu Jianzhang, the middle-aged team leader, because of his snoring, and moved instead into one of the women's tents. Although the move raised some eyebrows, it was accepted. But when Arsha moved out of the tent she shared with one of the women and moved in with a man, it caused more serious repercussions. She had already spent a lot of time with two male news reporters and fellow team member Zhou Hua, and freely admitted she preferred the company of men. One morning, apparently after tenting with him, she spoon-fed Zhou Hua, a social gesture that shocked the straitlaced Chinese squatting around the campfire—and embarrassed Zhou Hua no end. She later repeated this gesture with other men, including reporter Sha Yang.

Arsha quickly became the focus of gossip and controversy, and sparked the rage of several, including a middle-aged reporter from Guizhou named Xu Xinzhi. A former artist and dancer himself, Xu's own youth had been marked by as much controversy as Arsha's, for years earlier his fiancée had left him for another man. First he had beat his former fiancée, then he had approached her new lover, but held off attacking him when he saw that he was "a weakling." Now, in his mid-forties, he was the vice president of the Guizhou Video Company, and a hard worker, sometimes staying up well past midnight to file his reports; his main objection to Arsha seemed to be that her friendship with Sha Yang was affecting his work. Given his own background, there may have been a psychological element in his antipathy. But whatever the cause, it led to a bitter argument between the young dancer and the middle-aged reporter.

Another member of the first flotilla down the Tuotuohe was Kong Zhiyi. Like his father before him, Kong was a military man: for ten years he had served in the Chinese Army in the Qinghai-Tibet plateau. He had been cited for meritorious deeds five times, awarded the title of Hero, and elected a deputy to the People's Congress of Qinghai Province. Unlike most members of the Sichuan team, however, Kong did have river-running experience, on the Yangtze in fact: in 1976, he had made a solo rafting trip down the flatwater stretch of the Chang Jiang, from Chongqing to Wusong, the Shanghai suburb where the Yangtze flows into the sea. His experiences from the two-thousand-mile trip had made him a vital source of information for Yao Maoshu, and Kong had even tried to join Yao in his 1985 source-to-sea adventure. Military commitments had prevented him, and though he was saddened to hear of Yao's death, his determination to run the Yangtze had been, like that of so many other Chinese, reinforced by the tragedy.

While the main team floated down the Tuotuohe, the reputed source stream of the Yangtze, another team also sponsored by the Academy of Sciences in Chengdu set off down the Dam Qu. This is the more southerly river, with its headwaters in the Tanggula Mountains that mark the border between Qinghai and Tibet, which some believed to be the longer and larger tributary, and therefore the ultimate source of the Long River. Because of the speculative nature of their trip, many of the team members were scientists: marshlands researcher Sun Guangyou, geologist Tang Bangxin, glaciologist Pu Jiancheng, and others. The team also included a good friend of Arsha's from the training school at Luding on the Dadu River, an adventurous sailor named Wang Yan from Xiamen, the former British port city of Amoy in Fujian Province. Together, the team accumulated a wealth of information about the Dam Qu, which later proved to be valuable in proving that it was in fact the true source river of the Yangtze.

The Dam Qu group was far away when the main team encountered its first major rapids—which the Chinese invariably call "shoals," just as they call rocky shelves or passages "'reefs"—at a place known as Bawu Shoal. This is the gorge the Warren group later called Top of the World; the Chinese reached it on July 1, five weeks ahead of the Americans. The water level was near flood stage, 3.9 meters—twelve feet—higher than when Yao Maoshu passed through a year earlier. Neither the Americans nor Yao experienced difficulty in this section; but for the Sichuan team, running the gorge at flood stage, it would be a different story.

The river narrowed quickly, and the first drop looked dangerous to the inexperienced rafters. But boldly they entered it, first one boat, then another; by the time the seventh and last boat entered they were gaining confidence. It proved to be short-lived, as the boat hit a wave sideways and two men were swept overboard, the two reporters whose names had been romantically linked with Jiehu Arsha—Zhou Hua and Sha Yang. They were quickly rescued, but it was clear the Tuotuohe was no longer a friendly river.

Soon after they launched into the gorge the next day, July 2, the surging rapids had drenched nearly all the rafters. Though the sun was out, the water was freezing, and several of the rafters, including Dai Shan Kui, trembled from cold and fear. "We should have a stop, I cannot bear any more," he pleaded, and the boats pulled over to dry out before the morning was half over.

Suddenly shots rang out. Everyone leapt to their feet in astonishment. Yao Maoshu's diary, which nearly everyone on the trip had studied, spoke of bandits in this area, and the gunshots did little to soothe the nervous rafters. One of them spied a teammate, Yu Cheng, on a nearby ridge, however, and concluded that they were being warned about the coming rapid. The knowledge that they weren't being shot at would not be comforting for long: downstream was a drop of twenty-five feet, fronted by "a wild wave as if it were the gate of hell," as Dai Shan Kui wrote.

The first six boats began the descent into the rapid. The crew of the last boat quickly loaded up and started to follow, only to hesitate as they watched the first boats be swallowed by the water. On shore, Yu Cheng—armed with his pistol—gestured madly for the boats to hug the right bank. Then Dai Shan Kui's boat entered, and he felt himself submerged, released, and submerged again. He feared the raft had flipped, then marveled as it burst out upright. Then it dropped into a hole and rode halfway up the reversal on the far side, hung precariously for a moment, then surfed through. "When we survived I felt as if I had just escaped from hell," Dai Shan Kui wrote. The boats struggled to pull to the bank, to rest and recover their strength.

Perhaps he had come through hell on water, but the devils awaited on dry land. Two bandits came out of the bush, big scraggly men with scowls on their haunted faces. One held a club, the other hefted two stones in his hands; they stared at the rafters menacingly. Yu Cheng walked up to them, his pistol visible; it looked like a Tibetan standoff. Two of the rafters who knew some Tibetan tried to talk to the strangers, but their dialect was as strange as they were, and communication was sketchy.

Arsha thought they were growing "some kind of tobacco," an intriguing possibility indeed; others thought they were bandits pure and simple, who had thought the rafters would be an easy mark. But at last the two dropped their weapons and ran away, possibly realizing they were simply outnumbered by the sportsmen. Whitewater and bandits seemed to be conspiring against the Sichuan team, so they took a rest day to consider their course.

Downstream, a scouting group had discovered three major rapids in the next couple of miles, including one at the base of a fresh landslide. Some of the rafters thought they should pull out and go overland to the next section; some thought they should continue on the water slowly, carefully. But two strong voices spoke out for persevering no matter what, continuing on as soon as possible regardless of obstacles—Jiehu Arsha and Yang Bin.

Unable to stop them, Yu Cheng ordered a safety team to be set up beneath the first rapid. Before it was in place, however, Arsha, Bin, and a third boatman, Xu Ruisiang, shoved off into the current, eager to show the others how it could be done. Almost at once Arsha fell out, and Ruisiang reached out to help her; alone, Yang Bin could not pilot the paddleraft, and it drifted out of control toward the more dangerous landslide drop. Heroically, Yang Fan, a member of the rescue team, leapt into the water and helped Yang Bin wrestle the boat to shore, where they reached safety at the very lip of the rapid.

Somewhat chastened, the renegade rafters agreed to go with the group decision from then on, and from that point the seven rafts were tied together in three large rigs to provide more stability in the dangerous high water. It was a maneuver born of inexperience that was to be repeated by the Americans in the coming weeks. Two days later, on July 5, the team reached the Zhimenda Hydrologic Station, near the town of Yushu.

Here, the personal conflicts that had been simmering for the past three weeks boiled over. Arsha accused Yu Cheng of telling reporters she was having improper relations with some of the male rafters; to her defense leapt Wang Yan, a member of the Dam Qu exploration, which joined with the main team in Yushu. But the reporters, including the independent Xu Xinzhi, stood their ground, and Arsha became so infuriated she almost attacked the senior journalist. Zhu Jianzhang, the erstwhile leader of the team, proved unable to deal with the conflict, and finally Yu Cheng seemed to take command. He telexed the sponsors of the expedition in Chengdu, and they responded that Yu Cheng, Zhu Jianzhang, and five others were now the ruling committee of the seventy-person expedition, and everybody had better get in line behind them. Unity was all: there was rough water ahead, and division was not to be tolerated.

Meanwhile, as the Sichuan team followed the Tuotuohe through the sparsely inhabited plateau, the Luoyang team was about to launch its own expedition. Without the semi-official backing of the Academy of Sciences or the approval of CSS, the Luoyang team had a harder time earning the respect of the reporters covering the event. Many referred to the Sichuan rafters as "the China Team," a designation that irked the eight proud rafters form Luoyang. The city itself is one of the oldest in China, had been the capital of several early dynasties, and was said to be where

Confucius had his historic meeting with Lao-tzu, primary teacher of Taoism; in addition, the first Buddhist temple to be erected in China was situated in Luoyang, which by 400 A.D. had 1,300 Buddhist temples. But subsequent history turned Luoyang into an outback, and its population sank to fewer than 20,000 earlier in this century (though now 900,000 live there). As a consequence of their inauspicious homeland, their relative youth (average age was less than thirty), and lack of funding, the Luoyang rafters felt further that they were victims of prejudice in the national press.

The only way they could prove themselves was to succeed. They launched from Tuotuoheyan on July 2, and began the race to catch up with the so-called China Team four days ahead of them. At this point, while at least four journalists were traveling with the Sichuan team, none were with the Luoyang team. Details of their progress down the Tuotuohe are therefore missing, but they did arrive at Zhimenda on July 12.

Meanwhile the Sichuan team was still in Yushu, waiting to let its land crew reach the next supply point. Finally the competing river teams met and, with the shared experiences of rafting the uppermost levels of the Yangtze behind them, cautious friendships began to develop. Dai Shan Kui, who had known Luoyang team leader Lang Baoluo earlier, filed favorable reports on Lang's team, and soon all of China knew there was a race on its Great River, in which both lead teams were Chinese, while the Americans had yet to begin.

More significantly, perhaps, Wang Dian Ming jumped ship. An outspoken but apparently lethargic member of the Sichuan team, he decided to join the Luoyang group when his arrogance led to strain with his former teammates. On July 17, while the Sichuan team still waited in Yushu—growing increasingly nervous over reports that the Sino–USA Upper Yangtze Expedition was about to begin its float down the river, which it did on July 21—Lang Baoluo led Wang Dian Ming and his Luoyang teammates back onto the river to run the much-feared Tongtian Gorge, where Yao Maoshu had met his death.

Confronted with the first of the Yangtze's dangerous rapids, and possibly under the advice of Wang Dian Ming, the Luoyang team adopted the Sichuan team's technique of tying together their boats, including the black sealed rubber capsule, and rowing into the rapids in a single large rig. Before long, the capsule was leaking and taking in water, creating a tremendous drag on the large craft's maneuverability. Two boatmen, Wang Maojun (co-leader with Lang Baoluo) and Wang

Dian Ming, were swept off the raft. The water's tumult prevented them from climbing back on, and only after an hour of clinging to the raft as it swept through the whitewater of Tongtian Gorge could they recover. The big raft was rowed to shore, and the exhausted crew stretched out on the rocks, too tired to move. A day later they floated into Dege, now two days ahead of the Sichuan team. The upstarts from Luoyang were the first to raft the Tongtian Gorge safely, and they were ahead in the race.

By July 19 the members of the Sichuan team had finally resolved their differences and left Yushu; the next day they too confronted Tongtian Gorge. Again it was a day of drama and excitement. They did not tie their boats together, but rafted steadily through the challenges of the gorge until sunset, making nearly sixty miles in a single day. It was a pace Ken Warren would envy. The next day they put on the river early, eager to catch up with the Luoyang team. Soon, they had their own brush with disaster when two boats overturned in a rapid near the Kasong Ferry. One reporter lost three cameras and film, his map of the river, binoculars, and compass, while another who had quickly made it to shore had to hike for two hours to catch up with the rest of the group. He found them all sprawled in exhaustion on a big stone, its solid mass warmed by the sun. They camped there that night, and paddled on to Dege the next day.

Though the teams were both in Dege at the same time, their competition continued, and almost as soon as the Sichuan group pulled off the river the Luoyang group put back on, still eager to maintain its lead in the race. Then, at Baiyu, the Sichuan group—with a pared-down crew and fewer boats—leapfrogged over their Luoyang countrymen, hurriedly putting three boats on the river. Both teams were pressing to make it down the river as quickly as possible. Their maps showed no major rapids between Baiyu and Hutiaoxia, Tiger's Leap Gorge, nearly five hundred miles away. But once they got into the canyons between Baiyu and Batang, they soon found how wrong maps could be.

On July 24, the Sichuan team drifted down to the first major rapid on the Jinsha Jiang, some thirty miles below Dege, not far beyond the Sichuan town of Baiyu. The Warren expedition members would later dub this Three Boat Rapid, for it marked the first time they rigged their rafts together; to the Chinese, it was Kagang Shoal. "The cliffs on both sides of the river leaned out like upturned eaves and cast a big shadow on the river," wrote Dai Shan Kui. The river funneled into a big drop, so that even the relatively well-equipped rafters from Sichuan hesitated. And while they did, they were joined by the Luoyang team.

Confronted with a common adversary, the crashing waters of Kagang Shoal, the two teams at last decided to patch up their differences and unite. The men from Luoyang suggested the idea, for they had a "secret weapon" their countrymen did not—the enclosed boat, a black capsule that could hold four people and virtually guarantee a secure, if wet and uncontrollable, run through almost anything. Intrigued by the idea, the Sichuan group agreed to let two of their team share the capsule with two of the Luoyang crew.

The Sichuan group, now traveling in a considerably lighter flotilla with only three boats, decided to portage two rafts downstream to help retrieve the capsule after its run. Unfortunately, while they were lining the boats along the shore, one of the rafts got loose from its handlers and was washed away, unmanned but gone forever. So only one boat was stationed below Kagang Shoal when Lei Jiansheng and Zhang Jun of Luoyang and Wang Yan and Kong Zhiyi of the Sichuan team climbed into the capsule. The black boat was pushed into the current, and less than a minute later picked up below the drop by the safety raft.

Now the Sichuan team was confronted with a problem: they had ten people above the rapid, but only one boat, the other two having been portaged down, and one of those lost. Ironically, the Luoyang team—the impoverished upstarts—had three boats for eight people. Yu Cheng asked three of his teammates to go with the Luoyang rafters, but they refused: there was still resentment and competition between the two teams, and the defection of Wang Dian Ming two weeks earlier remained a sore subject. The two teams split up once again: four of the Sichuan rafters left the river, hiking out to join the land group for the overland haul to Batang; the other six crowded in the one boat and tried to make do.

The next day both teams set out, and after successfully rafting another twenty-five-foot drop and a number of other "shoals," they made a late camp together. The rapids they were facing had not been anticipated, and the gorge ahead seemed threatening despite the indications of their maps. Grudgingly, they admitted they would all be better off if they could again unite efforts and proceed the next day as one team—with fewer people and only two boats. Judging from their records, they may have been approaching the region of whitewater where Ken Warren and his diamond rig would later spin out of control for ninety hair-raising minutes.

The following morning, July 27, the fourteen remaining Chinese set out in their two rafts and the black capsule. There were rapids aplenty ahead, and soon the teams agreed to tie together one of the rafts and the capsule. At midday, they reached Yieba village and enjoyed their first proper meal in three days. There were some changes made in the personnel aboard the boats; some connected with the land crew to leave the river, and one boat was taken off the water. They left Yieba with five people in one raft and three in the capsule—Yang Honglin and Zhang Jun of the Luoyang team, and Kong Zhiyi of the Sichuanese, the young man who had ten years earlier floated solo from Chongqing to Shanghai. The next big rapid was Yela Shoal, with a single drop estimated at over twenty feet. In all probability, this is the rapid the Americans would later call the Buddha Hole.

"There are so many dangerous rapids and rocks ahead," Kong had told one of his teammates when they left Yushu. "I may die at any moment, but I'll never retreat." Kong was one of the rafters inside the capsule when it flushed over Kagang Shoal, but when they came to the rapids at the Yela Shoal, Kong wanted to ride in the open raft, dubbed the *Vanguard*, because he thought it would provide a more exciting ride than the enclosed capsule. Thinking he was holding Kong's best interests at heart—and the expedition's, for Kong had proven a hard worker and an inspirational teammate—Wang Yan ordered Kong back into the capsule.

"All right," Kong smiled, "but only this time."

As the linked boats crashed over the waterfall, all five in the *Vanguard* were flushed overboard; miraculously they managed to swim safely to shore. The capsule was held in the giant hole, torqued and twisted by the powerful reversal for half an hour. Finally the rubber boat was ripped apart, and the lifeless bodies of Kong Zhiyi, Zhang Jun, and Yang Honglin were swept downstream through the savage waves, never to be seen again.

The five survivors stood on the cliffs above the rapid and cried.

CHAPTER SIX

The Dream Is Realized

A good beginning is
half the victory.
—CHINESE PROVERB

With Ken Warren's various false starts over the years—his 1981 association with Jack Wheeler, his 1983 debacle in Chengdu, his inability in 1984 and 1985 to raise funds for the permit—he had gone through a Rolodex of team members. So when he got word his July 1986 trip was on, he was still trying to pull together his final crew. He would later admit the time factor proved important in misjudging the dedication of some team members.

For boatmen Warren brought along Ron Mattson, Gary Peebles, William "Toby" Sprinkle, and William C. Atwood. Mattson, thirty-four, headed Cascade Frames, an outdoor equipment manufacturing concern in Monroe, Oregon, which supplied frames and other rafting essentials to the expedition. He had been with Warren in 1983 for the abortive expedition, which was grounded by red tape in Chengdu. Sometimes temperamental and used to being his own boss, Mattson was a desirable team member because of his jack-of-all-trades, fix-anything abilities as well as his boating skills—skills which eventually would prove to be in short supply on the Sino–USA Upper Yangtze Expedition.

Gary Peebles, thirty-nine, a high school biology teacher in Long Beach, California, and former owner of West Waters Expeditions, a small rafting company on Southern California's Kern River, had made a $2,000 cash contribution to the Warren Expedition to secure a seat in 1985. "I believe in your dreams," Peebles told Warren, and that—along with the money—secured him a seat for 1986. Toby Sprinkle, twenty-four, of West Linn, Oregon, was a fishing guide and camp cook who was owed some $5,000 in back pay by Warren, and was promised payment, plus an additional $3,000, if he joined the expedition. Bill Atwood, thirty-four, of Beaverton, Oregon, was also a former Ken Warren Outdoors river guide, but he was currently working as a janitor at the nearby Nike plant. He had once proposed to Warren's daughter Kimberly, and for a while had called Ken "Dad." These, then, were the boatmen— Mattson, Atwood, Peebles, Sprinkle, and Warren himself, plus the three Chinese whom Warren had trained in Oregon. Including the rafts stored in a Hong Kong barracks since 1983 and the new ones being brought over from Oregon, the expedition numbered seven rafts.

Warren knew he needed more team members experienced in expedition conditions, and he found one in Ancil Nance. The forty-five-year-old mountain climber and freelance photographer showed up in May, less than two months before the trip was to begin, assigned by *Sports Illustrated* as photographer for a "Sideline" profile of the fifty-nine-year-old boater written by Franz Lidz. Nance and Warren had never met before the session at Ken's ranch in Tualatin, twenty miles south of Portland, but each found something in the other that he could use. During the photo session Ancil asked a few questions, a technique he liked to use to keep his subjects relaxed. His curiosity aroused, he finally asked if everyone had been selected for the expedition. When Warren answered that a climber from the Indian Army had just canceled, Ancil lowered his camera, grinned, and said, "I'm a climber." The next day Warren asked Nance to join as a climber, and to back up the expedition photographer he had already selected, David Shippee.

David Shippee had met the Warrens under similar circumstances. Born and raised in St. Paul, Minnesota, Shippee began his professional career while a student at the University of Minnesota. After graduating in the fall of 1981 with a bachelor's degree in photojournalism, he landed a job in Texas at the *Corpus Christi Caller-Times*, where he won several awards. But he and his wife, Margit, were outdoorspeople who loved camping, skiing, ice-skating, and mountain activities, so he applied for a job in the Northwest. In October 1984, he was hired by the *Idaho Statesman*, owned by the nation's largest media conglomerate, Gannett Co., Inc., which publishes *USA Today*.

In May 1985, the national daily decided to do a piece on Ken Warren, assigning Laurence Jolidon to write it. They asked the nearest Gannett paper to send a staff photographer, and David, who was considered by his boss to be "the most dedicated photographer I've ever worked with," got the job. He accompanied Warren and the three Chinese trainees down the Owyhee River, and loved the experience. Warren, in turn, liked the enthusiastic young photographer, and the following May he offered David Shippee the plum job of expedition photographer.

David wrote about his first reaction when Ken Warren called with the job offer: "My body was shaking so much that I couldn't speak . . . I paced the floor, dragging the phone off the counter until it crashed to the floor. I was incoherent." The Yangtze expedition looked like it would be the big break the young photographer needed. If all went well, his photos would appear in *National Geographic*, and Warren certainly seemed to know what he was doing. Besides, if he got the assignment he would be paid $2,500 for the privilege of participating. He couldn't believe how lucky he was. At twenty-nine, he would be the second-youngest member of a historic expedition. "I still feel like I am flying from excitement," he wrote a few weeks later "—like a kid getting ready to go to Disneyland for the first time."

He still had to drive to Tualatin for a job interview, and on the way he told his concerned wife, Margit, "If it's not safe, I won't go." At the interview Warren promised there would be daily radio contact between the river party and the road support team, and that helicopter evacuation would be available for emergencies. Warren gave David assurances that their travel schedule was designed to gain altitude at the accepted rate of one thousand feet per day.

"When I heard about the helicopter, I was really relieved," Margit said. "I had some real concerns about safety." Even so, after his return to Boise, David experienced anxiety as well as excitement about the upcoming adventure. "But the scary thoughts were replaced by thinking about the beauty of seeing 20,000-foot peaks, rowing by herds of antelope and meeting the people of different cultures," he wrote.

Strangely, an earlier Ken Warren photographer had met an untimely death while flying in a helicopter. Ralph Perry, whom Warren had chosen to go to the Yangtze on the abortive 1983 expedition, worked for the *Vancouver Columbian*—the local paper for a small town in Washington just over the river from Portland. While Perry was covering the aftermath of the volcanic eruptions of Mount St. Helens for *National Geographic*, the helicopter he was flying in crashed and he was killed.

Ken Warren had agreed with John Wilcox that there would be a medical doctor along for the duration of the expedition, even though Warren had his doubts about the contribution doctors had made to expeditions in the past. Warren later wrote, in the account of the 1986 expedition that he sent to newspapers for publication, "It has been documented in diaries of other major expeditions over years past that a Doctor can do more harm than good on an expedition, because they tend to overemphasize the medical dangers and overplay their role with team members. They can actually create more fear and at times paranoia." Still, he did recognize the necessity of medical expertise, and for the 1983 attempt had hired Dr. Cameron Bangs of Oregon City, a specialist in altitude and hypothermia medicine. Dr. Bangs quit after the 1983 debacle because "I felt he [Warren] would ignore my medical advice, and I didn't want to be medically responsible for people if he wouldn't listen to me. We had several conflicts on specific issues, and he overruled my medical advice."

Earlier in 1986 Ken Warren had written to MEI, a Fresno, California–based mountain equipment manufacturer, soliciting gear donations. The factory manager, Steve Pfeiffer, called Ken back to discuss the project, and in passing Ken mentioned he was still looking for a doctor. Pfeiffer immediately recommended his old college roommate, David Gray, thirty-six, the director of emergency medicine at Memorial Hospital in Corpus Christi, Texas. The two were soon in touch. Again, Gray met Ken Warren for the first time in late May, just over a month prior to departure.

Dr. Gray made the obligatory pilgrimage to Warren's ranch, where he spent the night and heard that the doctor before him was being dropped because he was a wimp with a weak handshake. Gray had no prior rafting, expedition, or high-altitude experience, but he was an avid sailor and had an extensive emergency medical kit. By the time he left for home, he was on board. Warren was soon proudly boasting, "We have gone all the way to Corpus Christi, Texas, to choose a man we felt would be the most qualified doctor for our Expedition." Gray, too, later signed a contract with Ken Warren that said, "In the event of the need for emergency evacuation, the Chinese have assured us we will have helicopter support."

With the financial support of John Wilcox came the promise of a television coup as the lead program on Mutual of Omaha's new "Spirit of Adventure" series to be aired on ABC. Marlin Perkins's longtime second-banana Jim Fowler would be the series host, and television sports announcer Bob Beattie would narrate the two-hour-long Yangtze television specials. Wilcox himself would accompany the group overland to the base camp at Tuotuoheyan, but then return to the United States before the actual rafting expedition began.

The toughest job in the television production would fall to the field crew, and for the actual shooting Wilcox chose Dan Dominy as director of photography. Dominy candidly describes himself as cocky, but points out that this characteristic is necessary for a good cameraman. Second cameraman was to be Kevin O'Brien, who had filmed Malcom Forbes's "Capitalist Tools" motorcycle trip through China by sitting backwards on a bicycle for long stretches to get the necessary footage of the wealthy renaissance man. He knew the hardships of a difficult shoot, but they were hardships of a decidedly different nature than those he would encounter on the Yangtze.

John Glascock was the soundman, as he had been in 1983, when Warren's expedition spent a month in Chengdu awaiting final permission. In many ways, Glascock was the odd man out—an American Buddhist who was looking forward to visiting the homeland of Tibetan Buddhism. Although he was not an outdoorsman and had not camped outdoors since high school, he was willing to give this expedition a try.

The on-river film crew was rounded out by Paul Sharpe, an expert kayaker who had made several well-regarded river-running videos. Sharpe had never before used the 16-millimeter film format, however, and spent the flight over the Pacific to Hong Kong huddled with Dan Dominy learning how to use a light meter—which he promptly left on the plane upon debarking. Dominy loaned Sharpe his own and used a backup, but had few other reasons to complain about the kayaker's double skills in the coming months.

In addition to the Americans and the official Chinese rafters, there was also to be a Chinese newsman, a different one for each of the four major legs, assigned by the government to report the expedition from the boats. Of course, these men had no whitewater experience—the only Chinese with river-running experience were running either with Warren or with one of the two teams already well downriver, a month ahead of the Sino–USA Upper Yangtze Expedition.

On July 3, 1986, Ken Warren and his crew rendezvoused in Hong Kong with three tons of expedition equipment. That gear was then combined with another six tons of gear that had been stored in a warehouse there since 1983, giving his enterprise a total equipment weight of 18,000 pounds. One thing the expedition could never be accused of was being undersupplied. Warren had spent years soliciting sponsors and suppliers, and he was proud of the fact that he had recruited 110 such sponsors, even if some of the materials provided never would be used.

Three days later, the American crew of the Sino–USA Upper Yangtze Expedition took the train across the border into Guangzhou. Chu Siming, Xu Jusheng, and Zhang Jiyue waited for Warren on the other side of the border, as did part of the Wilcox film crew—Dan Dominy, Paul Sharpe, John Glascock, and associate producer Barbara Boyles. The expedition was complete. All gathered with an entourage of Chinese officials at a fine restaurant in Guangzhou for a welcome banquet to kick off the expedition. Almost at once, the bad news began.

A month earlier, Xu had been knocked from his bicycle by a runaway car, and had broken his wrist. He had taken off his cast early, so Warren would not notice his problem, but the CSS representative, Kong Qingwen, felt obligated to inform the American expedition leader. That wasn't all—Zhang had just gotten out of the hospital after a severe bout of pneumonia, a condition that did not bode well for the coming weeks at high altitude. At least Chu Siming seemed all right, alert and eager to get to the headwaters.

Worse still was the news that no helicopter support would be available, despite repeated assurances by the Chinese that it would be. Warren, well aware of his crew's particular concern on this point, neglected to inform most members of his team of this news—he mentioned it to Ron Mattson, who in turn told Ancil Nance. "Guess I don't get a broken leg on this one," Ancil shrugged to himself. If neither Ken, Ron, nor Ancil seemed overly concerned, it was a potentially serious bit of information; it wasn't the last time Warren would decide not to call a group meeting to discuss a new situation.

Finally there was the news that could not be disguised: several all-Chinese teams had already begun to descend the Yangtze from its source, with the unofficial theme of "beat the Yankees down the river." They were predominantly college students, instilled with a tremendous amount of national pride, who wanted the Chinese to be the first down their own river, even though they lacked experience and proper equipment. Warren had gone to great expense to train his three Chinese boatmen, and he even called his expedition the Sino–USA Upper Yangtze River Expedition, in large measure to avoid any charges of "cultural imperialism." But primarily, Warren was upset at this news because he thought his contract with CSS assured him of exclusive rights to run the river—a claim he would still be making over a year later, when SOBEK set out to run the Great Bend. In addition, Warren feared that since he had sold a "first descent" story to John Wilcox and Mutual of Omaha, the news of the Chinese expeditions might cause him to lose his funding at the last minute. Desperate, he asked if the different expeditions might combine forces with his group, so he could still be part of the first descent. He received no clear answers from CSS, only assurances that the government had tried to stop the student rafters, but had been unable to do so.

The morning after the banquet, July 7, the Warren group was led across the tarmac of the Guangzhou airport to the plane they had chartered, an ancient Russian Ilyushin driven by four propellers. While the last of the gear was being loaded, Jan Warren reluctantly told John Wilcox about the Chinese trips already on the water. Wilcox's reaction was the opposite of what the Warrens had expected. The producer lit up. "Great!" he said. "Now we have a race!"

After an overnight stop in Lanchow, the plane landed smoothly on the desert strip ten miles from Golmud, in the southwest corner of the Qaidam Basin. The crew and gear trucked down a cobbled road, past ponies, sheep, bicycles, and camels, to a hotel in town where they would spend three days reorganizing and acclimatizing. Several people were already suffering from the sudden change in altitude; there were headaches, nosebleeds, bouts of diarrhea, and vomiting. The thin air was dusty, and many of the locals wore filtering face masks. But excitement was high that first night, and Bill Atwood plucked his guitar and sang until exhaustion took over.

Just two days later, Warren talked to the group. Dr. Gray and others recall Warren as saying, "The doctor and I had a meeting and he said that since everyone is acclimatizing so well to the altitude, we're going to leave a day early." Dr. Gray was surprised—he had never talked to Warren about leaving early, and in fact he thought it would be better to take more time to acclimatize properly, since experts advocated climbing only one thousand feet per day after the nine-thousand-foot level. Yet it was still the start of a great endeavor, and people were just getting to know one another, so Dr. Gray decided not to contradict the expedition leader. Instead, he helped load the gear onto two Army six-wheel-drive trucks. The crew then boarded a Toyota minibus and two four-wheel-drive Mitsubishi wagons, and headed southwest toward the source of the Yangtze.

The question of Warren's schedule was beginning to arise. In mid-June, a final itinerary had been sent from China Sports Service to Warren, outlining arrival times in Guangzhou and Golmud and the departure for Tuotuoheyan on July 10. The expedition kept to that schedule as best they could, even though gaining more than one thousand feet a day once above nine thousand feet is deemed unsafe by physicians specializing in high-altitude medicine. There was nearly a five-thousand-foot gain between Golmud and Tuotuoheyan, over 260 miles of travel in eight hours. But only by sticking to the CSS schedule did Warren stand any chance of meeting his goal of rafting 1,900 miles to Yibin by the beginning of September.

They drove the whole day through the spare, denuded landscape of the high-altitude plateau. The sun had not yet set when, at 7:30, they turned the engines off at their destination: Tuotuoheyan, a town at 14,500 feet consisting of a hydrometric station, a meteorological observatory, mud-walled workers' barracks, and a concrete bridge spanning the barren banks of the Tuotuohe, thought to be the longest source tributary to the mother river. The great river so often described by Ken Warren as "the deepest in the world" was, at this point, nothing more than a shallow series of mazed and murky streams, apparently wandering aimlessly in a bed eight hundred feet wide. One of the Chinese meteorologists said the area was suffering through a twenty-year drought, and the river was at its lowest known level for that time of year. That spooked some team members, who wondered aloud if the expedition might have to be abandoned. But Warren said no, nothing would stop them, come hell or low water.

Not even, apparently, the discovery that the English-language maps of the region had been forgotten (though Warren claims they were not permitted into the country). All they had were some incomplete Chinese topographic maps, which they couldn't accurately decipher. Warren told Dominy that Lewis and Clark didn't have maps on their river exploration to the Pacific, and John Wesley Powell didn't have maps on his first descent of the Colorado. Warren compared these historic expeditions to his own. The cameraman read his attitude as being, Why should the Sino–USA Upper Yangtze Expedition need maps?

John Wilcox judged Tuotuoheyan unphotogenic, and took off with Bob Beattie and a crew to film a Tibetan horse race; he later returned briefly to base camp, only to leave for the United States shortly thereafter. The rest of the expedition stayed behind to set up base camp on the northern bank, about a mile upstream from Tuotuoheyan. David Shippee pitched in with great enthusiasm and helped the Chinese prepare *jiaozi*, Chinese-style ravioli, for dinner. But the meal was not a great success—appetites were suffering from the rapid gain in elevation, some five thousand feet in a single day. After dinner, Shippee turned to his diary: "About half the expedition party is bedridden from the altitude.

Ron Mattson is in tears . . . David Gray is moving from patient to patient frantically trying to cure everyone's ills." Later, Dan Dominy would term that day, July 10, "Black Thursday" because so many fell sick.

The weather was another cruel lesson. In twenty-four hours one could encounter four seasons, including monsoon rains, dust squalls, and snowstorms. The temperatures varied from 90° F. at midday to 23° after nightfall, which in midsummer at this latitude fell at about ten P.M. The only stability seemed to come after dark, when it was always brittle cold, and the unearthly howling of wolves was carried by the biting wind.

Though Ken Warren was not immune to the effects of the elements, as expedition leader he felt driven to keep the show on the road. Surprisingly, his remedy for altitude sickness seemed to be to keep everyone busy, and four days later the equipment had been repacked and split up into two lots: one to go with a handful of members who would journey overland to the start of the river, then float in kayaks down to the Tuotuoheyan base camp; and one to accompany the main expedition as it proceeded from Tuotuoheyan downstream in rafts. A land support team would be created at Tuotuoheyan following the kayak trip; it would be led by Jan Warren and include photographer Barbara Ries and journalist Laurence Jolidon, both on leave from USA Today, and associate producer Barbara Boyles. Her ex-husband, Edgar Boyles, the director of photography for the land trip, and soundman Alan Becker would meet Jan and her land crew for the first time weeks later in Xining, Qinghai's capital. Several Chinese journalists would travel with the overland team as well.

Toby Sprinkle, one of the paddlers slated for the source leg, had been coughing and spitting blood, suffering from the altitude. At a meeting just before the source group left, he expressed his concerns about the elevation, the cold, even about the prospects of actually navigating the river from its source to their base camp, given the shallowness of the water. Finally he opted out of the source trip and chose to stay in base camp. Warren was irritated, no less so because he had warned Toby to cut down on his smoking and drinking well in advance of the trip, and now those bad habits, he felt, were showing their effects. But when Sprinkle bowed out, Jan Warren, who had never before paddled a kayak, volunteered to take his place. Her husband was initially reluctant—her parents had invested $30,000 in the expedition, with the proviso that Jan would not go on the river. But he was proud of her determination and realized that, of all the group, only she shared his dedication to the success of the expedition. He decided she would be the first woman on the upper Yangtze—not knowing that not one but four women were members of the Chinese rafting teams ahead of them.

Ron Mattson, though suffering from a severe headache, chills, and stomach spasms, said he would go, and began welding the frames, building floorboards and camera mounts, and repairing stoves, lanterns, and a camera. Mattson and Bill Atwood would paddle the two hard-shell kayaks, which Warren had initially decided not to take because Paul Sharpe, the most experienced kayaker, had been pulled off the source team when John Wilcox decided to use him as a photographer for the Tibetan horse race in the town of Yushu far downstream.

David Shippee also felt quite ill, and confided in Barbara Ries, the photographer on a leave of absence from *USA Today*. She urged him to see Dr. Gray, but the eager young Idaho photographer was hesitant. He described his condition in his journal:

> July 12: The Qinghai province is an interesting place to vacation. This morning I thought I might die of pneumonia. Yesterday morning, I felt like I was dying. I got up for breakfast and then went back to bed. I was very weak and had a tough time walking. My lips and fingernails were blue from lack of oxygen. I was seeing spots and couldn't think straight. Barb suggested I talk to the doctor about my ills. I was reluctant, because Ken was driving him and the rest of the team like horses, and I didn't want to interfere. I just wanted to hide.
>
> July 13: Now my head feels fine, but it is difficult to breathe, and my fingernails and lips are still purple from lack of oxygen in my blood. . . . [At] about 2 A.M. my lungs and breathing tubes began to growl every time I breathed out.

Finally Ries talked to Dr. Gray about Shippee's condition, and the physician made an examination. He diagnosed a "spot" of pneumonia, or a combination of pneumonia and pulmonary edema, a condition in which lack of oxygen causes the membrane in the lungs to leak fluid into the lungs. As the lungs fill, oxygen is unable to permeate the fluid, and the victim suffers oxygen starvation. Dr. Gray announced that his patient should head back down to Golmud at 9,500 feet. The decision didn't sit well with Warren. Shippee wrote in his diary that the leader had placed Dr. Gray "on probation until we get to Yushu because he overrode Ken's authority and sent me to a lower elevation when I was sick. Ken said from now on he makes all the decisions on what to do with sick expedition members because 'I have more experience than the doctor does.' "

At about the same time, Dr. Gray examined Ries, who was also complaining of the effects of altitude, and recommended she stay behind on the next leg of the trip, the truck journey to the glacial source of the Yangtze. Warren overrode the doctor's decision, and had Ries go on the trip to the source. The expedition leader's style was becoming more clear, and tempers were getting short.

In order to get its gear to the source of the stingy stream, the group took off in two six-wheel-drive trucks on a rainy July 14 and drove seventy-five miles to the west up a muddy road along the Qinghai-Tibet Highway. Along the way, the trucks became intermittently mired in marshlands and bogged down in fast-flowing streams, and they had to camp out in the empty tundra. The plan had been to meet a Tibetan yak-and-pony team at an abandoned quartz crystal mine twenty-two miles from the source on July 17, but when the pack team didn't show, Chinese liaison officer Li Jun and a Tibetan guide, Nyima, went off to find them.

The animals and their packers, led by Li Jun and Nyima, joined the Warren camp a day later. There were seven small Mongolian ponies and seventeen yaks, the primary pack animals of Asia. Yaks can carry up to 150 pounds each at elevations up to 24,000 feet, fueled almost exclusively by the sparse glacial grasses in the region. Nyima expertly loaded the gear from the trucks onto the yaks, and the beasts—bizarre beneath the huge coolers, kitchen boxes, and elongated kayaks—headed off across the tundra.

One of Ken Warren's dreams had been to be the first white man at the fountainhead of the Yangtze, and the yak-and-pony show was devised as a cinematic way to show the pioneers reaching their goal. In fact, vehicles could drive to within a mile of the source; the year before, a Japanese climbing team had arrived that way, and proceeded to climb Mt. Geladandong successfully. And the all-Chinese Yangtze expeditions had arrived weeks before Warren in a similar fashion. Now a Chinese news crew had decided to drive to the source ahead of Ken to get some establishing shots. Dan Dominy, who also needed such shots, talked the Chinese into letting him join their jaunt, and he was joined in turn by Laurence Jolidon, Barbara Ries, and Ancil Nance. They followed the tire tracks of trucks before them, the tracks left from the Chinese expeditions that had launched on the headwaters before Ken Warren. Dominy and company arrived at the source three days ahead of Warren, got their shots, then returned to the yak-and-pony train to record Warren's "historic" arrival.

The integrity of the Sino–USA Upper Yangtze Expedition versus the necessity for Mutual of Omaha's "Spirit of Adventure" to tell a story that would attract a television audience would become a recurring source of friction. The expedition would have two masters, each battling to achieve his own goals. Dominy's usurpation of Warren's "first white man" arrival at the source was the beginning of a fissure that would grow to Grand Canyon size before the summer was out.

It was a full-moon day, Friday, July 18, when the advance party finally arrived at the southwestern base of 21,723-foot-high Mt. Geladandong. A chorus line of glaciers fed the Yangtze in this area, but one major one drained the southeastern side of Geladandong, Jianggudiru Glacier, which fed into a tiny lake called Qemo. This had been identified as the source by China's Geographic Research Institute in 1976, and this was where the Chinese team from Chengdu's Institute of Geographic Research six weeks earlier, and Yao Maoshu a year before them, had begun their journey.

Throughout the area pieces of ice assumed fanciful forms. Some members of the expedition picked out what looked like a crowing rooster, a polar bear with head cocked skyward, a monkey paddling in the water, an old man on crutches. Dan Dominy envisioned Ken and some of the expedition members stepping along the dazzling glacial ice, passing these phantasmagoric shapes, peeking into snow caves, and argued that such a scene should be set up for the film. Warren and his boatmen said no. They weren't mountaineers, they weren't ice climbers, they weren't movie stars—and they weren't interested in glaciers. They were river runners, and they only wanted to get on the river.

Around the glacial pool, Gary Peebles noticed a wooden stela with the names and dates of the Chinese teams ahead of the Warren expedition and a five-gallon can with Chinese characters. He started to take some photos, but Warren complained, apparently irked that Gary was documenting evidence that others were ahead of them in the race down the Yangtze.

For Warren, reaching the source of the Yangtze was almost a religious experience, the fulfillment of a long-standing dream. While Dominy's camera recorded his actions, Warren knelt at the edge of the gray pool at the snout of the glacier, and with a voice fractured with emotion, delivered a prayer: "Oh beautiful lady of the Yangtze, we thank you for allowing us to be here—especially for being here at your birthplace, such an incredibly beautiful place. We ask that you take care of us . . ."

Working slowly in the thin air of 17,660 feet, the team used foot pumps to inflate the seven Sea Eagle kayaks they would use, along with two hard-shelled Perception Eclipse kayaks, to float this shallow stretch

190 miles back to the base camp at Tuotuoheyan. It was hard work, and their hearts beat as if they would jump out of their mouths. But at last their motivation was clear—the reason for the last twelve days of travel, and seven years of dreams, was now right before their eyes. The trickling waters of tiny Lake Qemo slowly gathered together into the currents of the Tuotuohe, headwaters of the Yangtze.

CHAPTER SEVEN

Down the River to Heaven

A cautious halt halfway brings good fortune,
Going through to the end brings misfortune.
—I CHING

During the two weeks the expedition traveled from Hong Kong to the headwaters of the Yangtze, most of the difficulties that would later plague the team had already surfaced. There was the matter of equipment—the sheer weight and bulk of the gear Warren had brought along necessitated elaborate means of transportation, leading to unnecessary expenditures of effort and eventually making the job of portaging large rapids a monumental task. The altitude had frayed nerves and shattered the already fragile health of some team members, most particularly David Shippee. Not even Ken Warren was immune to its effects, given the fact that at fifty-nine he was nearly fifteen years older than the next oldest team member, Ancil Nance. He suffered from a wracking cough, perhaps the result of a possible asthma condition or the lingering effects of the lung worm he had picked up years before. He also had only his left kidney, having lost the other in surgery in 1980, and he had high blood pressure and a slight hemorrhoid condition.

But the greatest problem lay in personalities. Ron Mattson, initially Ken Warren's most solid ally aside from Jan Warren, had erupted in anger at Warren's leadership, as had Bill Atwood, Dan Dominy, and Toby Sprinkle. David Gray was becoming increasingly concerned about the physical health of the expedition, while Warren was growing disgruntled with the doctor's seeming reluctance to help with hard work. The altitude surely had a great deal to do with these complaints: sleeping was difficult, headaches and diarrhea were common, both mental and physical reactions were slow. Warren acknowledged that the relatively quick assembly of his crew meant that potential personality conflicts had not been adequately evaluated, and the very status of his leadership had been endangered.

Still, there they were, at their first goal, the source of the Great River. The Sea Eagles were inflated and loaded, though a yak caravan was going to parallel the team downriver to help carry the bulk of equipment. The two Perception kayaks, manned by Atwood and Mattson, bobbed in the icy waters of Lake Qemo. Dan Dominy finally announced his cameras were ready, and just before two P.M. on July 21, the team unfurled their flags—the familiar stars and stripes, the celestial banner of China, red with five yellow stars, and the Explorers Club crest—and posed for the cameras. Then they launched the kayaks, the Americans singing their national anthem, the Chinese theirs. The fourteen adventurers started downstream towards Tuotuoheyan, 197 miles ahead of them.

In the low water of the uppermost river, the going was rough. They pitched over small waterfalls, broached against rocks, paddled against fierce upstream winds. They blistered in the intense sun one minute, battled hailstones the next, all the while fighting off the burning chest pains that come with exertion at high altitude. One Chinese guide fell out of his kayak into the icy water, but was back on board in seconds. At some places the river was a mile across but just inches deep. In others, the serpentine stream divided then divided again, and then again—up to forty braids, a riverine Medusa. It became impossible to pick the correct channel despite compass help, which kept them headed in the southeast direction toward base camp; Ken Warren insisted on leading the group, and too often he seemed to pick the wrong channel.

But no matter which way they paddled, they got stuck. Those in the inflatables could hop out and drag their kayaks, some of them loaded with eighty-four-quart coolers, over the shallows. But Atwood and Mattson, sealed inside the hardshell kayaks by neoprene spray skirts, couldn't liberate themselves as easily from their boats, so they took to "knuckling" their way to deeper water—placing their fists on the riverbottom and lifting their boats with their bodies inside, up and forward, up and forward, slowly bumping their way downstream.

In addition, the river corridor was often foggy, cutting visibility to a hundred yards or less, and stinging headwinds sometimes blew the boats backwards. Nights were always cold; boots placed inside tents were frozen stiff by morning and plastic water jars burst from swelling ice. Since it was treeless terrain, meals were fueled by propane stoves, and the basic fare was freeze-dried food that had been stored in Hong Kong since 1983. The spartan meals had Ron Mattson daydreaming about ice cream, spaghetti, French bread, and chocolate-chip cookies; he silently vowed to start paying more attention to the pleasures of life upon his return home.

During this period, photographer David Shippee had been recuperating in Golmud. When Dr. Gray had diagnosed pneumonia and altitude sickness, and recommended David be driven down to a government rest house at Golmud, Ken Warren had called the doctor "alarmist"—he didn't believe David was that ill, and he wanted David to photograph the trek to the headwaters of the Yangtze and the float back down to Tuotuoheyan. But David had known he was sick all right, and took the truck down to Golmud to rest.

After three days in Golmud, in a cell-like room that smelled of urine, David received a letter written by Jan Warren, and cosigned by herself, her husband and Dan Dominy, as the film crew's representative—saying he had two choices: "Based on how you are feeling you can return to base camp and await our arrival or head straight for home. You are not free to rome [sic] around China, and we be greatly upset to heard about it [sic]. Already this [your illness] has been an added expense."

The note shook David. He turned to his diary: "I don't plan to 'ROME' anywhere in the near future, expect possibly back up to base camp." Nonetheless, by the time David received the note he was feeling better. He had little Chinese money left, having used up most of his $100 carrying cash on two phone calls to his wife, Margit. But there was enough to pay his hotel bill and buy a ticket on a public bus back to base camp. He was determined to return and finish the expedition, to prove he wasn't a pansy.

Before hopping the bus, he wrote one last letter to Margit: "We have 2,000 miles of muddy water, mosquitoes, poisonous snakes, waterfalls, and dehydrated food ahead of us." He arrived back at the Tuotuoheyan base camp on July 19, and waited for the source team to arrive. With him were boatman Toby Sprinkle, photographer Barbara Ries, and Laurence Jolidon, who was to help the Warrens with press releases for the expedition. Shippee continued to record his thoughts: "July 23: Margit's and my wedding anniversary is tomorrow, and we are 10,000 miles apart. This base camp life is crazy as it is, without my sweetheart always on my mind. God, how I miss Margit and that easy Boise life. The physical aspect of being on top of the world becomes less challenging every day, but the mental strain of life on this dust bowl is something else. I maintain a level head by reminding myself that we are not stuck here forever." Shippee had taken the last of his antibiotics, but the lung ailment that had troubled him seemed to be returning. "I am sure it is the cold/flu that everyone else got while I had pneumonia. I was healthy for 1½ years before this trip, and now, boom."

Warren had scribbled a note back at Qemo to be taken to the base camp, instructing that additional food be packed and brought upstream to the kayaks if they didn't arrive by a certain date. The camp had received the note, and David and Toby set about packing a resupply run, thinking Warren just wanted some extra supplies to supplement an already ample main stock. For the first time, but not the last, Warren underestimated the time it would take to run a leg of the river, so on July 27 the pony pack team sent from base camp met them on the river with the resupply he had requested. It was woefully inadequate, overstocked with toilet paper, paper towels, and more pots and pans. The only food was a package of pancake flour, some honey, and Tang. Warren seethed, his mood already grouchy from the recurrence of what he called his "Preparation H affliction." But the resupply team assured him they had only one more long day on the river before they reached base camp, so the next morning after a breakfast feast of pancakes, honey, and Tang, they set off.

Late on the last kayak float day, Monday, July 28, the expedition paddled into a cheering camp under an afternoon sky as bright as their smiles. To nearly everyone's surprise, a healthy David Shippee, renewed by his recovery in Golmud, rolled up his pants and bounded into the knee-deep channel to help pull the boats ashore.

Ken Warren got out of his boat and was rewarded with cold Chinese beer. With cameras whirring, Ken and Jan spoke to their prospective audience: "Most difficult thing I've ever done in my life," Ken asserted.

"Easily the most difficult thing I've ever done, ever, in my entire life," Jan echoed.

When the cameras were turned off Ken's mood reverted, and he raised his voice as he leaned over David Shippee's slim frame: "Who put together that goddamn resupply? We starved up there. I wonder whose fault that was?"

David accepted the blame, but again turned to his diary to vent his feelings: "Everybody lost at least 15 pounds apiece. Ken and Jan were pleased they lost weight. They weighed themselves in front of everybody as if to announce that losing weight was a benefit rather than a fuck-up. The resupply was not part of the plan because there was no plan."

*   *   *

The next morning Ken Warren, wary as ever of group meetings, held face-to-face meetings with each expedition member, handing them written evaluations of their performance thus far on the trip. He had complaints about the attitude and performance of several, including Gary Peebles, David Gray, and David Shippee. Peebles had not been able to get himself in shape for the trip, and Warren was concerned that his physical condition might prove a liability. Warren claimed he asked Peebles to leave at this point, but when the California boatman and schoolteacher pleaded to stay, Warren relented. Peebles himself said that he was asked to stay on and act as liaison between Ken and the Chinese. In any case, Warren could ill afford to lose a trained boatman, and Peebles stayed.

The situation with Gray was more touchy: Warren later claimed he had nothing but complaints about the doctor's contribution to the workload, was disappointed in the emergency medical kit he supplied, and questioned his judgment about David Shippee's health. By his own account, Warren had already sent for a physician with a practice in Hong Kong, Dr. Wayne Moran, asking him to join the expedition at the next major resupply point, Yushu. But other observers recall the facts differently, noting Warren was not eager to call on Moran because the doctor was from India—and Warren was conspicuously anti-Indian following his journeys to the Ganges.

David Shippee wrote his wife, Margit, back in Idaho that Warren had given him a mediocre evaluation. The expedition leader was not pleased that the young photographer had become ill and missed documenting the first leg of the trip.

Finally, Warren was upset with Laurence Jolidon. The reporter had taken a leave of absence from *USA Today*, for which he had profiled the river runner, so he could join the expedition, file field reports, and hopefully work with the Warrens on co-writing a book about the expedition. Meanwhile Jolidon had an arrangement with Mutual of Omaha to produce regular news releases. To date he had written and sent out five, none of which he had shown to Warren for editorial approval— after all, Warren had been on the source team and Jolidon had not. Warren said he wanted Jolidon to stay with the road team, but the reporter argued he should be allowed to float the river. It was an impasse. The next day Jolidon hitchhiked to Lhasa to begin five weeks of traveling solo around China.

After two days at base camp, still sticking to the schedule that CSS had supplied Warren and Wilcox, it was time to start the next leg of the expedition. A crew of fifteen was picked to ride in seven boats, including the four orange Maravia PVC rafts stored in Hong Kong since 1983, and three new gray Havasu Hypalon rafts, each built on the traditional standard of whitewater rafts, with four independent air chambers in the outer hull and two inflatable thwarts in the middle. The newer Hypalons were considered the superior boats, and they were immediately snapped up by the top American boatmen. They also named the boats, Warren again calling his the *What's Next* after his boat on the Ganges and the first wooden boat down the Middle Fork of the Salmon. Bill Atwood had painted the name *Wet Tailed Fox* on his, after a saying of Confucius: "If you want to successfully cross a river, fox, you must wet your tail." Toby Sprinkle pulled oars on the *Proud Mary*, while Ron Mattson piloted one of the Maravias, optimistically dubbed *Piece of Cake*. To the Chinese fell the task of rowing the rest of the larger, more cumbersome Maravia rafts.

Ron Mattson, with his Cascade Frames business concern, had a clear advantage over most other boatmen in knowing the best equipment available. He had urged Warren to invest in self-bailing boats, which had only come on the rafting scene in 1983. These rafts are built with inflatable floors, lashed in by open grommets, to allow the bilge to drain water without bailing. This keeps them light and relatively manageable for the oarsman. Yet because they are light, some boaters think they are more likely to capsize in big water than closed-bottomed rafts. Ken Warren did not want self-bailing boats on his expedition. He believed the old-style bilge rafts would better serve his needs in the high volume of the Yangtze, as when crashing through big whitewater they would fill with hundreds of gallons of water, each gallon weighing eight pounds, adding tons of ballast. An old-style raft filled with water may be more difficult to capsize, but it can become so heavy it is extremely difficult, if not impossible, to control in fast water until bailed—a situation that could prove disastrous.

The other members of the expedition chosen to join the run down from Tuotuoheyan included Gary Peebles, Dr. Gray, Ancil Nance, and a considerable media crew—film cameramen Dan Dominy and Kevin O'Brien, soundman John Glascock and two still photographers, a Chinese sports journalist, and David Shippee. Shippee had convinced Warren he was fully recovered and eager to join the downriver expedition: he wouldn't miss it for the world.

Among the supplies packed on the rafts were seven propane stoves and their accompanying large tanks of compressed gas; big 1,500-watt power generators and the gasoline to run them; a supply of freeze-dried food;

and thirty-seven cases of camera gear, within which were stored six 16-millimeter film cameras (including three Beaulieus at $50,000 each), two waterproof camera housings, roughly 120 rolls of movie film, battery packs, light meters, lenses, filters, and sync-sound equipment. It would be 540 river miles until the next resupply point at Yushu, for which Warren allocated eight to ten days—an average of about 60 miles a day, a highly optimistic goal. Meanwhile Jan Warren and the road crew would have to drive 1,350 miles over bad roads to reach the same place—back through Golmud to Xining, the capital of Qinghai Province far to the northeast, across the upper Yellow River, and then back down to the southwest to reach Yushu.

On Thursday, July 31—right on schedule—Chinese soldiers and local Tibetans dressed in traditional costumes staged a sendoff ceremony for the Warren group. They presented each expedition member with a red triangular scarf sent by schoolchildren in a Boy Scout–like organization from Tianjin, China's third largest city, to the southeast of Beijing. The Tuotuoheyans also gave out *katak*, pieces of silk commonly used by Tibetans as greeting gifts, then toasted the adventurers with kerosene-tasting barley wine. Speeches were made and a poem read about the cooperation between the Chinese and American expeditioners about to embark. Shortly after noon, amidst an aural hailstorm of firecrackers, drums, and cheers, the next leg was launched.

The river had risen a bit with the recent rains, but was still shallow, and the lumbering rafts had to pick through the braids, fight the upriver winds, and be wrestled over gravelbars. Still, the float was impressive. Ancil Nance later described that first rafting day on the river: "This was the river on the top of the world, still close to 14,000 feet, cutting across a plateau without trees, without permanent settlers, but not without beauty. This seemed to be the place where all the world's puffy white clouds were born, up in the dark blue sky. This was where you could see the sun rise almost below you on an incredibly distant horizon, where the darkness rolled away each dawn like a gray veil slipping down the western sky."

In the lead boat was Ken Warren at the oars, with David Shippee and Dan Dominy in the bow focusing their cameras on the leader. As he had been doing since returning up to Tuotuoheyan, Shippee threw himself into his work, quick to leap from the raft when it became grounded to help heave it back into deep water. "The channels are braided like a rope," he wrote. "We had to drag the 18-foot, heavily loaded boats across about 50 yards of sand bar . . . the task was a killer."

That first night they camped on an island. The temperature dropped below 20° F., and it snowed heavily. A blue Oshman's tent, dedicated to the expedition by producer John Wilcox, leaked so badly during the night that the crew decided to leave it behind when they proceeded downstream. Up to this point, they cultural trash disposal policies had differed radically on the expedition. The Americans always buried their refuse, while the Chinese simply threw it in the river. Now, though, the two countries agreed to gather their garbage, stuff it into bags, and deposit it in the useless blue tent. A sign was hung outside the tent, designating the island Camp Wilcox.

On the second day Ken Warren mistakenly led the group down several wrong channels that turned into sandbars and required the crews to get out and push and pull. Behind the leader's back, curses were flung whenever this happened. "A shallow river is not hard to read, but an old man of the sea is tough to order around," Shippee wrote. Because of the hangups, they made only twenty miles that day, and it was clear they were falling far behind the schedule Warren had set.

Still, there were rewards: the scenery remained wildly impressive, and they were treated to a special wildlife sighting, as Shippee's diary recounts: "Three wild asses watched us float by from a hilltop. They were beautiful, graceful-looking animals. They looked like a cross between a wild horse, a deer and an antelope. They had white, short legs with dark splotchy bodies and long manes and tails. The asses looked as if they were laughing at us as we struggled through the shallow water below them."

There was a pain in David's chest as he wrote these words. He didn't know it, but they would be the last he would ever write.

The morning of the third day, August 2, the Tuotuohe was joined by the larger Dam Qu River from the south, and the combined stream started to take on some size, making floating easier. From the confluence of the Dam Qu until Yushu, their next goal, the river is called the Tongtian Ho, meaning literally "River Going Through the Heavens," or more simply "River to Heaven." The day began intermittently sunny, though an ominous black patch hung on the northern horizon and seemed to be rolling their way. That afternoon, about 3:30 P.M., the black patch swept towards their flotilla with frightening speed, and brought with it a blizzard.

Within seconds, nobody could see more than fifty feet in any direction. Snow collected on the rafts and life jackets, and the temperature plummeted. The raft carrying Chu Siming and Zhang Jiyue slid down a side channel and got separated from the others for a frustrating thirty minutes. Warren talked to the Chinese on his walkie-talkie, but it was impossible to determine their whereabouts or the distance of their separation. Finally the blizzard lifted, and they saw Chu's boat in a nearby channel, not half a mile from the main group. The Chinese rafters had found a deeper channel than the one Warren had chosen, and after the blizzard the Americans grappled their six rafts back upstream and across a connecting channel to join the Chinese.

The sky cleared as quickly as it had eclipsed, and the temperature soared to 70°F. But the blizzard had stung David Shippee, who now sank into relapse. That morning he had moved to Bill Atwood's boat and occasionally had taken a photograph, but his movements had been forced and slow. Following the blizzard he was clearly distressed, and an early camp was called.

That night the doctor listened to David's lungs and heard the telltale wet noises that indicated excess fluid—a sign of the beginning stages of pulmonary edema, a very serious form of high altitude sickness that can quickly lead to a victim's drowning in his own internal body fluids. The only known cure is immediate evacuation to a lower altitude. On the vast, two-mile-plus-high Tibetan plateau where they were camped, the only fast way to a lesser elevation was by helicopter.

The doctor alerted Ken Warren to the seriousness of the situation and urged action. It was about 8:30 in the evening, but the summer sun had not yet grazed the horizon. Warren had the 1,500-watt portable generator fired up, attached the expedition Icom radio for the first time on the trip, and tried to make contact with his road crew. But someone had forgotten to bring the coaxial antenna, and at first the radio only spat static. About a hundred feet of conductive wire was hurriedly rigged between two oars as an antenna, and at last human voices faintly crackled.

But the tinny voices coming over the radio sounded Russian, and there was no possibility of communication. Although some said that there were assigned frequencies and times for radio contact established before the expedition set out from Tuotuoheyan, Warren himself claimed there had been no plan for radio communication in this quiet-water section. In addition, there had been no base camp testing of the equipment prior to their launch, and this lack of a radio check made any contact a shot in the dark. As it happened, the radio in Jan's truck, also missing its antenna, was packed away, unavailable to receive broadcasts. She and the land support truck were perhaps three hundred miles to the northeast, and had no idea they were being called.

Later, Gary Peebles recalled in an interview with the *Idaho Statesman* that Warren "was in his sleeping bag very casually turning the knob to see if he could hear any English." Peebles added that Warren "declined to explain to him why he didn't have one of the Chinese attempt to call for help in Chinese," the *Statesman* reported. Peebles also asserted that Chu Siming had told him Warren had been instructed in advance how to make emergency radio contact with the Chinese air force. Warren, for his own part, said that he checked on Shippee himself, bringing the bedridden photographer a cup of hot tea in his tent and covering him with his own survival suit. Shippee, still anxious about pleasing the expedition leader, apologized repeatedly for being so much trouble, but Warren told him not to worry, just to get well.

Sometime that night, Dr. Gray went back to Shippee's candlelit tent and asked how the patient was doing.

"I feel strange; I feel weird," David told the doctor.

"Do you feel you're going to die?"

"Yeah, I do."

The next morning Shippee was weak, barely conscious, cyanotic, and congested. The expedition had to move on: the only way to lower elevations was the river, though it was to be an agonizingly slow descent. Dr. Gray laid Shippee out in his sleeping bag along the front thwart of Bill Atwood's raft, a tarp slung above him for shade from the burning sun. The doctor rigged up an intravenous line, both to administer antibiotics and to provide saline solution to prevent dehydration. Shippee became delirious; he babbled that he was in Minnesota, at his old pool hall hangout with his buddies. At lunch Ron Mattson's Maravia sprung a small leak, and the group pulled in for an early camp not long afterwards. They had traveled only about one hundred miles downstream from Tuotuoheyan in four days, far short of their schedule. David was so weak he had to be carried off the boat. Dr. Gray tried to give him an oxygen mask, but Shippee could barely breathe. By nightfall he had slipped into a coma.

That night David Shippee lay in his tent semi-comatose. The radio was tried once again, but no voices spoke through the static to the desolate crew. In desperation, Warren and other crew members tried to fly a kite with the jury-rigged antenna attached. It was lifted about seventy-five feet into the steely skies. "Breaker, breaker, Mayday, Mayday. This is the Yangtze River expedition, can anybody hear me?" Ken called into the microphone. There was no contact. The doctor took Warren aside and disclosed the worst prognosis.

At 11:24 P.M., August 3, 1986, the spirited redhead died. A tearful

Toby Sprinkle broke the news to Ken Warren, who was in his tent, pitched away from the others on a knoll. "My best friend just died, Dave is dead," he sobbed.

Although Warren must have been upset, Sprinkle remembers only a callous Warren brushing him off with "What are you crying for, Toby? People die on expeditions. You could be next."

About one hundred yards from the rushing waters of the River to Heaven, Gary Peebles cried as he stabbed the earth with a shovel, digging a grave four feet deep in the hard permafrost soil. It had dawned clear, and birds were singing as the sun rose and they put David's body into a yellow waterproof bag and lowered it into the ground. There had been talk of taking the body out with them, but questions about morale and sanitation led them to agree on a wilderness burial.

The team members took turns filling the grave. A single black and yellow oar with David's name and the date of his death, carved in English on one side, in Chinese on the other, was planted on the grave. Bill Atwood started to remove the large American flag from his boat to attach to the oar, but Warren vetoed the move, saying they needed the flag for the film. So instead China's red celestial flag was hung from the blade, and below it five tiny American flags, representing David's five days on the river—including that final morning. Rocks were piled high on the grave, like a traditional Tibetan cairn; wildflowers were placed beside it. Three shots were fired from the expedition carbine as a final tribute.

In a cold and somber mood, the expedition packed up and continued. Few words were exchanged; thoughts were kept private. Dr. Gray took to reading; Toby Sprinkle hooked up speakers to his Walkman and listened to music as he rowed. Bill Atwood was morose, withdrawn, and hardly spoke a word. Later, Ken Warren would say, "It cast a pall of gloom over the expedition, to say the least. You could cut the fear with a knife. Because people realized, finally, that yes this certainly was a real expedition and people could die."

Chu Siming, who had been ecstatic at his part in the expedition in spite of the poor food and cold weather, called Shippee's death "an unexpected shock. Before, it was like a party—we felt it was a very hard trip, but the scenery was beautiful. It was a vast land, and a privilege to witness it. But when someone dies, it changes everything. You feel helpless watching someone die slowly, that was the hard part. That's the part that got to most people—they felt so feeble, it could happen to any of us, sooner or later. And the biggest water was yet to come: this was only the beginning."

Gary Peebles recalled the scene: "There was a pall over the expedition from that point on. It started to hit us that Warren's decisions could determine our living or dying. It's hard to tell what's going on in a man's mind, but it seemed to us that Warren didn't care about Shippee's death. It was an inconvenience to him, and that's how we figured he would react if one of the rest of us got into trouble. He just wanted to get the burial over with so he could get back on schedule."

Not true, said Warren. "Just because I didn't get down on my knees and blubber like some people, doesn't mean I didn't feel anything. I was just trying to hold everyone together."

With widening cracks in the solidarity of the expedition, the rafts continued to drift downstream. They began to pass terraced oatfields, hanging monasteries wreathed in mist, Buddhist prayer wheels like huge umbrellas made of twenty-five-foot poles with spokes of rope running in all directions, draped with prayer-inscribed flags. Prayer flags flapped on the crags and cliffs above them. There were also countless *mani* stones, handcarved flat rocks stacked in cairns. Whether stones or flags, their message was always the same, to be carried far and wide by the winds—*om mani padme hum*, the Jewel in the Lotus, the cardinal mantra of Tibetan Buddhism.

As they drifted by small villages comprised of brown hovels of dried mud, timber, and stone, the inhabitants would sometimes rush out to the edge of the river, waving and yelling. Some people longed to stop and visit these villages, for they were, after all, in one of the most exotic lands in the world. Only at lunch or camp did the team meet Tibetans, when black-robed nomads would venture over the sand dunes down to the expedition, bringing tea, bread, yogurt, and butter. the Americans entertained the visitors with the official expedition yo-yos, Frisbees, and balloons, even with the beeps emitting from digital watches. The big Westerner Warren handed out Marlboros, but, eager to make up for lost time and return to his sixty-mile-a-day schedule, he refused to make extra stops.

The Tongtian Ho was now similar in size and character to the Rogue River in Oregon, a narrow, boulder-choked stream, with no more troublesome gravelbars and confusing braided channels, but many manageable rapids. The landscape was still stark, however, and great black vultures wheeled in the air above them. In the fast-moving current, Warren tried to accelerate the pace of the expedition, and complained about the slow pace of his oarsmen.

Once again, having fallen behind schedule, they were running out of food. The bag of fresh potatoes, someone realized, had been accidentally placed in the Wilcox tent as a trash bag. So in the evenings, Chu Siming would head out with his rifle to see if he could find game. After days of no luck, he and Ken hiked to a nearby village, bought a live sheep from a shepherd, and toted it back to camp, where Chu shot and Warren butchered it.

Personality conflicts began to dominate the flotilla, without a doubt exacerbated by the Shippee tragedy. Toby Sprinkle had run out of cigarettes, and Warren only reluctantly doled out some of his Marlboros, which he had brought to give to the Tibetans. Warren complained about the music coming over Toby Sprinkle's Walkman, Waylon Jennings and Willie Nelson as well as rock and roll, saying "That jive-ass music is an affront to the Tibetans, an affront to the river." He also objected to reading on the boats, a favorite pastime of Dr. Gray especially, virtually demanding that everyone pay attention to the scenery.

Camp chores also became a major source of friction, as Warren complained that he, Ron Mattson, and Ancil Nance were doing all the work, while the rest of the crew squabbled like children over who would do the dishes. The Chinese were grumbling that they were given the slavish task of pumping water through the blue First Need water purifiers, a boring effort that required at least 250 strokes over ten minutes per metric gallon (four liters) of potable water, four such gallons a day. Other less labor-intensive methods of water purification, including chlorine or iodine treatment, had been rejected. "I hate iodized water," Warren had complained to Dr. Cameron Bangs back in '83, and that was that.

Meanwhile the film crew was in a state of fission. Glascock and Dominy could barely speak to one another, Kevin O'Brien yelled at Chu and Warren for holding a map-reading session without a camera present, and nearly everyone had gripes about the film crew's reluctance to help with cooking or cleaning. Their attitude was that they were paid to film, not make camp; whether or not this is a normal expectation for film crews on expeditions—and it usually is—the attitude did not sit well with several other expedition members, especially Ken Warren.

All the while, the expedition's attitude towards its leader deteriorated considerably. Warren had brought a supply of hair mousse, and Gray mocked him behind his back, imitating his fastidious grooming habits. "Ken Warren, man or mousse?" became a running inside joke.

People wondered aloud why the expedition had six stoves, five large cooking pots, and a hundred glass bottles of MSG seasoning, but not enough food. The supply was getting low as the days rolled beyond the eight estimated to get to Yushu, and morale was so low people would steal food from the group food boxes and stash it away for private use. The cans of tuna became a prize object of theft: the oil in the fish was a natural laxative, and the freeze-dried diet had many team members grouchy and constipated. In brief, things were not going well.

Their sketchy maps and estimates of the river's speed indicated they must be getting close to Yushu, but they were still days behind schedule. To make up time, they rose before sunup, when they were treated to the light flashes and streaks of the mid-August Perseid meteor shower. Then they'd row all day, everyone sharing the task—except for Warren, who had made a personal vow to row every inch of the Yangtze. They'd make camp as late as they could, and retire to their separate tents and their separate thoughts.

Finally the character of the land changed—the weather noticeably warmed, small trees began to crop up in the lower elevation, and they entered a three-mile-long canyon, their first, which they named "Top of the World." It culminated in their first rapid of any size, a Class III drop which they christened with the same name as the canyon.

After fourteen days they arrived late in the afternoon of August thirteenth at the Zhimenda Bridge, about sixteen miles from the inland town of Yushu. Here they were greeted by the road crew, whose smiles of congratulation turned to tears on the news of David Shippee's death. Jan broke down in her husband's arms. Then she told Ken her own news: several Chinese rafters had disappeared somewhere downriver, between Yushu and Batang, and were presumed drowned.

CHAPTER EIGHT

Mutiny and Recovery

The credit belongs to the one who is actually in the arena . . .
his place shall never be
with those cold and timid souls
who know neither victory nor defeat.
—THEODORE ROOSEVELT

Inside the American embassy, in the quiet, well-guarded diplomatic quarter near the heart of Beijing, Dewey Pendergrass sat at his desk facing a pile of reports. Many of them were requests from American tourists for help in obtaining visa extensions, passport renewals, the sorts of things the American consul spent most of his days taking care of. The green screen of his computer terminal glowed, a half-finished letter displayed on the screen. The phone was ringing, but Pendergrass wished someone else would pick it up. Someone did.

"Dewey, it's Jim Abrams at the Associated Press. He says he's picked up a Xinhua wire service report saying an American river rafter died in Qinghai. He wonders if we've got anything on it."

It was the first word of David Shippee's death to reach the State Department, and Dewey Pendergrass was not pleased. Americans traveling in remote provinces of China often caused him trouble, and Qinghai was about as remote as you could get.

"It became a major issue around here," the young, bearded career diplomat recalled later, as he looked through the documents in the file on his desk. "There was definitely an atmosphere of excitement. Our main concern was to verify the means of death and to see that the remains were properly disposed of, since Shippee was an American citizen. But at some point we had to know more about the expedition—just who were these people, and what were they doing?"

Pendergrass first contacted the China Sports Service, listed in the wire service report as the sponsoring agency. There, Kong Qingwen told him a highly regarded American outfitter named Ken Warren was leading an expedition down the upper Yangtze, and that he had already gone more than six hundred miles—less than a third of his projected goal. He also said that the body of the dead rafter, who had succumbed of natural causes, was buried on the river, two hundred miles from the nearest road. Getting the remains out would not be easy.

Next, Pendergrass contacted David Shippee's family. Once he convinced them of the isolation of the riverside grave, the family agreed that, for the time being at least, it would be best if the remains stayed where they were.

Pendergrass learned something else from the CSS official, something that made him contact the Department of State consular officers in the western provinces. There had apparently been a mutiny of the crew in Yushu, and four of the party had left the expedition. Pendergrass ordered the DOS to find those four men, and figure out just what in hell was going on.

Bill Atwood compares it to *The Caine Mutiny*. Ken Warren likes to scoff at it as "ridiculous," but in one revealing statement he called it a "Captain Bligh sort of mutiny." A mutiny it was—a rebellion of the expedition's crew against their leader. At Yushu, after a heated pow-wow of team members, it was voted 13–0—including the three Chinese members—that Ken Warren step down as expedition leader; if he refused, the expedition would be aborted right there: everyone would just pack his bags and head home. The vote marked the first time the entire group had acted as a team.

Dan Dominy, who knew he didn't have a film yet, spoke up and suggested they consider going on without Warren. Someone pointed out that Warren would never accept that, as he had signed an agreement with Wilcox stating that Warren must complete the expedition—or make "a substantial attempt to raft beyond the base camp to Yibin"—in order to receive the final payment of $25,000. The news took many of them by surprise. Was Warren jeopardizing their lives for his own financial gain? Dominy proposed he find a way to buy Ken's rafts and gear for $25,000 so they could continue without the leader and get on with the film. Most of the group agreed with the plan, and Ancil Nance fetched Warren from his tent to join the meeting.

The first thing Ken Warren noticed when he approached the gathering was the cameras and sound gear, set up for filming. Drawing a deep breath, he entered the circle and said, "What's on your mind?" Acting as first spokesman, Ron Mattson told Ken Warren the group wanted him to abdicate as expedition leader and to leave the trip. Mattson was to be the new leader.

Warren was shocked. He refused the request, saying it was his and his wife's expedition, it was their equipment, and they would continue downstream with or without the crew. End of conversation. He refused to meet further with the team as a group, but instead agreed to talk to members individually in his tent.

When Ken Warren stalked away after hearing a few more words of complaint, Jan Warren took the ball, and lit into the assembled group with her own litany of complaint and accusation. She had evidently recovered from the shock of Shippee's death, and was once again acting in concert with her husband to preserve their mutual dream of conquering the Yangtze. In no uncertain terms, she asserted that no weak-willed, spineless, self-interested group of so-called whitewater jocks would stand in their way—or words to that effect. Warren later wrote of his pride in her frank and aggressive support of him in the hour of trial.

That night everyone debated deep into the evening, while the Warrens stayed out of sight. Faced with the collapse of the expedition, several team members reconsidered their vote, and by the time they met one-on-one with their erstwhile leader in his tent the next morning, the decisions were relatively easy to make after all. Bill Atwood said no matter what changes were made, he would not put on the river with Ken Warren. Since Ken was staying, Bill was going home. He didn't say another word to Warren until he left Yushu.

Gary Peebles pointed out he had a wife, two kids, and a good job, and threw in the towel, with the comment that he didn't want to be a part of making Ken Warren famous. "I just didn't trust him. Rather than put myself into a situation where I didn't know how Warren would react, I chose to leave the trip. I didn't want to put up any longer with the stress of Warren's undermining and manipulation, his divide-and-conquer kind of leadership," he said. Toby Sprinkle, the youngest member of the team and one of the more capable boatmen, also left the expedition, despite his ties as a former employee of Ken Warren Outdoors.

The decision on the future role of Dr. David Gray was perhaps the most difficult. In his one-on-one meeting with the leader, Gray demanded that Warren apologize to the group for his behavior, and said that if he left, the camera crew, the Chinese, and others would pull off too. Warren remained intractable, and when he refused to apologize, Gray announced his intention to leave. Though Warren still insists he fired Gray, the Texas doctor is adamant that his departure was motivated by professional as well as personal reasons.

"Warren had interfered with my medical decisions too many times, and I simply didn't want to be around the man any more," Dr. Gray has said. "We were going to be getting into the heavy whitewater in the canyon, and it was becoming very clear that he didn't care about the safety of the rest of us. He didn't know anything about leadership. He didn't know how to build a team. He didn't know how to keep a group together."

Ron Mattson, who had not yet been paid for the frames, tables, benches, and cook boxes he had provided for the expedition, reconsidered and decided to stay. Ancil Nance, who was as a mountain climber more experienced with expedition-style travel than many of the others on the trip, also decided to remain. The film crew was told they were not expedition members anyway, but under contract to John Wilcox and thus could not decide their own fates without breaking their contract. Kevin O'Brien had become quite sick with dysentery, however, and was concerned because there would be no doctor on the river and some of the best oarsmen were leaving. He announced he wouldn't raft, but would ride with the road crew to Dege, the next checkpoint, and then re-evaluate.

Then there was the matter of the Chinese team members, Chu Siming, Xu Jusheng, and Zhang Jiyue. By now it had become clear that the Chinese, Chu in particular, were a real asset to the expedition, their lack of rafting experience notwithstanding. Though the three novice rafters had their complaints about the expedition, Chu later pointed out that the Chinese attitude towards authority is more respectful than that held by Americans—and Ken Warren was the leader of the expedition.

Still uncertain on their course of action, the Chinese called Kong Qingwen at the China Sports Service headquarters in Beijing to see if they were still obligated to go on if everyone else left. It became irrelevant once it was clear that a smaller group would continue. The Chinese were proud men, and if the Americans were going to continue rafting, they would too, to prove they could. The loss of three trained American boatmen—Sprinkle, Atwood, and Peebles—made the Chinese role all the more significant.

The four retirees gathered their gear and the personal effects of David Shippee, including his journal, passport, and a quantity of exposed film.

Toby Sprinkle gave his three Chinese friends big hugs, and said in perfect Chinese, *"Gemen, zaijian!"* ("Buddies, bye-bye"). On August 15, the four began the long overland journey to Guangzhou.

With four members gone, the crew pulled together in perceptible ways. They consolidated their gear and rolled up three of the Maravia PVC rafts. The first two legs had run short on food: now they were resupplied with fresh vegetables, canned fruit, energy bars, peanut butter, Pringles potato chips, soda pop, even beer. Everyone pored over four 1:500,000 ONC (Operational Navigational Chart) quadrant maps Edgar Boyles had brought in, the best they had seen so far—charts available at $3.50 per quadrant in map stores in most American cities, but which somehow were not part of Ken Warren's expedition equipment. This next leg would be only 160 miles, as opposed to the 540 they had just suffered through. The Zhimenda Hydrologic Station had a gauge that indicated the river was running 12,500 cubic feet per second, a healthy but by no means excessive water level, considerably less than the Chinese had found when they passed through a month earlier. It was beginning to sound manageable.

John Glascock, the soundman for the river, and Alan Becker, soundman for the road crew, got out their respective radios, attached the baling-wire antennas, tested them, and wrote down frequency numbers and prescribed 8:00 A.M. and 8:00 P.M. as the times they would communicate. Ron Mattson agreed to take over the kitchen operations. It was as if the crew members were taking matters into their own hands, and it was becoming a better expedition for their efforts.

Ancil Nance, who had only rowed one river, Oregon's Sandy, a creek compared to the Yangtze, volunteered to pilot *Wet Tailed Fox,* which because of its initials and the expedition's progress was now referred to as *What the Fuck?* Chu Siming, who later spoke highly of Nance's courage in taking over the raft despite his lack of experience, qualified his admiration: "We used to say he didn't know enough to be scared." The four Chinese would row the single remaining orange Maravia, while Ron Mattson took over Toby Sprinkle's *Proud Mary.* Lack of rafting experience notwithstanding, it would be a more cohesive group.

The smartest move was the addition of a skilled kayaker. Paul Sharpe, thirty, the Aspen videographer who had been hired to help with the on-river shooting but had thus far not made a stroke in the river, asked to join the river team at this point. He was a tough, disciplined outdoorsman who practiced yoga and was fasting one day a week to keep his body prepared for stress. Though Warren was in principle against scouting, he knew he had to compromise to keep any control over his expedition—and he also knew that several Chinese had drowned in the waters ahead. So he agreed to allow the capable kayaker Sharpe to join the trip.

But Ken Warren had hardly undergone a spiritual reawakening. He told Paul Sharpe never to kayak in front of his raft, insisting that the *What's Next* never be next, but always first, the lead boat at all times. "Your kayak does not get ahead of the rafts, and once you're in it, you're in it. We're not going to carry you out." The first admonition made no sense to Paul Sharpe; the second was unnecessary.

There were other thorns in the bed of roses. John Glascock refused to ride in a boat with Dan Dominy, and the film crew as a whole refused to ride with the Chinese boatmen, or with Ancil Nance, because their skills were inadequate. Nance shrugged it off, acknowledging he was indeed a virtually untrained boatman. Chu was more irritated and, with the compacting of the three Chinese in a boat no one else would ride in—the scorned Maravia, to boot—he was beginning to feel racially isolated. Perhaps in retaliation, he requested that the three Chinese prepare their own meals and eat together.

On Sunday, August 17, they started on the third leg. The river was slow here, slow enough for Tibetans to ply in log rafts, slow enough for Ancil Nance to gain familiarity with the oars. Too slow for Ken Warren—he was in a hurry now. Shippee's death, the mutiny, the low water, and the tiresome filming process had put him far behind schedule. The CSS schedule showed them halfway to Batang by now, two days out of Dege, their next supply stop. And he had signed the contract with John Wilcox that made his final payment of $25,000 payable upon his "substantial attempt" to complete the expedition. He assumed that meant he had to be in Yibin, still over a thousand miles downstream, by the time his permit expired on September 15. Warren desperately wanted to make that date; he had staked not only his reputation and his self-image on this trip, but all his financial resources as well.

Pushing to meet his daily mileage quota, a figure that had now soared above sixty miles a day, he clashed repeatedly with Dan Dominy whenever the cameraman insisted the expedition allow enough time to set up cameras. In addition to river footage, Dan wanted to explore some of the villages they were passing for the cultural and human angles. From Dan's perspective, it would be a shallow film if they did nothing but railroad down the river. Ken Warren and John Wilcox were uneasy partners, each with his own reason for the expedition. To a large extent, since it was Wilcox's purse, Dominy felt his filmic requirements—for cultural angles, scenic shots, multicamera shoots of the rapids the boats ran—should carry some weight. When things started going wrong with the Warren trip, Dan Dominy, representing the film production, and Ken Warren, representing his own vision of what such an epic expedition should be, clashed repeatedly. Ultimately both were disappointed.

At one point Dan Dominy saw a gorgeous tributary he thought would make a wonderful backdrop for a float-by scene. He argued with Ken Warren to stop and let him film it, and this time Dan won. He had the boats pull over upstream of the tributary; he lugged all his camera gear down to the best vantage point while the rafts and crew waited; he set up the tripod and camera, and radioed for the flotilla to set out and drift past his lens. Then, as he pressed the operating button to set the film in motion, he realized he had forgotten one thing—the camera battery. Dan didn't have the heart or guts to tell the rafters, so as they floated past, Dan duly panned his camera and waved. When he returned to the boats, he never said a word.

On the eastern bank they crossed the border from Qinghai to Sichuan, while the western bank still fronted Tibet. The scenery slowly grew greener and more dramatic. Not far downstream they encountered their first Class IV whitewater, rapids that normally take some scouting when run for the first time. They were in Tongtian Gorge, where Yao Maoshu had drowned a year earlier. As they approached a bend in the river where white whips of water licked the horizon line, evidence of a significant rapid, Dominy argued for the umpteenth time about whether to pull over. Dan hoped to set up his camera; Ken wanted to barrel on through without scouting. Exasperated, Dominy suggested they make it a lunch stop, which may have appealed to Warren's sense of how to handle these things. He pivoted the raft and pulled in above what would be named "Lunchstop Rapid."

It was a noisy and formidable piece of whitewater, with several jagged rocks from a recent slide snapping the water like wolf's fangs. Ron Mattson stared at the boils and waves, easily big enough to flip a boat, and fumed that Ken had almost had them charge blindly into a major rapid. He screamed at the top of his lungs, "I will not die for Ken Warren! I will not die for Ken Warren!"

Warren, seeing no fault in his methods and no problem with the rapid they faced, pointed out a route through from the shore. Ron Mattson calmed down, and joined Ken and Ancil in the What's Next for a near-perfect run. Placated by the success of the run, Ron walked back upstream and went next, rowing backwards, a method he often preferred as it allowed him more power in his strokes. Ancil Nance then made his first big-water run, entering a bit off center so that he was completely inundated for a few tense seconds; but he emerged upright, and rowed happily over to shore. The last raft was piloted by Xu Jusheng, with Chu and Zhang riding the bow with their fists raised high above the white-tipped waves in joy. Finally Paul Sharpe made a sweep run in his kayak, and rolled over for a few scary seconds; he came through gasping but grinning.

Only four days below Yushu, on the windy, rainy afternoon of August 21, they reached their third checkpoint, Dege, a lumber town surrounded by flowers. The land support team, by now used to their being several days behind schedule, was surprised to see them arrive on time for once. But everyone was disappointed to hear that the new doctor from Hong Kong, Wayne Moran, had not yet arrived—he had apparently been blocked by a landslide on the road to Dege. So, while waiting for him to show up, they enjoyed the comforts of beds, hot food served on tables, and a telephone, though hot showers and sit-down toilets were still too modern for Dege.

By now they had found out more about the fate of the Chinese rafters ahead of them. There was said to be disorganization and fighting among the two main Chinese expeditions; boats had been lost and damaged; the expeditions had pulled out of the river in chaos above Batang. Although five of the missing eight rafters had been found, three were still missing and presumed drowned. A rumor spread that a sixty-foot waterfall loomed downstream, in the stretch they would be rafting next. But bolstered by their relatively cohesive performance between Yushu and Dege, and reading the map to mean it was only about ninety miles down to Batang, the team decided it would be worth the risk to travel the next leg even without the doctor. They would just pick him up at Batang, and he'd be on board for what everyone expected to be the worst section of the Yangtze, Tiger's Leap Gorge.

Meanwhile, John Wilcox was getting worried. Already somebody had died on the Upper Yangtze trip he had sponsored, and the crew had suffered an acrimonious mutiny that sent three of the most experienced rafters, plus the trip doctor, packing. Wilcox knew he had to have his Yangtze River film for Mutual of Omaha's new series: his career and reputation depended on it. So while the Warren expedition drifted between Yushu and Dege, John Wilcox called SOBEK Expeditions in

Angels Camp. The agitated television producer wanted to know if SOBEK could get on the river soon, that year, so he could continue to film the Yangtze for the "Spirit of Adventure" program.

Only a couple of days earlier, we had received a telex from China denying us a permit to raft Tiger's Leap Gorge and the Great Bend for 1986. I was puzzled: things had seemed all set when last I talked with the Chinese; we even had T-shirts printed up by our freeze-dried food supplier, AlpineAire. But Wilcox's call seemed to clear up the mystery behind the sudden Chinese denial of our permit: he told us that two Chinese expeditions had launched ahead of Warren, and four people were dead, including David Shippee. It was the first we had heard of these developments, though a flurry of newspaper reports began a few days later, focusing on the death of Shippee and the riverside mutiny at Yushu.

Ready to get back in the race, and incidentally to help Wilcox with his film plans, I hopped the first plane to Beijing. There I met with a dour Qu Yin Hua, a hero to Chinese athletes for his successful climb of Everest, and the assistant general manager of Chinese International Sports Travel. I asked Qu if there was any chance we could still run our expedition. He bowed, while a liveried attendant served green tea. Qu refused to admit any causal link between the four deaths on the Yangtze and the denial of our permit, but despite my entreaties and assurances of safety, his decision was final: there would be no SOBEK trip on the Yangtze in 1986.

Frustrated, I met with Jim Abrams at the Associated Press's Beijing office, to find out more about the Chinese rafting expeditions. He showed me a stack of Xinhua news agency clippings, told me what he knew, then suggested I go to the American embassy to see Dewey Pendergrass, the American consul. Half a mile away, the young bearded diplomat was in the midst of dealing with the gnarly case of the Warren expedition, and showed me several official reports, including the interview the Department of State had held with the four mutineers—Atwood, Sprinkle, Peebles, and Dr. Gray.

On August 22, according to the report, two Department of State officers who had been staking out the Guangzhou train station spotted the four American travelers and pulled them aside. Their first step was to take David Shippee's personal effects into custody—that was a job for DOS. Then they started to ask some questions, like "How did Shippee die?" and "What was going on with that expedition, anyway?"

David Gray was the most forthcoming. He stated the cause of death as "acute mountain sickness complicated by pneumonia," and outlined the steps he had taken to save Shippee's life. He mentioned the failure to make radio contact, and expressed bitterness that helicopter support had not materialized.

Moreover, the four had some strong words about the organization of the expedition. The DOS report telegraphed the next day from Guangzhou was addressed to the Secretary of State in Washington, the American embassy in Beijing, and the American consulate in Hong Kong. It read in part:

> The four expedition members told post they withdrew from the expedition because they were extremely dissatisfied with the "disorganized" and "reckless" handling of the expedition by American leaders Ken and Jan Warren. They believe the potential for further disaster is very great. All four stressed that, in contrast to the American organizers of the expedition, the Chinese support of the expedition has been exemplary, although the skills of the Chinese raftsmen are not good. The four feel that a further disaster could imperil future Sino–US expeditions of this type.

Following his receipt of the telegraph, Dewey called the China Sports Service again. "I told them I had heard a disaster was possible, and wanted to hear some assurances that their team is going to handle it." In reply, Kong Qingwen admitted that privately, they too were concerned, but had decided to honor their contract with Warren, and let him continue.

"A little while later," Pendergrass would say, "their concerns proved justified, when the expedition set out again and disappeared."

CHAPTER NINE

Into the Canyons of Sichuan

It is harder to reach heaven
than to get to Sichuan.
—CHINESE PROVERB

There had been no Chinese journalist on the Sino–USA Upper Yangtze
Expedition voyage from Yushu to Dege, but now Chen Qun of *New
Sports* magazine joined the Ken Warren group. Kevin O'Brien rejoined
the team, having recovered from dysentery thanks to a rural Chinese
doctor who had given him an elixir in a tiny vial. So eleven rafters, with
unspoken apprehensions about the reputed sixty-foot waterfall downstream, loaded up their gear and headed out on a cold and blustery
Sunday, August 24. Ken Warren boldly announced that the ninety-mile
trip would take three days; Dan Dominy pressed for extra food, four or
five days' worth, just in case. Warren agreed to six, making it sound like
a victory.

For the first thirty miles, until they passed the village of Baiyu on the
Sichuan side of the river, the going was smooth and quiet, still enough
for animalskin boats to cross the currents. The landscape grew extraordinary, with deep green terraced fields and steepening canyons. They
seemed to be floating into a stylistic Chinese silk watercolor. In the
middle of the second day, they began to see tens of thousands of inscribed
mani stones, piled in cairns around shrines. Then they met an old
Tibetan couple who carved the stones with Buddhist sutras, living in a
simple house nearly buried by their work. Their task was endless,
repetitive, but deeply satisfying as an act of devotion. Warren commented, "I just hope they don't all say the same thing."

Later that afternoon, they hit their first large rapid in a spot where the
river squeezed into a narrow channel, accelerated tremendously, and

107

broke into a monstrous roostertail that slammed against the far wall. The team speculated that it might be the place where one of the Chinese expeditions had lost three members, but judging from later research they may have been mistaken. This was more likely Kagang Shoal, which the Chinese had overcome by portaging two boats—one of which was lost in the effort—and running it with a black capsule. In any case, though it was no sixty-foot waterfall, neither was it a piece of cake. It was easily the worst rapid they had yet faced.

After scouting, it was decided to portage one raft around the *What's Next*. Not only does Warren not like to portage, he regards it as a contemptible way to get down a river; but here he agreed to do so, to show the others how miserable portaging really could be, thus to discourage the option down the river. It took four grueling, back-breaking hours in the hot sun to portage the first boat and its complement of coolers, boxes, oars, and camera gear.

The crew agreed it was time to reevaluate. Back in Oregon, Warren and Mattson had come up with a system of rigging four rafts together in a so-called diamond rig, creating a single boat twenty-four feet wide by thirty-six feet long. They decided to try to rig here, with three boats instead of four, resulting in a rig that was eighteen by twenty-four feet—big enough, they figured, to beat what they would name "Three Boat Rapid." A similar rigging, called the G-rig, had been developed years earlier by Georgie White in the Grand Canyon, but few other contemporary boaters had ever employed such a curiosity.

The rigging took two hours. It was getting late, the last of the sunlight was quickly sliding up the canyon's walls, and Paul Sharpe expressed the opinion that they should call it a day and try the run in the morning. But Warren didn't like the idea of camping above a major rapid and having to worry all night long about things to come. He ruled they would go for it, despite the late hour.

It was about 8:30 P.M. when the rig was finally pushed into the current. Ken Warren steered from the left, Ron Mattson rode the right boat, and Chu Siming, with a handheld walkie-talkie and a movie camera in a waterproof housing, was in the middle. They filled the boats halfway with water, reasoning they needed the extra weight to blast through the first wave. Together they plunged down the tongue and into the maelstrom, gathering speed until they reached what Warren estimated at close to twenty miles per hour. They hit a wall of water that stopped them, picked them up, spun them around, and tossed their huge raft into the eastern cliff as though it were a toy.

The impact bent the steel frame and cracked an oar, sending a report loud as a cannon echoing up the canyon. They crashed through another wave, careened through a series of giant boils and whirlpools that tipped the boats on edge, rode onto a shelf rock at the bottom, and finally drifted into the quiet water with a hole in one raft, two broken oars, and a punctured propane canister. Warren declared they had gone through "the biggest whitewater on this earth," and helped wrestle the tripartite rig to the left shore several hundred yards below the rapid.

At the foot of the rapid were stationed the other eight expedition members, including Paul Sharpe, whose kayak had been portaged down, and Xu Jusheng, who had sprained his ankle helping to push the triple rig into the currents. The portaged raft was pitching in a surging back eddy just below the rapid, and it looked like a shaky place to attempt to row out, especially since Ancil Nance, who was not an experienced boater in any sense, was at the oars. Paul radioed down to Warren to request assistance, assuming that the triple rig was just a couple of hundred yards downstream around the bend. He thought it would be an easy matter for someone more experienced to walk back up and help extricate the raft. In the meantime, Ancil, John Glascock, and the Chinese tried to haul the raft out of the eddy by pulling at various angles on the bow and stern ropes. But the eddy was too powerful, and they could make no progress—no matter how they tugged or towed, they couldn't negotiate the raft out of the surging eddy. After about half an hour of trying, Paul again used the walkie-talkie to radio down to the big rig. Warren answered, saying they had moved their craft some two miles downstream to find a good campsite, and were setting up for the night on the other side of the river. There would be no help forthcoming.

It was now dark, and no headway had been made in freeing the raft. The eight tired boaters decided they would have to bivouac at the site of the stuck raft and try to extract it the next day. They had no tents, just a couple of sleeping bags, and spent a miserable night in a fine drizzle among the shoreline rocks, huddled by a fire. The next morning, their resolve renewed, Ancil, Zhang, Xu, and John Glascock climbed aboard the boat to try again. The triple rig parked downstream was carrying the waterproof camera cases, so Dan Dominy, Kevin O'Brien, and Chinese journalist Chen Qun, all carrying cameras, agreed to hike downstream from their bivouac to a point about one hundred yards beyond the rapid and meet the raft in calmer water.

An eddy is an upstream-flowing current that usually recirculates water into the main current at its farthest point upstream. If an eddy is strong, the easiest exit is at that extreme upstream reentry point. But with Ancil straining on the left oar, and Zhang on the right, they still couldn't punch out of the pulsating eddy: they just knew too little about reading whitewater, and tried to row the raft out into the main current by punching through the middle section of the eddy. But that's where the fast-flowing downstream main currents meet the fast-flowing upstream currents of the eddy, creating a nearly impenetrable barrier called an "eddy fence."

Ancil and Zhang tried again and again. Each time the raft would take on gallons of water as the eddy fence sucked one side below water level. After ninety minutes of back-straining pulls, they wearily let the raft float towards the eddy top, and heaved on the oars one last time. It worked. They broke through the upper end, the weakest point in the eddy fence, and were swept into the main current.

Almost immediately, a breaking wave swept Zhang Jiyue overboard. The raft struck the same rock that the big rig had slammed into the evening before. Ancil's oar wedged under a strap on his life jacket, holding the blade at a steep angle downward. The current grabbed the oar; a suckhole caught the left tube. As Ancil reached out to grab John Glascock's hand, the raft spun off the rock, and abruptly flipped.

"At least we got the water out of the raft," Ancil yelled to John as they surfaced near the boat, with Xu nearby. The novice rafters had no idea how to right the boat, and the upside-down raft floated down to Warren's camp with three people riding on top of the floor, using the eleven-foot oars as paddles. Zhang was still missing, and when Warren radioed up to Three Boat Rapid that he had not appeared, Paul Sharpe quickly kayaked downstream and found the wet Chinese rafter catching his breath on shore.

Those who had opted to walk downstream now had to trek even farther to reach the main camp. Slowly, they worked their way down the left bank, until the walls became too sheer to continue. So Paul Sharpe paddled back upstream and ferried one camera across the river, then another, then the rest of the gear, and finally the crew, one by one. Once on the right bank, they started to negotiate downstream, but soon the boulder-strewn shore on that side grew narrower, and finally transformed itself into an imposing and impassable sheer canyon wall, polished by millions of years of floods.

Once again, Paul Sharpe became a ferry, loading one camera onto his deck and paddling a mile down to camp. Then, using the eddies and still water next to the shore, he paddled back upstream to repeat the ferry with the second camera. Dan Dominy, Kevin O'Brien, and Chen Qun waited at the base of the cliffs until, with coaxing from Sharpe, they jumped in the now relatively tame river and floated to camp—first Chen Qun, then Kevin O'Brien, and finally Dan Dominy.

Everyone was reunited, but the full extent of the damage had not yet been determined. Turning the flipped boat over, they discovered several missing oars, but worse yet, when they turned on the shortwave radio for the evening transmission, something shorted out, and acrid blue smoke wafted out. They were now, once again, out of radio contact with their land team. It was not a cause for celebration.

That night everyone huddled next to a fire in an abandoned Tibetan stone house near the river. Though Warren didn't apologize for failing to help Ancil's crew when it was in trouble, he did publicly praise Paul Sharpe for his competent assistance, and asked the bearded, bespectacled kayaker to act as scout from then on, paddling downstream ahead of the rafts to radio back reports on the upcoming rapids. Some thought it was a large and humbling concession coming from the big man.

Somewhat recuperated and repaired, they set out the next day, August 27, under sunny skies, and made forty quick river miles before a charging tributary burst into the Yangtze, swollen from monsoon rains and brick-red with silt. They called it the River Red, and it significantly boosted the volume of the Yangtze while staining it a rust color. Soon after the muddy tributary, Paul radioed back to the rafts. "You guys better get pulled over. This is definitely the biggest whitewater we've seen so far.'"

It was about six P.M., the end of their fourth day down from Dege, and they guessed they still had twenty or thirty miles to Batang. The rafts were pulled over to the left side, in Baiyu County, Sichuan, beneath a tributary trickling over a ledge and into the mother river. The crew scampered up the bank to scout the rapid ahead. One look at the giant haystack waves rolling at least a hundred yards downstream convinced them something drastic would have to be done.

Rather than attempt another late evening escapade, they pitched camp and decided to cook up a big meal to enjoy before tackling the rapid the next day. They fried up the last of their potatoes and onions and some canned chicken and rice, and feasted. Ron Mattson suggested this as the place to rig the four rafts together in the unconventional diamond shape. The next day he went about the rigging, strapping the various D-rings and frames together and wrapping four lengths of 11-millimeter static line beneath the center. The result was a Godzilla raft, huge and seemingly unflippable. And, as it was to prove, virtually uncontrollable.

It was Thursday, August 28, their fifth day beyond Dege. While Mattson finished rigging the boats, Ancil Nance led Dominy, Sharpe, and O'Brien on a difficult trek to the top of the cliff overlooking the rapid so the cameras could be positioned for the best possible shots. Each carried a forty-pound pack filled with various cameras, tripods, walkie-talkies, batteries, magazines of film, and a survival kit, in case they became separated from the rig. Over four hours later, long after the rigging was done, Dominy finally radioed down to the boats that they were ready.

Ken Warren was positioned on the left oar, Ron Mattson the right. Xu and Chen rode in the center, where John Glascock wielded a handheld camera; the other Chinese, Chu and Zhang, shared the oars in the rear boat. After four anxious hours of waiting, they made a final check of their rigging, life jackets, and oars, then dropped into the white hell of the cataract.

It took them just forty-six seconds to plow through the rapid. The television film of the rapid shows the big boat dwarfed by the scale of the rapid, but it also seems to show a sizable area of relatively shallow, slow-moving water along the right bank, where a single boat might have been able to make a harmless "cheat run." Warren, however, elected to attack the rapid down the middle, through its heart, through waves Ron Mattson estimated at twelve feet high, Warren at fifteen feet or even higher. Chen was washed out the back, his camera ripped from his neck, but he managed to hold on to a rope attached to the raft for the rest of the ride. But the big rapid was run, and safely.

Paul Sharpe watched the huge boat as it was swallowed by the roaring waves of the river. Then he left his camera with Ancil, walked back upstream to his red kayak, slipped into the seat, sealed the spray skirt, and pushed off. He headed straight into the heart of the monster rapid, and slipped between, into, and through its waves with experienced ease.

But the chaotic water took its toll on the diamond rig, which filled up with water and became so uncontrollable it drifted for two miles before the four oarsmen managed to pull into an eddy fronting a sandy beach. Ancil Nance took Paul Sharpe's camera, Dominy and O'Brien took their own, and they started scrambling down the pathless, rocky cliffs towards the distant beach. Three hours later, sometime after four o'clock, they finally joined the diamond-rig crew, and found a furious Ken Warren waiting. From his point of view seven good hours of potential rafting time had been spent capturing forty-six seconds on film. They had made just two miles so far that day, and had a thousand miles to go. The pace just couldn't cut it. He insisted they get back on the big rig and head out downriver. Dan Dominy was too beat to change the film in the cameras.

So into the early evening they rowed, Paul Sharpe scouting out front with walkie-talkie in hand. It was to prove a mistake. Even Warren later admitted it was virtually impossible to pull over the heavy four-boat rig and stop, should there be danger downstream. Not long after they started again, Sharpe called back on the walkie-talkie. "You better pull over on the left. I can't see around the corner, but I can see a horizon line with spray kicking up and it could be bad."

By this point the rafts had bounced through a few small rapids and were already burdened with water in the bilges. Now, more than ever, the self-bailing boats that Mattson had urged would have proven their value. The rig was too heavy and unwieldy to pull over at such short notice. They hurled around the sharp corner, bounced off a rock the size of a house, and continued pell-mell downstream—dropping into holes, hurtling through haystacks, out of control on the Great River.

CHAPTER TEN

Four Oarsmen of the Apocalypse

When the going gets tough,
the tough get going.
—VINCE LOMBARDI

The waves downstream were so powerful that stroking through them took all the strength the rowers could muster. In order to pull on the oars with both arms while staying in the boat, a system was quickly improvised by which Kevin O'Brien sat next to Ron Mattson, holding him in; similarly, Ancil Nance held on to Ken Warren. Warren yelled orders over the chaos, a General Custer surrounded by savage waves. Everyone worked like demons as the barge nipped the corner of one enormous keeper hole, then dropped into others. Chu Siming and Zhang Jiyue were washed out of the diamond rig in some of the big rollers, but both were quickly pulled back in. Dan Dominy grabbed pieces of broken frame, twisted them off, and threw them in the river before they could puncture the rafts or passengers. He jettisoned the bulky propane canisters that kept getting in their way: they weren't cooking with gas anyway, but using wood fires.

Ancil was thrown into an opening between the lashed rafts, where he lay for a second in the eye of the storm; then he scrambled back to his post. Warren was launched to the bow of his raft, but in lightning time leapt back to his oar. "Hang on!" Warren bellowed, and Ancil grabbed him securely. Warren braced his feet, wrapped his big hands around the oar handle, and put his back into a mighty stroke. His stroke was more powerful than white ash—with a crack the oar snapped. Ancil briskly unlashed the spare oar, and Warren fitted it into the oarlock and began stroking again.

The recollections of the crew are both vivid and sketchy, deeply imprinted and random. They barreled past Paul Sharpe, riding his kayak in a surging eddy. Their wild ride down the Yangtze continued, past bend after bend in the river, through rapid after rapid, for an hour and a half of madness. The boats were constantly full of water; it was impossible to bail in the chaos, and the floors of the rafts sagged from the weight in the bilge. Controlling the cumbersome craft was out of the question; it was like trying to row the *Titanic*. "It was like getting on a train without any stops," summed up Chu Siming.

When they finally managed to pull over at a sandy cove, they took stock of the damage. A Pelican waterproof camera case had been crushed, a camera housing smashed. Frames were bent and broken, a hole yawned in a Havasu, two gashes tore open the Maravia. Ron Mattson had lost his favorite river hat. Incredibly, despite scratches, bruises, torn muscles, and general stress, no one was badly hurt. "Altogether, not too bad," commented an exhausted Warren, "considering the *amazing* water we just went through."

A cheer went up as he spoke. Paul Sharpe had come into sight, for the first time in half an hour. For him, it was an equally reassuring moment: in an eddy near a hole a few miles upstream Paul had found a broken oar, and feared the worst. Ironically, in his comparatively tiny kayak, Sharpe did not have such life-threatening problems. He could work with the currents, pull into the eddies when he needed a respite. Later, Ken Warren estimated they had dropped 150 feet per mile in this stretch; Paul Sharpe hesitantly guessed 50 feet, at the most. Warren gauged the water flow at 100,000 cubic feet per second, on a par with the glacial-draining rivers of the Northwest, like the Frazier; Sharpe thought it was closer to 20,000. Sharpe later said of his solo kayak run of the stretch, "It wasn't so tough. It reminded me of the Colorado through Cataract Canyon." Cataract's flow usually peaks at around 40,000; its whitewater section drops 14 feet per mile, with one three-mile-long stretch of 29 feet per mile. In any case it was big water: the Yangtze was flexing its muscles.

The next morning they rose stiffly, licked their wounds, dried out their gear, and slowly worked up their energy for the day. Mattson and Nance set to work fixing up the big rig again, strapping together the broken frames and patching the torn tubes. Warren blamed the Maravia's rips on the PVC material, feeling it was not tough enough for the weather extremes of high elevations and the enormous pressure put on the material by the Yangtze rapids. Others noted that the oarlocks had not been removed in this cumbersome rig, and it could easily have been the pins that punched and tore the tubes. There was ample patching material, however, and nobody was too worried about the boats—until Ron Mattson confessed that somehow, back at Yushu, with all the confusion of the mutiny and consolidating the gear for the four boats and everything, he had forgotten to bring the repair material for the PVC boats.

Stitching together the fabric and using Hypalon swaths, they did manage two makeshift patches, though they knew the repairs could not be relied upon to hold. Running low on food as they were, and believing their wild ride down the river must have brought them within striking distance of Batang, at three P.M. everyone climbed back on the rig, and they pushed off into the current. Everyone felt lucky to be alive, and agreed there was no way they could ever afford to get out of control like that again.

As they were preparing to launch, Ken confided to Paul Sharpe he had a gut feeling they'd been through the biggest of the rapids. Paul didn't answer, but silently he disagreed. It was August 29, the sixth day out of Dege. Though they had tried to conserve their food, they had only packed enough for six days and were now dangerously low on supplies.

They continued downstream into the canyon. It got narrower and steeper with each mile. Again Paul Sharpe kayaked ahead, alone, maneuverable, out of sight; he radioed back reports to Warren and crew in the ponderous barge. After a nervous hour of travel through a handful of sizable rapids, Paul called in to report a very bad rapid ahead, with an enormous hole yawning across the river. At first he got no response, and wondered if anyone had heard him. Then the walkie-talkie spat to life. The big diamond rig was close.

Luckily, the four oarsmen were able to pull the massive raft over. Warren climbed up the bank and scrutinized the rapid. The water roared and twisted like an angry dragon, then dropped into the mouth of the monster hole, which swallowed up half the river, chewed it up, then spit it and hungrily reached out for more. Somebody dubbed the maw the "Buddha Hole," perhaps because it promised pain and suffering, and Nirvana was on the other side. Although we may never be able to ascertain this without doubt, it seems this was known to the Chinese rafters as Yela Shoal—the rapid that had held the enclosed capsule recirculating in its midst for half an hour, drowning its three occupants.

But the Chinese had been through a month earlier, at higher water; and the Americans were unaware that this was the fatal rapid. The accumulated wisdom of the party's boatmen perceived a slot on the right side of the Buddha Hole, and Warren felt positive the diamond rig could make it. So, after silent prayers, the four oarsmen rowed into the impending apocalypse. The raft slid down the dragon's tongue, transmigrated down the side, skirted the edge of eternity, and slid through to safe reward.

After the Buddha Hole the expedition stopped, scouted, and ran two more large rapids. The water then ran calm for about a half mile, but around five o'clock Paul Sharpe's voice once again crackled over the walkie-talkies in the diamond rig: "Ken, I am not kidding. You better get pulled over to the left. There is monster whitewater ahead. There is no way on this earth you're going to get through this."

Sharpe's call came too late. The diamond-rig crew started trying to move their huge boat to the left shore, but the water accelerated too quickly, and the rig was too unwieldy to catch the small eddies against the rocky left wall. The boatmen could see the plumes of waves cresting beyond the river's horizon line. The current pulled them ever closer; they gave up trying to pull to shore and straightened the boat for the rapid. Then they dropped over the edge.

Warren's raft careened into a boulder near the left shore, tearing a fifteen-foot gash in the double-layered floor; then it pitched over a ten-foot waterfall created by a jagged shelf. The underside ropes connecting the rafts snapped and the rig spun sideways, plunging into a savage chaos of whitewater. They rode over the first wave, which unceremoniously hurled Chu Siming and Zhang Jiyue overboard. A lateral wave punched Ron's boat and lifted it up on its side, tossing Ron and Kevin all the way across the center raft into Warren's. Then, almost comically, Warren's boat was lifted up, and Ron and Kevin flew back over the middle again into Ron's boat. With another wave, the left wing of the diamond rig was wrenched over and folded entirely underneath the other three boats, and the world dropped out from beneath Ken Warren and Ancil Nance.

"What's happening?" Ancil screamed.

"I don't know," Ken sputtered. They were in the water, clinging to the twisted frame of their flipped boat as it climbed and dropped through the mountain range of waves.

Dominy tried to pull them in, but couldn't reach them in the chaos. The huge lame rig was being swept towards a wall on the left bank. John Glascock was certain the left side would get smashed into the wall; Chu Siming saw no way the two helpless men clinging to their sunken boat could survive the collision. But somehow they swept by the cliff—

perhaps a pillow wave pushed the boats back, perhaps the Yangtze was merciful at last—and Ancil Nance and Ken Warren missed death by inches. They hung on for an agonizing ride through a hell of whitewater, until the rafts at last dropped into slow water, where the crew was able to pull the rig into an eddy just two hundred yards above another huge rapid. Once again, they had been out of control for over an hour.

"The turbulence, the awesome power of the Yangtze River was tossing our big thirty-six-foot raft around like it was a toy," recalled Warren. "This had a drastic effect on the people, no question about it. By the time my boat was turned underneath the other boats, there was definitely apprehension and fear created by what had happened to us. They were realizing the power of the Yangtze River, they were feeling the power of the Yangtze River."

They parked the wounded rig in a rocky stall. They'd been on the river only a few hours that day, and nobody would hazard a guess at the miles they'd run. They unloaded the rafts and set up a desperate camp on the narrow rocky ledge, then rigged up a pulley system to turn Warren's damaged raft back over. When they took inventory, they found little missing: a couple of tripods, a life jacket, Ancil's orange survival suit, and most seriously, some of the precious food. The condition of the boats on the whole was not encouraging. Many of the tubular steel frames were badly twisted, and two of the four boats were badly damaged. They had started the trip with twenty oars, and were now down to nine—enough for one spare among the four boats. "I saw more stuff torn up in two hours than in twelve years of river running," Mattson said.

Everyone was shook up by their latest chaotic rush through the canyon. Most suffered minor injuries, scrapes and bruises on knees and ankles. John Glascock was in tears; Ron Mattson was close. Suddenly the rumors of a sixty-foot waterfall downstream resurfaced—perhaps they hadn't yet seen the worst of the whitewater, perhaps they'd never make it to Batang. The hungry, exhausted rafters could see how, if they continued in this headlong, anarchic fashion, they too could be swept over the falls to their doom.

Not Ken Warren. Consulting the rough Chinese topographical maps he still had, he noticed they were closer than ever to Chinese airbases. Warren said he had another gut feeling, that helicopter support would be arriving soon, arranged by Jan Warren and the land crew. In fact, he suggested, he couldn't figure out why helicopters hadn't arrived yet. "I can imagine that she's having tremendous problems or else we would have some support in here," he told Dominy's camera during a campsite interview the next day. "And I don't know what those problems are. I have no idea. I talked to Chu at some length this morning. They [CSS] have gone through everything that is needed for helicopter support that I can see. Somehow we're not getting that support. It's far beyond me. I know Jan, and I know that she is raising all kinds of the devil to get us some support, I'm positive of that, but I can't understand, really truly understand, what's going on and why we haven't gotten it. We should have support right now," he concluded, looking around at the silent stone walls.

Ken Warren had complete, if unrealistic, faith in his wife. A couple of months earlier, while making final preparations back in Oregon, Warren had written to John Wilcox of his wife's talents. "She is the boss. Jan has gotten along with all of the Chinese extremely well and Kong Qingwen [of CSS] likes her very much. Chinese respect women and Jan will get more done with her blonde hair and all-American good looks than any male could dream of accomplishing." Even if this were true, the Warren equation did not factor in a critical item: helicopters just were not available.

Warren had been told this upon his arrival in Guangzhou, nearly two months ago: China Sports Service had not been able to get helicopter support from the government. He neglected to inform all of his crew of that information, however, and when things got tough—as David Shippee lay dying, and again when the shattered expedition lay exhausted on the rocks in the depths of a canyon in the middle of Baiyu County—Warren offered the chimera of helicopter support. Perhaps he thought that since his expedition was sponsored by the state sports agency, when an emergency arose the government would come through with a rescue. Perhaps he thought his wife's good looks would come through in a clinch. Perhaps he thought that as an American, he deserved rescue. Whatever he thought, he was wrong.

He tried to convince his crew to keep the faith, but found finally that the leader had no followers.

Paul Sharpe listened to Warren's promise of helicopter rescue, and didn't believe a word. He had spent the last two days kayaking alone, and decided he would continue downriver to Batang and try to arrange for a rescue party. The next morning he paddled his kayak down to the next rapid, just two hundred yards downriver, then pulled over and thought about it. Not knowing what was around the bend, traveling alone down an unrun river was never good wilderness technique. He decided he'd have a better chance on the ground, so he paddled back to camp and announced he was going to hike out and see if he could recruit a rescue mission.

Warren tried to talk him out of it, unwilling to see his expedition break up, perhaps sensing that any cracks in the veneer of their hard-earned solidarity would be followed by others. But Sharpe was determined. Chu wrote a note in Chinese for Sharpe to show anyone he found: "American with Sino–USA Yangtze team—need food and help and repair kits." Then Sharpe kayaked over to the Sichuan side of the river, pulled his red Perception up into the rocks above the high water level, and climbed hand-over-hand out of the canyon. He headed south, wearing a cap and a waterproof dry suit with a blue wet suit top, carrying only a fanny pack filled with two cans of tuna, a small water bottle, a water purification pump, a spare sweater, and a pair of binoculars. He was used to fasting, and could move quickly with little gear. It was Saturday, August 30.

Shortly after Paul left the canyon, the rest of the group sighted a bear swimming down the river. The black beast crawled out on the Sichuan side, at almost the same spot where Paul had hiked out, and stood there dripping, as if trying to pick up a scent. It seemed a bad omen.

That same morning Ron Mattson, Ancil Nance, and Chu Siming hiked downstream on the right side to scout the rapids while Warren stayed behind, trying to repair the floor of his ripped boat with Xu and Zhang's help. In the afternoon, the scouting group returned and Ron announced that the rapids ahead looked runnable. But just two hours later, Ron changed his mind and told Warren that the river ahead was not necessarily runnable at all. Instead, he said, he and Ancil should hike farther down the river and make a more thorough survey. If the river looked impassable they would continue to hike out for help; if it indeed looked runnable, they'd be back to ready the boats for the continued expedition.

Warren, skeptical of Ron's change of mind, decided to see for himself what the river held in store. So after Ron and Ancil left on their second downriver survey two days later, on September 1, Warren told Dan Dominy he was going to hike downstream and judge once and for all whether the upcoming rapids could be run or not. Dan said he would join him for at least one day to film the expedition leader's hike. In preparation for the purported overnight scout, Warren packed up an enormous backpack that included his exposed film, a lightweight

Mountain Safety Research stove with a quart of gas, the rainfly for his North Face tent, a sleeping bag, a survival blanket, a full-body pile suit, Gore-Tex raingear, and a microcassette recorder, into which he would record his impressions. He searched the expedition's gear several times, possibly for one of the pumps to purify drinking water, but apparently couldn't find one. He settled instead for two large water bottles.

Ken Warren detests backpacking. "I believe that mules and donkeys and those kinds of animal were put here on earth for packing things," he has stated. Nonetheless, he hefted his bloated pack onto his back, and started to hike out of the canyon on the right side of the river—the Tibetan side, opposite from where Paul Sharpe had exited. Dominy, carrying a film camera with one lens, extra film, energy bars, some water, and one of the film crew's two water purifiers, hiked with him. Hence, the details of the next few hours are based on Dominy's recollections.

Since Ron and Ancil were somewhere scouting downstream, close to the river, Warren figured it would be better to take the high road, where he could get a broader vantage, so instead of heading directly downstream, he began to lead Dominy upward. Halfway out of the canyon, they passed a spring, where they replenished their water bottles; soon, with his lighter load, the cameraman easily passed and then beat the fifty-nine-year-old boatman to the canyon rim, where he waited and rested for a few minutes. Then Dominy began to hike back down the trail to see what had become of Warren. As he approached, Dan yelled out to locate Ken, and heard the boatman bellow back, "I can't go on without water!"

His voice rang through the canyon, fueled by urgency. When Dominy reached Warren, he offered him his half-full water bottle, one of two small ones he had brought along for the hike; Warren reached out and downed it all. Dominy got mad, and suddenly the two men found themselves arguing over the most basic of physical needs, and their already strained relationship seemed close to the breaking point. Dominy turned angrily and went back to the top of the canyon.

But as night approached, Dominy began to worry that Warren had not yet appeared. He hiked back down again, and found the big man stumbling up the trail without his pack.

"Where's your pack?" asked Dominy.

"Down there," answered Warren, and they both walked fifty yards downhill, where the pack lay open, its goods strewn about. Warren grabbed a can, one that had lost its label, opened it part way, drank the liquid—then spat it out distastefully. It was canned Chinese asparagus, not the kind of liquid relief Warren expected.

Dominy decided he should help Warren carry his backpack up the hill. He hefted it, and almost buckled under its weight—he guessed it to be close to a hundred pounds, though Warren said it was seventy-five. But there was no way to measure it, and really no reason to; Dominy trudged up the hill, and Warren followed.

When they reached the top, Dominy gave Warren another half-full water bottle, which the boatman immediately drank dry. Warren told Dominy to go ahead and fix himself dinner from the backpack's supplies, then he pulled his sleeping bag out of the pack, and with his own two large empty water bottles headed back down towards the spring.

Dominy opened the bulging backpack and was astounded by what he found there. In addition to cans of tuna and asparagus, dehydrated soup, instant coffee, and sugar—all of which might be considered necessary for survival—he also found two sets of kitchen utensils, two pairs of binoculars, an extra pair of boots, a can of Raid insect repellent, a glass decanter of hand lotion, and a toilet mirror.

In the morning, Warren appeared, but without his sleeping bag—he had left it at the spring, returning only with the water. Dan said he was heading back to camp to make arrangements to get the camera gear and crew out. Then Warren dropped a bombshell: he told Dominy he was going to hike out by himself, to get "braver boatmen" and "bigger boats" to complete his journey. He urged Dominy to join him and continue on out, but the cameraman said he had a firm commitment to his crew to return.

Warren started to pack up his gear, abandoning some of the clearly extraneous goods, but picking up Dominy's water pump and putting it into his pile of things to take. Dominy objected and took it back, saying it was the film crew's, not the expedition's, and he didn't know what kind of gear was left back at camp. Warren went about packing, but a few minutes later slipped in the water pump again. Again Dominy took it back, angry and unwilling to share this one piece of survival gear that Ken Warren seemed most urgently to crave.

Finally they split up for the last time, and Warren walked away, to the south. Ken Warren had abandoned his expedition, without a word of parting to the crew he had led into the depths of the Yangtze's unknown canyons.

CHAPTER ELEVEN

"To Have Tried Is Enough"

> Fortune brings in some boats
> that are not steered.
> —WILLIAM SHAKESPEARE

When Dan Dominy got back to camp later that morning, the crew was astounded to hear that Ken Warren was hiking out. Astounded, perhaps, but not really surprised. Warren's credibility had been steadily eroding, and his position as expedition leader, while still accepted, had become almost titular. Whatever happened from here on in, in any case, the ragged band would have only itself to answer to—or to blame. Besides, hiking out just didn't seem like such a bad idea. Chu Siming, for one, gave high marks to Dominy for even returning himself.

Ron Mattson and Ancil Nance had returned the night before after a ten-mile second reconnaissance, and were ready now to make a try at the river. Several crew members were sick; the pots and pans hadn't been cleaned, flies were buzzing. Their nine tons of equipment had been reduced to a few hundred pounds of worn and broken gear. The original crew of twenty-nine at the Tuotuoheyan base camp was now just nine. They had only run two days of big rapids, but it looked like the exhausted last hours of the Hundred Years War. They had no leader. Here were the remains of the Sino–USA Upper Yangtze Expedition.

The group called a series of meetings, and argued as to whether they should hike out as well, or try to raft on. Their scarce food was dwindling, but until the sick team members got better they couldn't move. Ron and Ancil began to get impatient, and threatened to launch downstream together, but Chu talked them into staying, sticking together as a group no matter what happened. On the fourth day at the rocky camp, they finally agreed on something: they blew up a life-size, anatomically correct

125

inflatable female doll that Warren had brought along as a joke. The Chinese were worried about the propriety of the doll, so the team dressed her in a jacket and Speedo swimming suit. On her cheek, she bore the message *THE BOYS NEED HELP.* Since she would float on her own, they sent her downstream. Surely she would get attention, if anyone ever found her.

On Wednesday, September 3, they decided to proceed cautiously downstream, one rapid at a time, one raft at a time, scouting everything, with no leader to tell them otherwise. For the first rapid, just two hundred yards down from camp, they emptied the orange Maravia, strapped on a swamped camera and its broken housing, then cut the craft loose and kicked it into the current, sending it downriver with no driver or passengers. A ghost boat.

The ghost made a perfect run of Five Day Rapid, then disappeared around the corner, on its lonely solo voyage downstream. Ron, Ancil, and the Chinese followed in the three other rafts, while Dan Dominy and the film crew decided to walk around and film. Ron had an oar torn from his grasp by the river, Ancil's boat smashed into the cliff, and Chu was flushed out by a wave. But all survived, and the rest of the crew boarded the three rafts and headed downstream for a four-hour roller coaster ride. They made camp that night, feeling oddly exhilarated at their progress.

By noon the next day they had rafted about nineteen miles from Five Day Rapid, and began to think they might actually reach Batang, whose name by now had all the glowing connotations of Oz. Then they came to another rapid—a huge souse hole roaring and spitting at the end of a tongue, a fiendish keeper that leered across the middle of the river, daring the foolhardy to try their luck.

The boatmen stared at the hole, and stared some more. It looked tough to miss. They set up camp. They talked of lining the rafts down the side of the hole. Ron Mattson hiked downstream to scout, and returned saying he thought the boats could be wrestled over the basketball-size rocks on the far side. The Chinese rafters thought the current was too strong to get to the other side; the film crew didn't want to run it at all. Only Ancil Nance, with his "Damn the torpedoes, full speed ahead" attitude, thought they should go for it.

Nobody could agree. They debated and argued, adding up figures from the sketchy map that Chu produced: this fourth leg was to be ninety river miles, and perhaps they had done seventy-five. But the map indicated they had at least one hundred river miles to go. They figured they could hike the overland route in six days, seven at the most. Surely they would meet people, find food. But if they headed into the narrow gorge ahead and got into trouble, that would eat up time, and it might take longer to get out—if they could. And what about that sixty-foot waterfall? It was a specter that wouldn't go away.

They were down to coffee, noodles, rice, and pancake mix. This section was remote. They hadn't seen any villagers in six days. Nobody had emerged as a leader; nobody was making decisions. They argued incessantly. John Glascock became sick, then Ancil Nance, up until now the strongest member of their group, came down with dysentery. The others had come to look up to Ancil as a group touchstone; Ron Mattson took special care to bring him purified water, hoping to revive the downed climber. Finally, after a wasted day of debate and delay, they agreed to abandon the rafts and hike out.

The decision disturbed Mattson the most. He had been on the aborted 1983 expedition, and it had been painful to return to inquisitions about the expedition's failure. He didn't want to undergo that ordeal again. But he found solace in a book he was reading about General Joseph Stilwell, who commanded Chinese troops in the Second World War in Burma. The book included a quote from Erasmus, the sixteenth-century Dutch philosopher: "In great things, to have tried is enough." It became Ron's internal credo.

The three rafts were hauled up onshore and tied to the rocks by Ron Mattson. They attached notes to the boats, in both English and Chinese (they knew the only language spoken in the area was Tibetan, but nobody knew any Tibetan), saying they were hiking to Batang. Since they wanted to travel light, most agreed to leave behind their extra clothes or accessories, and even sleeping bags, taking just the light inner bag liners. They carried one stove and some fuel; a few soup and noodle mixes, their last six meals; and two walkie-talkies, one for the lead hiker, one for the rear.

Dan Dominy filled an orange 50-millimeter waterproof ammo can with the exposed film footage from this fourth, and last, leg of the expedition. The footage was invaluable: it included virtually all of the whitewater the team had encountered, the crux of any adventure film to be made from the expedition. But the film in its canisters weighed close to seventy-five pounds—too heavy to carry—so Dan proposed they divide it up among the nine of them, each carrying five reels. The others refused; by now the film for John Wilcox had dropped considerably on their list of priorities. So the cameraman left behind $200,000 worth of camera equipment, and the still more valuable exposed film, stashed in his North Face VE-24 tent, erected well above the high water mark.

On September 6, their fourteenth day downstream from Dege, a full week beyond their six-day food supply, they began to hike out.

For the first three and a half hours they picked their way through clusters of brambles, sometimes crawling on all fours. Then they came across a narrow but well-worn trail. They figured it must lead to Batang, and set out in the downstream direction with some relief. The trail climbed up a 1,500-foot ridge, then back down to the river, then up another 2,000-foot escarpment, and down again to cross a raging tributary. Finally they came within sight of the first populated village they had seen in a week. It looked enormous, as if tens of thousands of people lived there, its wide green fields manicured and inviting; but it was on the far side of the river, in Tibet.

Again, they disintegrated into argument. Some wanted to descend to the Yangtze and swim across; others wanted to continue trekking, believing Batang had to be close. Finally they chose to continue, hiking on until sundown, when they made camp.

The next day they set out with a schedule—walk for fifty-five minutes, then rest for five. Then it was hike forty-five, and rest fifteen. And then hike sixty minutes, and rest an hour. The Chinese ended up taking the lead positions in the hike, while the rear was brought up by John Glascock.

He had not been feeling well for days, and early on in the hike said he couldn't carry his orange waterproof river bag, which he was using as a pack. So Ron Mattson volunteered to carry it along with his own. At some point Glascock said he couldn't even carry the walkie-talkie, his by dint of his position as last hiker. As they continued, he lagged farther and farther behind. Finally, the group had to wait two hours for Glascock to catch up. When he finally trudged up to the group, screaming they should travel at the pace of the slowest member since it was dangerous for him to hike alone, Ancil exploded as well. He grabbed Glascock's pack from Ron Mattson and began to empty it, cursing, and prepared to divide up the contents among the hikers.

Out spilled a Walkman and tapes, batteries, cameras, film, a full Gore-Tex rainsuit, and a full sleeping bag. Ancil told John Glascock that if he wanted to take a sleeping bag he had to carry it himself. Glascock shrieked "Fuck you," and snapped up the bag. Just then, a wiry Tibetan walked into view, a puzzled look on his face. He was the first other human they had seen in nine days.

His name was Bamatsireng, and he was out gathering wild grasses with his two children and two horses. By gesture and the occasional words of Mandarin Chinese the Tibetan understood from Chu, the ragged rafters told him their destination—Batang. The group was sure it was just one more day down the trail they were following, parallel to the river. Bamatsireng shook his head and waved his hands, No, it was five days this way, over the mountains. Down that trail, he seemed to be saying, the canyon closes off, the trail disappears, the river goes over a huge waterfall.

Bamatsireng let the lost and exhausted hikers load their packs on his animals, and led them up a faint trail away from the Yangtze. They followed him for five miles to his village, Shanyan (Rocky Hill), reaching it at about 8:30 that evening. Bamatsireng's family fed the ravenous group *tsampa*, the pasty barley mush that is a staple of the Tibetan diet. It tasted terrific. Then they collapsed in sleep in Bamatsireng's towering mud and timber house. They slept most of the next day, waking only to eat *tsampa* and attend to their functions, then falling again into exhausted sleep.

At the end of his first day of hiking, Paul Sharpe had run into a group of ethnic Tibetan villagers. He must have presented a weird sight, a tall ghostly figure in a brightly colored wet suit, with a small pack hanging from his butt. "It was eerie. I could tell they'd never seen a white man before," he later said. "Luckily, they didn't feel threatened by me." Once the initial shock was over, they led him to their small village for the night. The next morning he mimed the use of a telephone, so the village headman took him to a nearby town where there was indeed a phone.

It didn't work. A new guide from the second village took over the responsibility of hiking with Paul, and together they traversed a snow-covered 17,000-foot pass. Occasionally they'd stop in homesteads, where they refreshed themselves on yak butter tea and *tsampa*. They picked one wild onion on the trail and shared it; they ate raw flour. Unknowingly, about halfway through his trek, Sharpe passed within two hours' walk of the small mountain town of Shanyan. Continuing on, they finally reached the terminus of a logging road, where Sharpe waited until he met up with a lumber truck headed for Batang.

The morning of Wednesday, September 3, Jan Warren and the road crew woke to another day of waiting. It had been ten days since the expedition had left Dege, and since then there had been little reason to hope. A couple of days earlier, a bloated body had floated onto a gravelbar right in front of the cliffside town of Batang, and it was with a mixture of relief and fear that Jan learned it was not one of the team. Still, it seemed like an evil omen. The only word they had had of the lost group had been the finding of the ghost boat, with its note saying they needed food and supplies, which had floated down to a village upstream. No one ever found the inflatable doll, or no one would admit to it.

To relieve the tension, cameraman Edgar Boyles and soundman Alan Becker of the land crew went for a walk to the outskirts of Batang. To their surprise, an approaching logging truck slowed and stopped in a cloud of dust; a lean and hungry Paul Sharpe leapt down. Edgar grinned. "We knew it was going to be you, Sharpe."

It had taken the young kayaker five days to hike out from the riverside wreckage of the Warren expedition, but he quickly helped organize a rescue party of horses and men to go back into the mountains on horseback, carrying food and supplies to repair the damaged rafts. Reluctantly, Sharpe declined to join the rescue party—his urine was a dark brown color, and he feared something was wrong with him. Later, he found the dark color was the result of severe dehydration.

It was the second day of September when Ken Warren began his solo trek through Gongjue County, Tibet. On his second day of hiking along the canyon rim above the river, he said he saw a rapid nobody would run, so in good conscience he continued hiking toward the southeast to find help. He met some Tibetans who fed him fly-filled yogurt (which Warren dislikes, even without flies), turnips, tea, and bread.

At certain points in his trek, Warren was hiking through clouds over passes 14,000 feet high. Dehydration hits quickly at high altitudes, and Warren stopped as often as he could to fill his water bottles. Near one village stream, an old woman stopped him as he bent towards the water and led him by hand to a freshwater spring. In gratitude, Warren gave her one of his signature red bandannas, an American version of the *katak* scarves Tibetans use as gifts. The old woman tied it on, tapping her heart in thanks.

Near one village, Warren met up with a dog he described as having "huge, enormous jaws and a big, massive chest. It looked like a small mountain lion. It was the biggest, meanest dog I'd ever seen in my life." The dog bared his teeth; Warren said, "Nice doggie," but the English-language reassurance didn't faze the Tibetan canine, who growled deep in his throat. With menace in his eyes, the beast started towards Warren. Ken threw a baseball-size rock that hit the animal alongside the chest, knocking him over. The dog got up and, like a creature in a horror movie, picked up the rock in his teeth and began to chew it.

Warren slowly backed up, but the dog lunged. Again Warren struck the animal, this time with his five-foot walking staff, and knocked him against a woodpile. The dog lunged again, snatched the staff out of Warren's hand; Ken Warren, his cumbersome pack on his back, took off running. He splashed across a stream, hurdled a stone wall, and finally escaped the mad dog. As he sat atop a nearby ridge to catch his breath, a Tibetan man came up and, in sign language, indicated the animal was his, and apologized for the dog's behavior.

Later, Warren met a Tibetan horsepacker who shared some wine with him, and took him to his village. There he led the silver-haired boatman to a storehouse, and showed him the orange Maravia raft and its frame stashed inside. It was the ghost boat the crew had sent down Five Day Rapid several days after Warren had left the group, and Ken didn't know what to make of it. Had the rest of the expedition perished? There was nothing he could do except continue hiking.

Ken Warren hiked for six days, close to one hundred miles by his reckoning, before he finally found a dirt road indicated on his map. It wound sharply up a steep mountain. He needed a rest before tackling the high incline, so he set up his rainfly tent to sleep under gathering clouds. When he awoke, a group of Tibetans was peering inside the flap, watching the big sleeping man with the shock of white hair. Warren looked up to see fresh snow on the high pass. So he rubbed his belly, hoping the Tibetans had some food.

They brought back a bowl of meat stew for Ken, then led him to their village near the road. The wood-walled compound reminded Warren of a fort from the Old West, so he dubbed it Fort Savior. They fed him again, introduced him to several people who were teaching Chinese to the Tibetans, and gave him a bed.

After a good night's sleep, they led him back to the road, where Warren finally found a truck. He rode for a day and a night to a good-size village, where he was put under arrest for two days—he had no passport or official papers, and Tibet is unused to wandering six-foot four-inch boatmen. Then, along with an interpreter who spoke a few words of English, he was taken to another town, where again he was led to the police station for questioning. Then it was back on the road, where he was stopped and searched at the Tibet-Sichuan border, at a bridge over the Jinsha Jiang, the Yangtze he had come to conquer. Finally he was on the road to Batang, where his wife Jan waited.

*   *   *

On their second morning in Shanyan—Tuesday, September 9—the nine hikers awoke renewed. They poked through the village, laughing, eating well, communicating with the curious villagers through sign language, enjoying themselves for the first time in days. The women were fascinated by Ron Mattson's hairy chest, awed by his balding head, both male characteristics absent among Tibetans. The Americans ventured out into the nearby countryside, a soaring granite landscape draped with grasses and pines that Dan Dominy compared to Yosemite Valley. The next day, the search party led by Zhang Xiaozhu, a reporter for *Sports Newspaper*, stumbled into Shanyan with ten horses, a doctor, medicine, and guns, as well as cookies, crackers, and soda.

It was a lucky find: the search party hadn't known the nine missing boatmen were encamped there and had been looking for them for three days, ever since Sharpe sent them down from Batang. Zhang said there were two 15,000-foot passes they had to cross to reach Batang, so they rounded up all the available horses in the village, packed the gear on wooden saddles, and headed southeast.

It was a spectacular hike, one they couldn't help but find awe-inspiring, even when it began to snow and they felt the chill through their one set of worn clothing. The first night they camped in a large cave, where John Glascock built a fire and was proclaimed the winner of the Most Improved Camper award by his companions. They were cold and weak, but their spirits were starting to climb. They hiked steadily the next day, through snow and mud, until they reached a lumber camp on a dirt road. There they piled into the bed of a truck and rode the final forty-two miles to Batang.

Ken Warren and his ten teammates had left Dege at midday on August 24. A week later, on September 2, Warren had begun his solo hike out. Four days after that, the remaining nine crewmen had begun their trek out, as much as thirty miles downstream of Warren's departure point. Uncounted miles of tumultuous river and a thousand miles of dusty roads later, at just before six on the evening of September 11, Ken Warren bounced into Batang aboard a lumber truck. Less than half an hour later, the nine weary teammates came in from the other direction. They had finally made Batang nineteen days after they left Dege for a four-day float. Reunited and relieved after their epic three-week adventure, they pored over Edgar Boyles's ONC map to check their route. They found that it was not ninety river miles from Dege to Batang but over two hundred. There was, at least, a small comfort: also in Batang was Dr. Wayne

Moran, the physician who had finally arrived from Hong Kong to replace Dr. David Gray.

"My eleven-day trek was the toughest thing physically I've ever had to do in my life," Ken Warren said. Still, he insisted he wanted to go on. With the exception of Paul Sharpe, the entire team refused. Warren began to talk of joining up with the Chinese expeditions ahead of him, combining his expertise with their forces through the treacherous Tiger's Leap Gorge, but the Chinese said no, thanks anyway.

On Saturday, September 13, two days before the official end of Ken Warren's permit, Beijing announced it would not be extended. The Sino–USA Upper Yangtze River Expedition was over, two and a half months after it had begun, nearly 1,200 miles downstream from the river's source, over 800 miles short of its goal, and 300 miles away from Tiger's Leap Gorge.

On Monday evening, September 15, the final day of the permit, the three rafts that had been securely lashed to the rocks upstream were seen floating by Batang under a full moon, upright and empty, stripped of their frames and bowlines, ghost boats passing in the night.

Paul Sharpe, rested and recovered, led a Tibetan posse upstream to retrieve the cameras and exposed film stashed in Dan Dominy's tent. The salvage mission took another ten days—they really had no idea where the tent was, as the reduced team had gone on for two days after Sharpe left the river. But the search was a success: "Challenging China's Yangtze," produced and directed by John Wilcox, aired on ABC in two parts in April and May 1987. It was nominated for Emmys in the Sports Documentary category, for Best Program and Best Cinematography.

In Minneapolis, a Dave Shippee Memorial Fund was created at the University of Minnesota's School of Journalism and Mass Communication, to award scholarships for promising students.

In October 1987, Margit Shippee and her mother-in-law, Elizabeth Shippee, journeyed to China to retrace David's last weeks. Accompanied by Chu Siming, veteran of the Sino–USA river team, the two women went to Golmud, where David's sixty-five-year-old mother caught a bad cold. Margit and Chu continued on to the Tuotuoheyan base camp, where Margit floated wildflowers down the river, one for each member of the grieving family.

Several months earlier, in July, the Shippee family had filed a $1.1-million wrongful-death suit against Jan and Ken Warren and television producer John Wilcox, maintaining that promised safety precautions—including helicopter support and reliable communications systems—were not provided. The suit also alleges that Warren ignored and overrode the advice of Dr. Gray and was thus responsible for David Shippee's death.

Ken Warren, for his part, filed a $1.2-million suit against the four men who left his expedition—Gary Peebles, Bill Atwood, Toby Sprinkle, and Dr. David Gray—claiming breach of contract and character defamation. Warren also threatened suit against several other people related to the trip and its aftermath, including a reporter who wrote an account of the trip that Warren perceived as unfavorable.

Warren's relations with other members of his team remain strained. Many will not speak with him. A couple, notably Ancil Nance, continue to support him, lauding the achievements of the expedition rather than dwelling on its failures. But at least one boatman, formerly a staunch supporter, now proclaims, "I wouldn't go with Ken Warren to the fucking 7-Eleven."

Immediately after arriving back in the US, Ken Warren declared, "We were very, very successful," and said he had been invited back to China the next year to finish the expedition. He did not return in 1987, nor in 1988, though he still vows to do so.

He has given a series of slide shows during which he announces his intention to return with newly designed twenty-foot rafts that have a "secret weapon" to help negotiate the huge rapids yet to be run, including those of Tiger's Leap Gorge. In one slide presentation, to a University of Montana audience, he announced he was looking for people to join him. His criteria: "You have to be very, very brave and strong . . . and stupid. We don't really want a lot of brains."

Ken Warren's words of personal philosophy ring in echo of another great helmsman, Mao Zedong, who once said: "If you read too many books, in the end they will petrify your mind."

CHAPTER TWELVE

Trial in Tiger's Leap Gorge

All Chinese are Confucianists
when successful, and
Taoists when they are failures.
—LIN YUTANG,
My Country and My People

While the Ken Warren expedition was slowly working its way down the braided channels of the upper Tuotuohe, on July 24, 1986, the land crews of the Chinese teams from Luoyang and Sichuan arrived in Batang, a thousand miles downstream. They expected their teammates to arrive in another three or four days—the maps indicated very little drop in the canyon lands between Dege and Batang, the first leg of the two-thousand-mile-long Jinsha Jiang, as the river is known once it becomes the border between Xizang (Tibet) and Sichuan provinces. The experience the Chinese crews had gained in rafting the Tongtian Ho, the River to Heaven, should have left them well prepared for the upper waters of the River of Golden Sands. So the news that arrived on July 30 by telex from Baiyu was a shock—the boats had been swept away, and the whereabouts of the eight rafters was unknown.

Over the following days, the story slowly came together, and the loss of life was tabulated at only three: five of the rafters had climbed out of the river canyon and were surviving in the mountains—eating roots, snails, and leaves, finding help from the Tibetan villagers, slowly making their way towards the roads to Batang. Still, the loss of three occupants of the ill-fated capsule, including the popular and heroic Kong Zhiyi, was a severe blow to the morale of the Chinese. Clearly it was time to reevaluate the techniques, and perhaps the purpose, of rafting down the Yangtze.

But rafting down the Yangtze had come to mean more in China than just another escapade—much more. "Many died in the past revolutionary wars," stated Zhiyi's father, Kong Kong. "Zhiyi died in the war against nature. I'm proud of him." *China Sports* magazine echoed the sentiment: "Chinese have laid down their lives in rafting adventures on the Yangtze for an ultimate cause associated with the national effort for modernization." The drowned rafters were not just casualties, but heroes, martyrs for a higher purpose. At the same time, David Shippee lay dying on the banks of the Tuotuohe, but his death on August 3 evoked none of the nationalistic sentiments in America that the Chinese expressed for their own. The American and the Chinese attitudes towards rafting the Yangtze were more than half a world apart.

For nearly two weeks, the two Chinese teams held steady in Batang, nursing their psychic wounds, wondering what to do next and how to do it. Wang Dian Ming, the member who had started out with the Sichuanese but joined the Luoyang team at Yushu, was asked to leave the river effort altogether—his concern following the disaster at Yela Shoal had been primarily for his money and film, not his drowned comrades. He stayed in Batang, hoping for an opportunity to get back with one team or another, until he finally gave up and left in mid-August for Chengdu. Two of the remaining six Luoyang team members—Wang Maojun and Lei Jiansheng—opted to join permanently with the Sichuan rafters. But Lang Baoluo was against it. The slight but strong-willed young shoemaker had committed more than his time and energies to this effort. In some ways, he had committed his life. And he was not willing to give that up for another team's effort. Their own team already had lost all three boats, and two of the three who drowned at Yela Shoal were from Luoyang, he reminded his teammates; they owed it to their dead friends to continue.

It was a time of hesitation and doubt, finally resolved from the outside. On August 13, the deputy director of the Academy of Sciences at Chengdu arrived in Batang with two civic leaders from Luoyang. In a frank meeting, they firmly reminded the Luoyang rafters that they were not sponsored by the government, and virtually ordered them to return home. Lang Baoluo and his teammates, including Wang and Lei, were furious. They had not set their aim, invested their funds, and left their families just to take orders from others. Three days later they left for Hutiaoxia—Tiger's Leap Gorge—vowing to run it ahead of the "official" group. Relations between the two teams once again collapsed.

Finally, there was the news from upstream: the Sino–USA Upper Yangtze Expedition, headed by Ken Warren, had safely reached Yushu, and was poised to head downstream towards Batang. At all costs, the Chinese wanted to keep ahead of Ken Warren: they feared his greater experience, his more sophisticated equipment, his better chances. On August 16, the same day the Luoyang squad left for Tiger's Leap Gorge, and the day before Warren left Yushu, the Sichuan group decided to start rafting again. Dreading a return to Yieba and a second try at the dangerous rapids in Baiyu County, they decided to skip that section and start at the confluence with the Baqu River, between Batang and Shigu. If all went well, they would beat Ken Warren through Tiger's Leap Gorge and on to Yibin and Shanghai; then they would think about making up the skipped sections.

Meanwhile, young Jiehu Arsha had once again been passed over by the team leaders for a spot on the Jinsha Jiang leg. She believed she had proven her worthiness on the Tongtian Ho, and though she had wanted very badly to be part of the small crew that entered the canyons of Baiyu County—and that met there with disaster—she had acquiesced to her team leader's wishes. Surely her willingness to work within the rules of the larger expedition would pay off, and she would be chosen to return to the river once they left Batang.

When her name was again left off the roster, she was deeply disappointed. But rather than react with anger, she came up with a plan. She disappeared from Batang before her teammates headed for their Baqu River put-in, and camped out on the banks of the tributary. Two teammates agreed to pick her up once the trip was underway—she would join the group when it was already on the river, leaping aboard in the middle of nowhere, and a place on the crew would be hers by default.

She lay down in a grove that night, watching the moon. While others doubted her ability to face danger, the press treated her as a heroine; but for all that, she had still been denied a place on the river. She didn't want to be a public figure, an example for China's young women: she only longed to challenge the Yangtze. Her experiences thus far had hooked her. She wanted the thrill of whitewater. She wanted to be on the top of the wave.

When she awoke, her teammate Wang Yan was shouting out her name. "Arsha! Arsha! Come back, everyone knows your secret!" The Sichuan rafters were searching for her in the woods along the river, and when they found her, her plan collapsed. She would have to wait to get back on the river's flow. Her dreams had once again turned to disappointment.

The Sichuan team did not anticipate much difficulty in running the stretch between the Baqu River and Hutiao Gorge. It was more open country than the canyons of Baiyu County, and the gradient less steep. Thinking it would be a good time to revive China's interest in their effort, they invited Li Mingfu of Sichuan Television to film their descent. For twenty miles, the decision seemed to be a good one: they floated quietly through the scenic countryside, passing from Sichuan into Yunnan Province. When they came to the only major stretch of rapids, at Longguo, they boldly conquered the upper drop, then threaded their way through the reefs of the second Longguo Shoal. It looked good on film, and they confidently planned their run down the next rapid, Wangdalong Shoal.

There was no easy way through Wangdalong; the rapid dropped steadily from top to tail. The crew in the lead boat started from the left side and paddled hard towards the middle, but something went wrong as the boat dropped through a wave at the end of the tongue: the boat slipped sideways, washed into a reversal, and capsized. Three of the crew immediately swam to the riverbank; the other two were swept through the rest of the long rapid, finally reaching shore, exhausted but safe, several hundred yards downstream.

The film, as broadcast nationally on television the next day, did indeed serve to galvanize the public, but the publicity was not all favorable. Some wondered if such senseless confrontation with the elements was the best use of China's young people, and if a death on the Yangtze was really preferable to national service. Some saw that only by such striving could the coming generation find its own voice. Still, China's attention was once again focused on the men and women trying to conquer the Yangtze. Danger and fear were simply an inseparable part of their challenge to the river; and the greatest challenge lay ahead.

By the time the Luoyang team arrived at the town of Qiaotou, at the confluence of the Xiaozhongdian He, they were over 1,500 miles downstream from the headwaters of the Yangtze. The passage over those miles had been filled with heroism and cowardice, challenge and romance, and finally death. Controversy dogged their course, but more than half the river was yet to be run. Of the 2,500 miles remaining, the last 1,700 would be the home stretch—well-traveled currents down from Chongqing, through the historic Three Gorges, and along the powerful flow through the broad valleys of the Yangtze River Basin to the ultimate goal, Shanghai. The intervening 800 miles held the dangers of the big rapids at Jingangbei Shoal near Luzhou, of Laojun Shoal east of Dukou, and the hidden mysteries of the Great Bend. But the biggest danger was just ahead—Hutiaoxia, Tiger's Leap Gorge.

On August 22, two days before Ken Warren left Dege for his final push into the canyons of Baiyu County, the two Chinese rafting teams arrived at Tiger's Leap Gorge. They sent separate scouting squads down the gorge trail to view the tumultuous rapids and figure out a way to run them. The gorge was horrifying: the midsummer flow was enormous, perhaps close to 100,000 cubic feet per second, boiling over the rocky shoreline with a vengeance. The gorge is only twelve miles long, but in that short distance it drops over 600 feet, perhaps as much as 1,000 feet according to some estimates—50 to 80 feet per mile. The three main groups of rapids are broken up into twenty-one discrete rapids, by the Chinese count. Mountains tower on either side of the gorge, including the glaciated 18,899-foot summit of Jade Dragon Peak, Yulong Shan, just ten miles southeast of the 6,000-foot river. In places the walls are so sheer that even to walk on the riverside is impossible, and to climb out in case of an emergency would be out of the question. To enter the canyon is to commit to running it, to do or to die. Shanghai never seemed so far away.

Two weeks slowly passed. Nearly every member of the two teams hiked down the high, narrow trail, viewed the rapids, and returned to Qiaotou discouraged. Fifteen percent, or at most twenty, were the estimated chances for success. One in five was not good odds, and some rafters considered the effort suicidal. But several of the Chinese argued that they must go through Tiger's Leap Gorge—to do otherwise would be fraud, for to run the Yangtze one must run Hutiaoxia. Some pointed out that the Americans led by Ken Warren were coming down the river after them; they would surely run the narrow gorge even if the Chinese did not—and they were getting closer every day.

On September 3, a new enclosed capsule arrived for the Luoyang team, a smaller but hopefully more secure model, just seven feet in diameter and four feet high. It was only big enough for two people, lying on their sides, but it was equipped with an air-filled pillar to allow the passengers to breathe in the raging waters. The team immediately took it to the first drop, Upper Hutiao Shoal, with its huge pyramid rock fronting a sixty-foot drop in two main pitches. The next day, to test the capsule, they put a dog inside, attached an oxygen mask to the animal's muzzle, lashed the capsule shut, and sent it over the falls. The capsule bobbed in the quickening water, then accelerated and careened over the white chasm into the maelstrom below. A few minutes later it flushed into an eddy, and the rafters eagerly clambered over the rocks to fish it out of the water.

The craft had been badly damaged in the falls; the door had been wrenched open, and the dog was gone. No one had thought to put a life jacket on the animal, and it was never seen again. Surprisingly, when the rafters reviewed the videotape of the run, they perceived good news: the drop had only taken a few seconds, the boat had floated through it all, had not even been caught in any of several large reversals. Perhaps if one made sure the door was secure, and tucked oneself in the corner of the capsule and held on tight—the dog did not have the benefit of two hands and the awareness of what lay ahead—the odds of survival might rise to a more reasonable 50 percent. The seriousness of purpose the Chinese had for their effort is measured by this incident: their experiment had killed their involuntary subject, yet they regarded it as a success and decided to try again—with humans this time.

By September 10, the news arrived from Batang that the Warren team was days late and presumably having trouble in Baiyu County, but for the Luoyang rafters there was no turning back. They chose two of their members to ride the capsule—a squat black stack of giant tire tubes, like a compressed Michelin man—through the first drop. Lei Jiansheng, one of the survivors of the disaster at Yela Shoal in Baiyu County, was a thirty-four-year-old high school history teacher, while Li Qingjian, thirty-two, was a boiler worker at the railway station in Luoyang. Both had young children at home, but both bravely said they had their family's support.

When Lei Jiansheng was interviewed moments before the challenge to the big drop at Upper Hutiao Shoal, he had some advice for his countrymen. "I think China is one of the greatest nations, but its development is hindered by some with backward ideas. We should encourage the opening up of minds, and the spirit of adventure. Rafting the Yangtze is a very small wave in the long river of history, but it is worthwhile if it can help move forward the development of our country."

The two men from Luoyang put on their life jackets and got into the cabin of the black capsule. The newsmen trekked down to the bottom of the drop and waited. Half an hour passed, then more; people began to wonder if the two had backed out at the last minute. The truth was stranger than the supposition: the capsule, without any steering mechanism, had drifted into a powerful eddy a quarter mile above the drop, and could not be pushed out. Meanwhile the two men were still inside, breathing through the oxygen tanks, slowly using up their hour's worth of air.

As the end of the hour neared, the capsule finally broke out of the first eddy, just to be drawn into another. Lang Baoluo tied a rope around his waist and jumped into the Yangtze, swam to the capsule, and kicked it out into the main current.

The capsule was sucked over the falls next to the pyramid rock, disappeared for an instant in the white chaos, then rode another wave into the second big drop. In a matter of seconds, it was over; the capsule drifted to shore, and the elated team members pulled the grinning Lei Jiansheng and Li Qingjian from the enclosed boat. For the first time, people had run a rapid in Tiger's Leap Gorge, and they had survived.

The success of the Luoyang Expedition for Sailing and Exploring the Yangtze captured the imagination of the nation. Seventy reporters converged on the ten-thousand-foot-deep Hutiaoxia, making the legendary canyon a scene of modern history. The Luoyang team, which had been ignored by the press a month earlier, suddenly became the team to beat—a group of independent workers who had taken on the challenge of rafting the Yangtze without official support and against orders from the authorities who wanted them to stop. Their sudden glory eclipsed the Sichuan team, and once again resentments between the two flared up.

The next day, September 11, Wang Yan and Li Dafang of the Chengdu Academy of Sciences team rode their own capsule over the falls of Upper Hutiao Shoal. Their craft—an enclosed maroon capsule covered with ox-skin, which in turn was covered by a nylon shell—dropped from near the top of the pyramid rock. The impact of the plunge burst their oxygen bags and wrenched open the capsule's door, flooding the two rafters. But when four teammates jumped into the water and pulled the boat to the riverbank, Wang and Li were ready to continue floating—they wanted to do the Middle Hutiao Shoal, and take the initiative away from the upstarts from Luoyang. Fortunately, wiser heads prevailed, and they put off their conquest for another day.

Meanwhile, Wang Dian Ming—the proud rafter who had left the Sichuan team to join the Luoyang rafters only to be fired from the Luoyang squad—appeared in Qiaotou with his own capsule. On September 12, he too made the plunge over Upper Hutiao Shoal. Three days earlier it had seemed impossible; now, five men had made history. And, to the nation's pride, they were all Chinese: Ken Warren and his crew had been stopped in Baiyu County, and on September 13 it was announced that their effort was officially over.

But the greatest challenge of Tiger's Leap Gorge was yet to come. Between Upper Hutiao Shoal and Middle Hutiao Shoal, there were two sets of rapids known as Liangjiaren and Yachajiao. Somehow, the black Luoyang capsule was set adrift above the rapids with no occupants; perhaps it was sent down as a "ghost boat," perhaps it just got away from its handlers. By the time it was recovered, it was close to the start of Middle Hutiao Shoal, and a rapid known as Mantianxing—Star-Studded Sky, or Meteor Shower Rapid. Two other team members climbed into the capsule, and on September 12 Lang Baoluo and Sun Zhiling plunged into Middle Hutiao Shoal. "Someone says that there is only a twenty-percent chance to succeed in rafting the Hutiao Gorge," Lang Baoluo had said. "I'd like to say that we should give one-hundred-percent effort, even if there is only one-percent chance to succeed." He would be called upon to give that 100 percent, and then some.

The Luoyang capsule had been torn in two places during its first test, over Upper Hutiao Shoal; it had been hurriedly patched to keep the squad ahead of their rivals from Sichuan. When it made the mad drop into Meteor Shower Rapid, it split apart. Both rafters were flushed out into the rock-studded currents, Sun Zhiling never to emerge. His bloated body was found nine days later well downstream, the fourth casualty on the River of Golden Sands.

Lang Baoluo, miraculously, was swept into an eddy on the right side of the river, barely conscious; most of his clothes had been ripped from his body by the river's power. He crawled onto a rock and retched. Then he fell into an exhausted daze, only to fully waken as the day's light began to fade. He looked around and realized his situation: he was on the wrong side of the river, beneath a sheer 3,800-foot wall with no means of climbing out, and certainly without the strength to do so. In front of him, the Yangtze roared past like an endless railroad train, destination Shanghai. Swimming was unthinkable. His only clothing was a flimsy T-shirt and his water-logged life jacket. He was stuck, almost naked, without food, with no way out.

Soaked and shivering, he spent the night gazing at the bonfire across the river, a distant beacon of hope less than a mile upstream, but oceans away.

By noon the following day Lang was eating bitter grass to stave off hunger. Then, at three P.M., he looked up to see his friend Lei Jiansheng, one of the survivors of the upper run, positioned on a ledge 350 feet above. Lei and two others had crossed the river upstream in the quiet water, and had negotiated along cracks and toeholds to this precarious point above Lang. They lowered ropes, and Lei rappelled down to a meager outcrop 200 feet above Lang.

From the estrade Lei tossed two ropes to Lang and began trying to pull him up. But fifty feet up the cliff face, one of the ropes broke; Lang dangled clinging to the other, twisting in the wind. He was lowered back to the river, where he spent another cold, fitful night, relieved only by the food Lei managed to send down to him.

That evening, as the reporters who witnessed this heroic rescue attempt from the left side of the river hiked back to their base camp at Yongshengxiang, a small rock slide plummeted down a side stream, and bounced across the trail just as Wang Ming passed by. The twenty-four-year-old reporter for *Youth World* magazine of Sichuan was hit in the head and chest, and fell halfway down the canyon wall before coming to rest in the tributary. The shallow water was stained red by his blood. Sichuan team member Yan Ke, a male nurse from the hospital at Yibin, gave artificial respiration as soon as he reached him, but without success. At eleven that night, Wang Ming became the fifth casualty of the Chinese efforts to run the Yangtze.

One more desperate day and night passed as every attempt to rescue Lang Baoluo failed. An army helicopter with a special rescue team was dispatched from Dali, in Yunnan, but a storm turned it back. The Sichuan rafting team and the Chengdu Regional Military Outpost also lent their advice and assistance, but to no avail. The nights were becoming colder, and Lang Baoluo was still far from safe.

Finally, on September 15, the third day after the attempted run of Middle Hutiao Shoal, Lei Jiansheng and his companions lowered a handcrafted ladder of vines and tree branches, barely long enough to reach Lang's rocky cove. The slight Luoyang shoemaker climbed up a few rungs, then a few more; slowly he was hoisted to safety, and carried out of the canyon on the backs of his teammates. The photographs show him grinning, glad to be alive, with perhaps a few more percentage points of effort left in his exhausted frame.

The competition between the two Chinese teams continued to cause controversy, all the more so now that the Sino–USA expedition had failed. The national press picked up on the fact that it had been the

Luoyang team that had first rafted the upper and middle sections of Hutiao Gorge, and downplayed the skipping of the rapids between. While the drama of Lang Baoluo added further fuel to the fire of Luoyang's glory, at the same time it exhausted the efforts of the young independents. Furthermore, their only capsule had been lost in the Meteor Shower Rapid. So it was perhaps a tactful decision for Wang Maojun to make when, on September 17, he agreed to unite the two teams yet again.

The new united front would preserve the name of the Sichuan group, the China Yangtze River Scientific Observation Drifting Expedition, while Wang would become deputy director, and Lei Jiansheng would be named co-leader of the rafting team. Since the Luoyang rafters had passed through Middle Hutiao Shoal—albeit not without tragedy—the decision was made to raft the Lower Shoal as a united team. But it was two members of the Sichuan team who were chosen for the heroic final plunge, not one of each. Almost at once, suspicions arose in the Luoyang camp. Was their success in running Meteor Shower Rapid being appropriated by the Sichuan rafters, and their future efforts undermined?

Once again, it was only a matter of days before the alliance broke down. By September 19, there was no more talk of cooperation, and Wang Yan and Yang Xin of the Sichuan team successfully rafted Lower Hutiao Shoal in their capsule. Two days later, the Luoyang team repeated the effort in a makeshift capsule. So by the first day of autumn, all three major drops had been run, though not all three successfully, nor by both teams. Middle Hutiao Shoal remained the bone in the throat of the Chinese conquest of Tiger's Leap Gorge, the one section that had eluded a successful run.

On the rainy morning of September 24, Wang Yan and Yan Ke, the male nurse from Yibin who had attempted to resuscitate the dying reporter Wang Ming, entered their skin-and-nylon-coated capsule and were pushed into the waters just below the first big drop, Upper Hutiao Shoal. Ahead of them lay the unrun rapids of Liangjiaren and the three shoals of Yachajiao, and the fatal Mantianxing—Meteor Shower Rapid.

The maroon craft pitched and pranced through the narrow gorge as its inner-tube buoys were stripped off one by one. Liangjiaren and Yachajiao were passed through without incident, but at Mantianxing the craft tumbled over and over, and its occupants were knocked black and blue. By the bottom of Middle Hutiao Shoal, the door was badly damaged and beginning to leak, but the rescue team could not get to the boat in time to stop it. The currents of Lower Hutiao Shoal drew the crippled craft onward; these rapids had been run before, but not by a beaten crew in a battered raft.

Miraculously, when the capsule was salvaged in the calm waters beneath the town of Daqu, at the end of Tiger's Leap Gorge, Wang Yan and Yan Ke were still alive and conscious. The two were pulled from their roost like astronauts from a space capsule, and cheered as national heroes. They had managed to run nearly the entire length of Hutiaoxia in a single day, and one of them—Wang Yan, an occupant of the Sichuan team's capsule over Upper Hutiao Shoal—thus became the first man to run all of the treacherous gorge successfully. While some compared the capsule attack method of running the river to the proverbial barrel over Niagara, or to the helpless astronauts in the early space shots, in some sense at least the Chinese had done what they had set out to do: they had conquered Tiger's Leap Gorge.

But from Daqu to Shanghai is still more than half the length of the Yangtze. There were still unknown reaches of river, such as the Great Bend, and stretches known to be dangerous. The most celebrated of these was Laojun Shoal, a compressed canyon with hundreds of reefs alternating with big waves. Over the centuries dozens of fishermen had met their death here. Neither the Luoyang rafters nor the Sichuan team took Laojun lightly; neither did they intend to skip it.

Since it was a glory spot on the river, both teams raced to get there, and in so doing bypassed the section between Daqu and Jinan, the so-called Great Bend. On September 30, less than a week after Wang Yan and Yan Ke were pulled from their maroon capsule at the end of Tiger's Leap Gorge, the Sichuan team was ready to challenge Laojun Shoal. It lay just beyond the riverside city of Dukou, Sichuan, in Huidong County, some three hundred miles downstream. The first thing they did was to choose their team, and at last Arsha got her chance: Song Yuanqing, Yang Bin, and the feisty dancer Jiehu Arsha were chosen to ride the capsule through Laojun Shoal.

The plan was to have a safety boat at the end of Laojun Shoal, manned by four teammates, which would motor out to midcurrent to pick up the rudderless, unsteerable capsule after it had floated through the rapids. It was a safety measure they immediately appreciated: as soon as the capsule entered the rapid, its three occupants could feel the pressure of the waves battering the flimsy craft. It seemed to suck their breath away, and they grabbed for the oxygen masks. But they couldn't get enough to breathe, and from the motion of the craft and the airless atmosphere, first Song Yuanqing then Arsha vomited. Still, the rapid continued; they were pitched about and flushed through unseen waves and over blind reefs again and again.

At last the water calmed, and they could hear the sound of an outboard motor, their rescue boat. The four rescuers—including Wang Yan, veteran of Tiger's Leap Gorge—tried to pull the capsule to shore; but in a curious twist of fate, the powerful currents of the Jinsha Jiang began to sweep both boats on down the river, slowly at first, then faster and faster. The force of the river twisted the rescue boat sideways, and water poured in, flooded the engine, and began to fill the bilge.

The four men in the open boat tried to bail, but as soon as they saw they were losing the battle, they abandoned ship and climbed on top of the capsule, watching the rescue boat sink.

Song Yuanqing, hearing some disturbance outside, stuck his head out of the capsule. "Why are you sitting on top of us?" he asked.

"Our boat has sunk!" The three capsule rafters climbed out to join their erstwhile rescuers on top of the enclosed boat, and together the seven rafters drifted for twenty miles down the Jinsha Jiang.

It grew cold as the daylight faded; they saw several fishing boats and people on shore, but each time as they were able to make their predicament understood, the fast-moving current swept them out of reach. Finally, a second rescue boat was sent out from shore, but it was too small to carry all the stranded rafters. Instead, it took only the three poorest swimmers—leaving four still on the boat. Downstream the whitecaps of Baihe Shoal could be seen, spitting skyward.

"You three swim to shore," Song Yuanqing ordered. "I'll mind the cabin myself." Arsha and two of the men leapt into the fast-moving river and made a mad swim for safety, reaching land just yards above the big waves of Baihe Shoal.

Song Yuanqing stayed aboard, riding the capsule through the rapid and on into the night. Before the trip he had vowed to ride the capsule as long as it would float, remembering the wild run that Wang Yan and Yan Ke had made through Tiger's Leap Gorge. But as midnight came and went, he wondered about his decision to stay aboard. Finally, just after one o'clock in the morning, a string of lights onshore told him he was nearing a village. Well-lit towns are unusual in remote China, and Song realized they must be looking for him. He called out as a boat came near, and was finally rescued after floating seventy-five miles down from Baihe Shoal over three counties, alone in the night. When he woke up the next morning, it was October 1, National Day, and Song Yuanqing was the latest hero in the Chinese conquest of the Yangtze.

On November 12, 1986, the Luoyang Expedition for Sailing and Exploring the Yangtze reached Shanghai. Over the past eight weeks, from the time they reached the end of Tiger's Leap Gorge on September 21, the bold and determined men had forced their way down the Yangtze, sometimes attaching their rafts to motorized boats to speed their progress. They had bypassed sections of the river in order to stay ahead of their Sichuan rivals; they had lost Lei Zhi, their fourth team member and sixth to die on the Yangtze, in a rapid at Qiaojia Ferry, where Song Yuanqing had ended his midnight odyssey. But there they were in Shanghai, grabbing the headlines for all they were worth.

The Sichuan team was sore, and deservedly so. Though they were some days behind on the slow thousand-mile flat-water run through the Yangtze River Basin from Gezhouba Dam at Yichang, they at least had made an effort to run all of the river, and the parts they had been unable to run they were making up with a second-unit crew. These sections included the Great Bend, the stretch between Yela Shoal and the Baqu River in Baiyu County, and a twelve-mile stretch called Moding Shoal, at the junction of Yunnan, Sichuan, and Xizang provinces.

Unwilling to be considered cheaters, the Luoyang team put together their own makeup crew. Throughout the rest of November, both teams battled it out in the backwaters of the Yangtze, returning again to Tibet, to Sichuan, to the tumultuous rapids they had been forced to bypass. Another Luoyang team member died upstream of Baiyu County, in Tibet—the fifth member of the eight-man team to meet death on the Yangtze. Between November 7 and November 10, the Chinese Academy of Sciences team rafted most of the Great Bend, surviving a flip and an emergency bivouac shortly after leaving Daqu. Meanwhile, three members of the Sichuan team were said to have completed the stretch between Yela Shoal and Batang in Baiyu County on November 16. Two days later, they made a successful run through the short but difficult canyons of Moding Shoal, where the Jinsha Jiang enters Yunnan, thus completing a major missing leg. Finally the Luoyang team gave up their attempt to finish making up their missed miles, and it seemed only a matter of time before the race went officially to the Sichuanese.

At 2:30 on the afternoon of Tuesday, November 25, the China Yangtze River Scientific Observation Drifting Expedition reached the East China Sea, ending their four-thousand-mile adventure. Just a few hours earlier, as they neared Shanghai, they had received shocking news: three of their teammates had been unable to reach shore after rafting through Moding Shoal and had capsized in the next, and last, big rapid. They were all drowned. The final toll stood at an even, fated dozen—nine Chinese rafters lost in 1986, plus one journalist; David Shippee, the American casualty; and Yao Maoshu, the first to raft the Yangtze, and the first to die, in July of 1985.

The successful yet grieving members of the Chinese rafting team from Chengdu, Sichuan, dropped a bottle into the ocean as they completed their epic journey. It contained the team's flag, the signatures of all the team members who reached Shanghai—including Wang Yan, conqueror of Tiger's Leap Gorge, and Jiehu Arsha, at the end of her own personal odyssey down the waters of the Long River—and the following statement:

"Comrades and friends: Today is November 25, 1986. We, the China Yangtze River Scientific Observation Drifting Team, have rafted 175 days and finally completed the rafting of the Yangtze River. Here we drop this bottle so that it will always accompany our teammates who died in the rafting. If one day you find this bottle, please respect our wish and put it back in the sea."

PART TWO

1987 — The Year of the Hare

CHAPTER THIRTEEN

Manning the Ship of Fools

All you have done
is for nothing, all is lost,
without any reward.
—CHINESE PROVERB

As 1986 drew to a close, and news reports of the Chinese teams' running of the Yangtze from source to sea began to filter through to the West, a strange feeling of release took hold. The great race had been run, and SOBEK had not even left the starting gate. The sound and the fury had passed us by, but somehow that seemed all right, for we were now free to explore other pursuits. My partner at SOBEK, John Yost, moved on to another year of battling the adventure travel wars, overseeing the commercial tours we offered in the rest of the world; Christian and I took off to Indonesia to work on a book. Still, even while climbing volcanoes or dancing with headhunters, images of the Yangtze would return to me: a snow-rimmed gorge bisected by a mighty river, purling white between sheer limestone walls.

Sam Moore, the Kentucky kayaker who had worked so hard with us to get the Yangtze permit for 1986, decided to take advantage of the time he had set aside for the expedition to travel in Yunnan Province, and in October, with his wife and four friends, he headed to China anyway. He and his companions each paid $1,500 to the Tibetan Tourism Authority in Lhasa for the privilege of traveling overland to hike Tiger's Leap Gorge. But, once there, they were informed they would not be allowed to hike the famous gorge without "special permits," which were not forthcoming no matter what the cost. However, once in Lijiang—the mountain meadow city at the base of Yulong Shan—they traveled to the entrance of the canyon, where they ven-

151

tured a short distance into Tiger's Leap Gorge on an aqueduct trail running along the right bank.

Sam and geologist Bob Casaceli walked ahead of the rest of the group, which included their Chinese guides. They found a farmer with a small boat, who agreed to ferry them to the other side of the river—despite their lack of official permission. Once across the river, they hiked several miles downstream on the Chinese tourist trail until they could see what they thought was the last bend in the gorge, at the bottom of seven huge rapids. Since they were carrying a ½-inch videotape camcorder, Sam and Bob shot the raging rapids they could see. The tape was crude but effective: the rapids looked monstrous, but maybe, just maybe, runnable. Then they turned back and rejoined the rest of their group.

A couple of days later, they all traveled to the small farming town of Daqu at the end of Tiger's Leap Gorge, and from there they hiked up the Daqu side to the base of the last rapid—which they assumed was the seventh rapid they had seen from afar, at the other end of the canyon. When he returned, Sam called us with the good news: at the low water he found in October, there were only the seven major rapids, two of which would probably have to be portaged—but five of which he guessed could be run.

We knew the Sino–USA expedition had faltered, stalled out a thousand *li* above Tiger's Leap Gorge. We knew the Chinese teams had run the gorge, though not without loss of life and certainly without finesse. But had they "rafted" the gorge, or merely "barreled" through it? And, whichever verb they deserved, did they really run the Great Bend itself, that long hairpin north of Daqu that arcs around the peninsula created by Yulong Shan?

The published reports of their efforts left room for doubt: they had reached Daqu on September 24, and less than a week later put on the river almost 300 miles downstream, in Huidong County, Sichuan— almost too far to float in that time, but about right for driving with their truckloads of gear. Later, they went back with a makeup team and ran much of the Great Bend—150 miles in three days, a rapid run if ever there was one. But details about this leg of their journey were sketchy: the best estimate of their progress suggests they took out at a lonely bridge somewhere to the southeast of Lijiang, at a place called Jin'anqiao. Our maps showed no such town.

Maybe we could salvage a first out of it all, and claim a first descent through the entire Great Bend—to Jinjiang, where the Yangtze embarks on its final eastward sweep. Or, if not that, the first Western descent. But as time went on, the "first" aspect of the expedition began to seem less important: something about the geography, the history, the spirit of the place called out to me, and said, with Yu-Pe-Ya, "Let me journey down on the Great River . . . 'twixt gorges of the hills." Come, I seemed to hear an inner voice call, let's raft the Yangtze. Not for the glory, but for the cultural, scenic, and adventurous aspects of an extraordinary river in an exotic land. For the fun of it.

I was in Java in January, between climbs of its forest-robed volcano gods, when John Yost reached me via telex at a beachside hotel. The Chinese requested I come immediately to Beijing to discuss terms for a new permit to run the Yangtze. I caught the first flight, though it wasn't direct—Indonesia and the People's Republic severed diplomatic relations in 1965, during a Communist-led coup attempt against Sukarno, and they have not been on speaking terms since. Instead I had to fly through Bangkok to reach Beijing, but at last I met once again with Qu Yin Hua of China International Sports Travel.

The associate director of CIST now beamed happily, and while his attendant served green tea, Mr. Qu presented me with a glossy new contract. Same terms as last year, only this one was inviolable: if we paid the agreed fee, we would definitely be on the river come October 1987. All we had to do now was assemble a crew—and enough willing passengers to help come up with the $100,000 fee.

The crew looked like the least of our worries. After a decade and a half of leading whitewater tours around the world, SOBEK had assembled an enviable stable of professional river guides eager to make the journey down the Great River. We were proud of our guides: they had tens of thousands of miles of wild river experience on whitewater all around the world, years of experience in handling the unexpected, passports stamped and restamped in a profusion of countries obscure and well known.

And therein lay a problem. It may have seemed that our roster would be top-heavy on talent; but much of that talent was a bit worn around the edges, a little rusty, with the faint creak of age audible beneath the roisterous barks of congratulation. There was John Yost, thirty-five, my partner in SOBEK, who was once considered something of a daredevil on exploratory raft trips, having flipped on several international expeditions. He was now married with three children and two mortgages, and he spent his weekdays rowing a desk, directing the far-flung operations of SOBEK Expeditions from Angels Camp. But after years of sharing the dream with me, he would not be denied a chance to raft the Yangtze.

Like Yost, my own stake in the river was too great: I had doggedly pursued the permit halfway around the world time and again, and had managed to land a contract to write about the Yangtze with co-author Christian Kallen. But Christian and I were in the same leaky boat: both thirty-seven, we had given up active guiding for writing, and despite weeks of regular morning runs, middle-aged midriff was a stubborn partner. Christian too had a family, with two kids younger in months than he was in years, and with each change of diapers, his commitment to rowing seemed to wane.

Skip Horner, at forty, was in the best shape, having spent the last fifteen years guiding international trekking and river expeditions with few interruptions. Dave Edwards, forty-five, our appointed expedition photographer, was fresh from his thirteenth consecutive full season on the Colorado, and was tuned as tight as a boxer half his age. But things started to droop from there. John Kramer, thirty-seven, once one of SOBEK's most daring and skilled guides, who had pioneered runs from Pakistan to New Guinea and trekked across jungle and tundra, also had a family of three children. In anticipation of his inevitable responsibilities he had rekindled his training as a geologist and was returning to graduate school. Although he was our designated equipment and food-supply manager, he had a recurring back problem, and his skills could not be relied upon once we got to the river.

Jim Slade, like his longtime buddy Skip Horner, had a career as an adventurer that spanned nearly two decades. A Columbia law school escapee with a razor-sharp mind, SOBEK's senior guide was looking ahead to his next birthday, the big four-oh, and had spent the last couple of years guiding less rigorous trips. He too was battling a weight problem, and had "a little rust on his sticks," as the oars are often called by professional guides.

Breck O'Neill once served as a Hollywood stuntman, whose biggest role was playing Rock Hudson's foot in a train fight scene in "McMillan and Wife." He had also been an active Colorado River guide, but that was ten years ago. Now he mostly managed the operation of Mad River Boat Trips from behind a desk in Jackson, Wyoming, and only occasionally got on the local scenic reach of the Snake River. Breck too was overweight, probably by twenty-five pounds. And he was afflicted with otosclerosis, which left him legally blind in one eye; in one ear he was partially deaf.

Not the crack team we were a decade ago.

But the roaring waters of the Yangtze called to us, its snowy peaks beckoned, and none of us considered giving up our slots to a younger, bolder crew. Joseph Rock's records and photos of his years in the Great Bend kept reverberating, as if a land so well loved might hold some secrets still. If the river was "the last great first," it would be our last great first too.

As the date for the Great Bend expedition drew near, our list of clients for the trip began to firm up. There were Ray Hubbard and Gerrit Schilperoort, our two sturdy seniors who, like Dick Moersch, a heart surgeon, had joined several previous SOBEK first descents; and orthodontist Jon Ingleman, who had responded to a news item in *Outside* magazine about our plans. Several former passengers on earlier SOBEK trips signed up—including balding and bowl-bellied Larry Krasnow, from San Diego, and chain-smoking Ken Jarkow, a paradigmatic New Yorker. Our other New Yorker, Sonny Falack, shared Jarkow's career in children's clothing, but there the resemblance ended: at twenty-five, Falack was a self-professed stud, who had the heavy-lidded looks of a Stallone to work for his success.

On the other side of the spectrum was Julia Amaral, a forty-one-year-old real-estate investor from Marin County, and our trip's only woman. Though she had at first balked at being the sole female, she finally realized that the once-in-a-lifetime opportunity would far outweigh any considerations of sexual politics. The client list was rounded out by big Jacques Vroom, forty-three, who owned a mail-order catalog consulting business and a computer training school. Despite his European, New Age name, Jacques was from Dallas, though like Jim Slade and John Kramer he had gone to school in western Massachusetts, and a Williams versus Amherst tension was never far from the surface when the three shared a boat.

That gave us nine clients, eight boatmen, and a kayaker—a ratio that put us woefully short of the $100,000 we needed to pay the Chinese. Christian and I agreed to put in $10,000 each; Breck O'Neill and Dave Edwards put in several thousand more apiece. By August, when we owed the final payment to the Chinese, we were still in bad shape. Looking at the roster and budget, I figured we were too old, too heavy, and too poor. I confided to Christian that I didn't believe the expedition would actually go. There had been so many false starts, and our financial situation seemed so shaky.

Then Joel Fogel called. He wanted to come kayak the Yangtze, and he offered to pay the nine-thousand-dollar kayaker's fee we had advertised to join us. That could make the expedition happen. Yet, if there were one person in the world I didn't want to have with us on the Yangtze, it was Joel Fogel.

I had met him fifteen years earlier when we were organizing our first SOBEK expeditions to Africa. Having returned to the United States nearly broke after several months of exploratory rafting in Ethiopia, I was looking for clients to join what would be our first commercial rafting tour of the Omo River, plus an exploratory down the nearby Baro River, a major tributary of the White Nile. Somehow Joel Fogel heard of our efforts, and tracked me down in Arizona, where I was about to embark on a Colorado raft trip. As I listened over the pay phone, Joel told me he wanted to join our proposed expeditions down the Omo and Baro rivers, and that he thought he could arrange for film money, a book advance, magazine assignments, a grant from the Explorers Club, perhaps even corporate sponsorship, plus he would pay for passage as well. He wanted to meet me, and offered to send a plane ticket to his home in New Jersey.

Our fledgling adventure travel company desperately needed clients and funds to survive. Joel was promising almost everything I had dreamed for SOBEK. And to that point in my life nobody had ever offered to fly me anywhere; that alone was terrifically seductive. Nonetheless, I agonized over the decision, then decided there was always the hint of chance that Joel was for real. I called Joel back and accepted his invitation.

Within minutes of arriving at the airport, a bright-eyed young man in a polyester leisure safari suit presented me with his four-page brochure: "Joel S. Fogel—Writer, Scientist, Adventurer, Ecologist." It told of his exploits kayaking from New York to Miami, of motorcycling ten thousand miles from Alaska to South America, of sailing solo six thousand miles through the South Pacific, of traveling for nearly two months along the White Nile. It was filled with pictures of Joel in action, skin diving, kayaking, sitting in a glider plane, straddling a motorcycle.

I had never seen such a blatant expression of ego, of unbridled megalomania in print, and I was amazed at the audacity it took to hand this self-advertisement to a stranger within the first few minutes of meeting. I was appalled, but strangely, I was intrigued; almost everything cited in the brochure was something I wanted to do—exotic travel, adventure sports, films, lectures, publishing, endorsements from the famous and powerful. It was as though Joel, who was just five years my senior, had manifested my secret fantasies, but had gone too far, had crossed some circumspect line of discretion and modesty. Joel was a living oxymoron, repulsive and attractive simultaneously. I wanted to turn my back, but I got stuck as if staring into a funhouse mirror.

I spent the next week with Joel, traveling to New York and Washington, DC to meet with publishers and filmmakers. I was impressed. Joel was a hustler. But nothing came of it all, except for cordial good lucks. Nothing, that is, except Angus MacLeod.

Joel introduced me to his neighbor and friend, a twenty-five-year-old professional soccer player who was ready for a grand adventure. Joel wanted Angus to join us on the Omo as a paying client, and on the Baro as a participant, on a share-the-cost basis. I already had misgivings about Joel, but Angus, I learned, had no whitewater experience whatsoever. Yes, he was in excellent shape, and Joel had taken Angus surf kayaking several times, but I knew it would not be prudent to allow a tyro on such a risky escapade. Nonetheless, Joel was relentless, and the lure of money was strong. Angus sold his sports car to raise the funds, and I accepted his donation to our share-the-cost exploratory.

A few days before our departure to the Baro, Joel met the rest of the group in Addis Ababa, Ethiopia, and read us a press release dated a week hence. He had arranged for the various wire services and news stringers to receive this report a few days after we would be on the river. It was meant to be a dispatch from the front lines of exploration. It spoke of huge rapids, of a raft being turned over and punctured by a charging water buffalo, and of our discovery of a tribe of Amazon-type women living along the banks of the river. This was all too fantastic to be believed. The room was stunned when Joel finished reading his master-piece. No, no, no was the consensus in the room—Joel could not release such flagrant fantasy as a report on our expedition. If he did, the group warned, he would be kicked off the expedition immediately.

On October 5, 1973, we arrived by public bus at the put-in for our Baro River exploratory, deep in a rain forest in southwest Ethiopia. The Baro was to be a prelude to the Omo, an exploration down a previously unrun river that, after having perused the maps, we thought might have commercial potential. Of the eleven people to attempt the Baro, Angus would be the only one with no rafting experience.

The current was high and swift, with an awful rust color. A hundred yards below the bridge the river doglegged, then pitched over a cruel waterfall into a corridor dark with jungle overgrowth. One look at the river and Joel knew he was in over his head, and he made the wise decision. He told the group it was too much, and he caught the next bus back to civilization.

That left a group of young rafters, heady and overconfident. And it left Angus MacLeod.

Angus was taciturn and wide-eyed as he boarded my raft just before launching. I went over the safety procedures with him, and when the other two rafts were loaded and ready, we pulled into the current. It was stronger than I had expected, and it snapped the raft around, propelling it towards the waterfall as though turbo-charged. I pulled on my oars to achieve some measure of control, but in seconds we were ripped around the bend and hurled over the waterfall. The raft crashed into a reversal, folded in half, spun, and did a dire dance. The frame shook like a railroad trestle. A wave punched from the side, and we were capsized.

It's a cold and desperate feeling being spun around beneath the surface of a rapid. I grasped for a handhold on the raft, and surfaced in swift water next to the upended boat. My glasses were gone, snatched from my face in the squawl. I looked back through the blurry billows to see Angus trailing ten feet behind, his face ghost-white in panic. His eyes telegraphed horror, incomprehension. He screamed for help.

I could see he was caught in the stern line from the raft, a strand wrapped about his chest. "Use your knife!" I yelled. Like all of us, he was wearing the requisite sheathed knife on his belt for just such an emergency. But Angus didn't respond—he was in deep shock, paralyzed with fear. I swam back to him, pulled my own knife from its sheath, and sliced the rope that had pinched his chest.

"Swim for shore, goddammit!" I screamed, and he looked at me with a glimmer of understanding. I nodded in return, then swam back to the raft to try to pull it to shore.

I was unsuccessful. I was swept through two more large rapids, and in the second I lost my grip and was sucked to the bottom of the river in a whirlpool. Barely conscious, I was pitched to the surface, where I managed to grab a tree branch and pull myself to shore. I collapsed and blacked out.

When I came to some minutes later, it sounded as if the river were making obscene swallowing noises. I found that a second of our three rafts had capsized, and both boats had been borne downstream, around the corner into the unknown. Everyone was accounted for, except Angus MacLeod.

We spent the next ten days in a massive search and rescue, using a helicopter and hundreds of locals, but there was no trace of Angus MacLeod. We returned to Addis Ababa broken, defeated, and despondent. There we discovered that Angus held a British passport, and when

I went to the British High Commission to inform them that our search had yielded nothing, I was handed a copy of a newspaper clipping from the *Atlantic City Press*, a report sent by Joel about the death of his "best friend," Angus MacLeod, on our expedition. But the article quickly turned into an account of the anthropological and entomological purposes of the expedition, describing Fogel as the reputed leader, and claiming that the group had encountered tribes that rarely make contact with the outside world. "I believe the tribes we have met so far have had little or no contact with Western civilization," Fogel was quoted as saying.

The report angered me. Joel's exaggerations and delusions of grandeur had at one time seemed harmless, even amusing. But now he had turned a tragedy into a travesty, using Angus's death as another way of getting his name in print.

Angus's death haunted me for years. I blamed myself for the senseless drowning of a young man. I had been greedy; I'd been brash; I'd been foolish. But a part of me also blamed Joel, and I despised his conduct and reactions to the accident.

For years Joel was parked in the furthest backlot of my mind. He would occasionally send me published articles about his latest exploits, or drop a note with an update about his covering of the Nicaraguan civil war for the *New York Times*, or his two-month, two-thousand-mile trip by cigarette boat from Fort Lauderdale to St. Martin. But I couldn't bring myself to believe any of it, or to respond.

Then one summer day Joel Fogel made me smile. I picked up a copy of the *San Francisco Chronicle*, and there was a small item with a catchy headline on an inside page: JUDGE SOCKS IT TO CHEEKY FELLOW, the title read, and the piece went on to say that one Joel Fogel had been arrested while parading down a New Jersey beach wearing nothing but a sock over his private parts. Joel had become a "naturist," a proponent of a clothing-optional life-style, and was making some sort of statement. As always, he was trying to glean as much exposure of himself as possible.

Not too long after, in the fall of 1983, Joel showed up on my office doorstep in Angels Camp, with his current girlfriend and a red Subaru crammed to overflowing with recreational gear, including a windsurfer, a surf kayak, two pairs of cross-country skis, and a ten-speed bike. Joel said he had been traveling across the country on a mission "to live with the homeless affected by the recession and write about their lives." Within hours of his appearance, he cornered one of the SOBEK secretaries and told her of his idyllic life at Club Orient, a nudist colony in the French West Indies, and invited her to come live with him—he would pay her air fare and expenses.

Shortly afterwards he confessed to me he was broke, and wanted to know if I could lend him a hundred dollars so he could continue. "Can't you use a credit card?" I asked. He said he had none. "Collateral?" I asked. He said I could call his father, a wealthy businessman, the founder and president of the Fogel Commercial Refrigerator Company. I did, and the senior Fogel wearily consented to pay me back if I would help out his son. I did, and Joel drove off to continue his mission of mercy. A few days later I received a hundred-dollar check from New Jersey.

Now a circumstance hauntingly similar to my initial encounter with Joel Fogel, fifteen years earlier, was presenting itself: an expedition was short of funds, and Joel was offering what we needed to make our dream happen. Memories of that first round were still painful. I just couldn't. . . .

John Yost took a different tack. He proposed we draft a contract forbidding Joel to publish anything concerning the Yangtze expedition without express written permission from either John or myself. The penalty for infraction: $25,000 per occurrence. John figured if Joel would sign the document, and send a cashier's check for $9,000, we'd have nothing to worry about, and our expedition could at last happen. We were so close to actually getting to the Yangtze, I couldn't let my personal animosity bar the way. I finally agreed.

And so we had our ship of fools, nineteen souls ready to challenge the Yangtze. In mid-October 1987, the Year of the Hare, we boarded a United Airlines jet in San Francisco and began the journey that would take us to Yunnan Province, deep into the unknown canyons of the Great Bend of the Yangtze.

CHAPTER FOURTEEN

The Land
of Stars and Horses

> This was Rock's country,
> from Yunnan to Tsinghai, a land
> of mountains that rival Himalayas,
> foaming rivers, jungle in the south and,
> beyond Lake Kokonor—the Northwestern Sea
> of Chinese folklore—windswept steppes,
> all unknown in America and Europe save
> for the writings of a few hardy adventurers.
> —S. B. SUTTON

One of the most stimulating aspects of remote river running is the contact with isolated cultures, be it the Nilotic tribes of northern Africa or the Papuans of New Guinea. In the Great Bend region where we were bound, there are two major ethnic groups, both of them related to the larger Burmo-Tibetan cultures. One of them, the Yi, are among China's most illustrious minorities. Known until 1949 as the Lolos, their homeland was so dangerous to travelers that it remained unsurveyed until after the revolution. The Lolo were long known as "iron peas," for they could not be assimilated into the stew of Chinese culture, as other minorities were more willing to be. Independent and warlike, the Yi were given to slave-taking and settling arguments before they began, in the tradition of America's own Wild West; their reputation for violence was unparalleled in historical China. It is even said that Chiang Kai-shek, after pursuing the Red Army all over southern China's Hunan, Guizhou, and Yunnan provinces, breathed a sigh of relief once they crossed the

Yangtze into the so-called Land of the Lolos. The tribespeople had such an unrelievedly evil reputation that Chiang was sure the Long March would end in ignominy in the wilderness of Lololand.

He was wrong, of course: the Communists managed to engage the sympathy, respect, and even a measure of support from the much-feared Lolos, as they did with tribal people throughout their march. Probably their first gesture towards accommodation was in not calling the people "Lolos"—the name is derived from the word for "basket," so the term is perhaps akin to calling a proud gypsy a "bag lady." This derisiveness used to be common among the Chinese: Joseph Rock noted that the Chinese characters for many minorities are prefixed by the radical or ideograph for "dog," to show contempt for the aboriginal people. "Yi" is the current name for the five-million-strong minority, and within the larger whole there are several smaller tribal groups. Those who live in the Great Bend region are called the Nosu; they are a tall and handsome people, dressed in long capes of gray or black. The women wear silver jewelry and headdresses of folded and stacked blue cotton, and enjoy a certain magical power—it is regarded as bad luck to touch a woman's skirt, and if a fight begins, a woman can end it by placing herself between the contestants and waving her skirt. One visitor to the Lololand of today, Jeff Chop of the National Geographic's 1985 expedition to the source of the Yangtze, said the Yi reminded him of the Indians of the American Southwest: "The style of their dwellings and the appearance of the people—their features, complexions, and costumes—were very reminiscent to me of those of the Southwestern United States. Large stretches of land in this area have the stark beauty of Arizona." His observation echoed that of Joseph Rock, one of the first Westerners to visit the region, who wrote sixty years earlier, "The villages here reminded me much of those of Hopi Indians of the American Southwest, with their flat roofs on which yellow Indian corn is dried."

It is to Joseph Rock, the peripatetic botanist whose articles for *National Geographic* first alerted so many to the spectacular gorges of western Yunnan, that we owe nearly all of our information about the other major ethnic group in the Great Bend, the Naxi. Numbering about a quarter of a million, the Naxi have been encountered by several other Westerners in the past 150 years, but they proved the special province of the Austrian-born scientist. In large measure, Rock devoted his life to the Naxi; the culmination of his study was the hefty two-volume tome for Harvard University, *The Ancient Na-khi Kingdom of Southwestern*

China, published in 1947. (A brief digression on phonetics: according to the old Wade-Giles transliteration of Chinese, *Nakhi* is correct; the new pinyin style has it *Naxi*. The pronunciation to Western ears, however, is "Nashi"—the spelling used in Rock's old *National Geographic* articles of the 1930s.) Thus, no current inspection of the Naxi is possible without a curious sideways look at the eccentric explorer of the Great Bend, Joseph Rock.

Born into a servant family in Vienna in 1884, Joseph Franz Karl Rock was never happy with his station. He lost his mother when he was only six, and his father never offered the emotional support the younger of his two children needed. School bored him, and as soon as his secondary education was completed he hit the road, in an extended *Wanderjahr* that lasted far beyond the traditional twelve months. He was twenty-four before he returned to Vienna, for the funeral of his father: by that time he knew some Hungarian, French, Italian, Greek, Arabic, and English in addition to German. Clearly, languages posed no problem for Joseph Rock, and this facility was to serve him well in later years, when he ventured to Asia.

In 1905, after his father's funeral, he went to America, working his way slowly westward until, in 1907, he had come to Hawaii. It was here that the first career of Joseph Rock was born. He talked himself into a job as a natural history teacher. Within a year, he developed tuberculosis, a disease that encouraged him to pursue his outdoor studies. With characteristic boldness, he approached the head of the territory's Division of Forestry, told him that Hawaii needed a herbarium, and had himself appointed its chief collector.

For the next twelve years, until 1920, Rock was a hardworking, almost driven botanist, first for the Division of Forestry and later for the College of Hawaii (now the University of Hawaii). He wrote many technical papers and three books, including *The Indigenous Trees of Hawaii*, which is still the standard reference on the subject. But his wanderlust had not deserted him: in 1913 he made his first trip to China, a country that had grabbed his imagination as a child. Suddenly Hawaii seemed too small, too isolated from the great civilization of the Orient. In 1920, Rock resigned his post and accepted an assignment with the US Department of Agriculture that would take him to Burma.

The assignment also led to another career, as a writer for *National Geographic*. The magazine published his first article in its March 1922 issue, by which time he had an appointment from the National

Geographic Society to investigate the natural history of Yunnan. Rock made his way to the center of the Naxi tribal area near Lijiang, in the heart of the Great Bend. His description of the area is so full of romantic enthusiasm it is easy to suspect that, perhaps for the first time in his adult life, Joseph Rock had found his spiritual home.

> As the castles were the strongholds of the knightly clans of the Middle Ages in Europe, so we may look upon the great snow range in the center of the Nashi Kingdom as the cradle and rallying point of a gradually vanishing tribe. Dragonlike, this mighty range, pierced by the Yangtze as by a giant's sword, extends toward the borders of Szechwan, crowned by three peaks whose turrets know eternal winter only. On the slopes and miniature plains—ice lakes in bygone days—are scattered the hamlets of the Nashi, living happily, as if in the Stone Age, for flint and edelweiss as tinder still take the place of matches, and pinewood torches are used instead of lamps.

Rock discovered that the Naxi were a lost civilization, a once-great kingdom whose vast empire had been reduced, once by Kublai Khan's invasion and again by the intrusion of Han Chinese. In many ways, however, the ancient culture of the Naxi survived. For the next twenty-seven years, despite his continued travels and diverse interests, Rock undertook comprehensive study of the Naxi, their writings and their culture.

The Naxi are one of the Ch'iang tribes that harassed the Han Dynasty from Tibet over two thousand years ago. The imperial armies finally dispersed the Ch'iang in nine directions, according to tradition, a diaspora reminiscent of the tribes of Israel; one of those directions was south to the Great Bend. The Naxi were said to have crossed the Yangtze and taken possession of their current stronghold, at the base of Yulong Shan, from the still more ancient P'u tribes. Chinese records mention them first during the Tang Dynasty, about 796 A.D., but by 1260 their independence was lost to the invasion of Kublai Khan.

After the fall of the Yuan Dynasty, however, the Naxi kingdom once again asserted itself, and early in the seventeenth century the Naxi ruler Mutienwang controlled not only the Great Bend but eastward over the Mekong River into Tibet and at least a hundred miles northward to the kingdom of Muli. Many mud watchtowers of the Naxi kings remain standing today throughout the region between the Yangtze and the Mekong, some of them still in good condition. By the rise of the Manchus a hundred years later, Chinese authority became established in

Lijiang, and the Naxi kings submitted to the emperors of the Qing Dynasty.

The Naxi are clearly of Tibetan origin, as shown in their myths and language as well as physical characteristics. Unlike most non-Han people in China, the Naxi had not one but two written languages, an elementary set of characters and a unique pictographic literature that Rock spent decades deciphering. The legends of this literature, known as *senjiulujiu,* or "markings on wood and stone," include tales of the Naxi migration from Lake Manasarowar and Mount Kailas, the most sacred region of Tibet. Four major Asian rivers originate in this region—the Indus, the Ganges, the Sutlej, and the Tsangpo or Brahmaputra; it is somewhat ironic that the Naxi now make their home on an isolated peninsula surrounded by another great river, the Yangtze.

Naxi legends tell of their former life as nomadic herdsmen, living in yak-skin tents on alpine meadows, and of their "elder brothers" the Tibetans. Some Naxi ancestors can be related to the gods of the Indian pantheon, and they claim that their heroes came from magic eggs produced from the union of mountains and lakes, pines and stones, snake spirits and women—origin myths highly reminiscent of Tibetan tales.

Even the landscape of the Naxi fits into the Tibetan cosmology. Although the Lijiang region is dominated by Yulong Shan, the long glaciated peak so visible from the Yangtze as the river approaches Tiger's Leap Gorge, the most sacred peak in the district is Shangri Moupo, a 14,000-foot pyramid south of Lijiang. Shangri Moupo is one of the dwelling places of the gods in Tibetan lore.

Foremost among Naxi deities is Saddo, a mountain-dwelling god whose lineage Rock traces directly to Satham or Sadam, a Tibetan folk god often represented as a cave-dwelling demon. When the Naxi traveled to the Great Bend region, Rock postulated, the cave-dwelling Sadam became Saddo, a mountain god who lived in the majestic peaks of the Great Snow Range. For the Naxi, Saddo was a warrior spirit, a cultural hero dressed in white armor, with a white helmet and white spear, riding a white horse. The white hero was said to appear in every major battle the Naxi fought, leading them to victory; in a guileless shift of allegiance, he even was said to have fought with the invading Kublai Khan against the Nanzhou Kingdom of Dali. Saddo's identification with the Naxi is so strong that Tibetan nomads, according to the nineteenth-century geographer Colonel Henry Yule, called the town we know as Lijiang by its Tibetan name, Sadam.

The Naxi world-view was, however, catholic in the largest sense of the word. Only the paranoid restrictions of fundamentalist Christians failed to become assimilated into the Naxi cosmos. Peter Goullart, a Russian-born Frenchman who became a Chinese public servant during the Nationalist period, noted in his book *Forgotten Kingdom* that the Naxi accepted a multiplicity of scriptures, as long as they did not interfere with the Naxi view of a happy life. Goullart identified the Naxi ideal in terms that are difficult to refute:

> It was best not to take chances on future joys but to enjoy oneself to the hilt whilst on this plane. The happiness, which every Nakhi should strive after, was described as the possession of plenty of good fields and fruit orchards, cattle and horses, a spacious house, an attractive wife, lots of male and female children, barns chock full of grain, yak butter and other edibles, multitudes of jars with wine, abundant sexual strength and good health and a succession of picnics and dances with congenial companions on flower-strewn alpine meadows.

Not all is flower-strewn meadows in the Naxi cosmos, however. The tribe was long notorious for its high suicide rate, especially prevalent among young lovers. Goullart estimated that 80 percent of Naxi suicides were pacts between adolescent lovers who found their passionate natures frustrated by the proscriptions of Chinese-style arranged marriages. Other rationales for suicide include unhappy marriages, tangled love affairs, and loss of face. But the psychological tensions inherent in Naxi suicide probably have their roots in the fairly recent cultural shift from matriarchal to patriarchal social structure—an ancient Naxi world-view layered over by the more rigid social regulations of the Han Chinese. Although the Naxi are ostensibly patriarchal, and have apparently accepted Chinese customs and Confucian patriarchy, most public business is conducted by women—they run all the shops, conduct the market, and in general call the shots in daily life.

While most Naxi live within the Lijiang "peninsula" of the Great Bend, some, such as the matriarchal Moso people, live above the Bend. Rock called this region Yungning, though the Naxi know it as Yuli. The Naxi of Lijiang, and many outside commentators as well, look upon the Moso as a separate tribe, but there are significant cultural similarities between the two groups that suggest a fairly recent split. Far more so than the Naxi, however, the Moso are matriarchal; and it is their matriarchal sexual practices that have drawn the most attention, both from visitors and from the ideologues of the Chinese revolution.

Before the revolution, their homeland was quite popular with male traders, who found among Moso women a degree of sexual receptivity verging on the ideal. From their early teens on, girls were allowed to sleep with their lovers in their own rooms, in their mother's house; they were also allowed whatever lovers they chose, and any children that resulted were theirs to keep. The young men of the Moso usually returned at dawn to their own mother's house, though when "marriages" did take place, couples might live together—as long as the woman thought it suitable. These relationships were known by the term *azhu*—each partner calls the other "*azhu*," friend or partner, though this year's *azhu* might not be next year's, or last year's. Men were expected to provide a certain economic security as long as they were part of the *azhu* relationship, but once it ended their obligation ended as well.

Jeffrey Chop noticed that government authorities were reluctant to discuss the Moso. Although women are clearly the heads of the households in Moso society, Chop observed that the only government officials they met were men, who emphasized the number of monogamous Moso relationships. Chinese writers also emphasize the "successes" of modernization over its failures. One book admits that the matriarchal family system is "fascinating to social scientists, but with the advancement of productivity, there will be an evolution into a higher stage of social development." If this sounds like Marxist-Leninist-Maoist dogma, perhaps it is.

Naturally, the Moso are protected by a mountain goddess, who dwells in the so-called Lion Mountain (more properly, perhaps, Lioness Mountain) which looms above the lake called Luku Hu; she takes her mates freely from the mountain gods of the surrounding ranges.

But the land of the Moso is not quite the paradise that the passing traveler would have it. Goullart noted that Moso women, despite their sexual attractiveness, were particularly shunned by sensible travelers and the Naxi because of their high rate of venereal disease. While in Lijiang, Goullart acted as an informal and untrained medical authority, as missionaries and government agents often do in remote areas. He recalled examining a Tibetan merchant who said he felt ill, and giving him the unfortunate news that he had a "confidential disease."

" 'No, no!' he cried. 'It is only a cold!'

" 'How did you get it?' I asked.

" 'I caught it when riding a horse,' he replied.

" 'Well,' I said, 'it was the wrong kind of horse.' "

On the other hand, it was noted even by Rock that suicide, of the type so prevalent among the Naxi, is all but unknown among the Moso.

Presumably the psychological tensions between the desirable and the unattainable are not nearly so strained.

Since the Naxi arrived in the Great Bend region several centuries before Padmasambhava brought Buddhism to Tibet, the religion of the Great Bend is, in some ways, even more ancient than that of Tibet. Subsequent contacts with their "elder brothers" the Tibetans have established Tibetan-style Buddhism, or Lamaism, in the Naxi area (as elsewhere in Yunnan and Sichuan). But the role of the local shamanistic cult, presided over by priests known as "dtombas," is stronger. Dtombas receive their legacy from the founder of the Bon sect, Dtomba Shilo (or Tompa Shenrabmipo, *tompa* meaning teacher). Although the dtomba shamans may wear the yellow cap of Lamaism, their rituals hark back to a still more ancient era of religious belief than that shared by their "elder brothers"—an era where blood sacrifice and spirit possession were the norm rather than the exception.

Today, the Naxi are concentrated almost entirely in the Great Bend region—in particular the area to the south of the Bend's apex, centered around the regional capital, Lijiang. Growing barley in terraced fields and raising even-tempered chestnut horses known throughout Yunnan, the Naxi have adapted well to life in Communist China. Their homeland is called the "land of stars and horses," and their women's traditional dress reflects this symbology: a sheepskin cape, fastened by wide bands across the front, features seven embroidered circles along the back, with leather tassels hanging from each, representing stars and their light rays. In earlier times, each shoulder of the cape was embroidered with a larger circle, symbolic of the sun and moon, but these are rarely seen today.

Yet it is not only the cultural richness of the Great Bend that continues to attract travelers, and that has time and again led to comparisons with that most mythic of lost horizons, Shangri-la. Nearly every journeyer to the Great Bend takes pause to stop, look around, and smell the rhododendrons. Peter Goullart's *Forgotten Kingdom* is rife with descriptions such as this one, descriptions that can only give a distant breath of the glorious atmosphere of the land of stars and horses.

Almost all the days in Likiang [sic] were glorious days. It was the land of spring eternal. . . . The beauty of this paradisiacal valley was never static or stale. It was renewed every day and something fresh and marvellous was added to it. The Snow Mountain was not a dead and stereotyped agglomeration of crags, ice and snow; it was a living goddess with her own way of life and moods. It never remained the same for more than a few minutes. It veiled and unveiled itself, trailed bands of white vapour around its base or shot a while plume of snow into the azure sky. Its crown, in the form of a vast, opened fan, shot out rays of gold and silver. The gurgling of rushing streams mingled with the songs of larks and cries of herons. Flowers changed their colours and variety with each day and always the air was heavy with fragrance. Everything seemed to scintillate and sparkle in this wondrous valley; nature visibly breathed and moved and smiled. Every walk outside the town was an excitement and a revelation: there was intoxication in the warm breeze and a hint of dancing in the undulation of green mountains, the streams twisting and bouncing and the birds and butterflies flitting in the air. The people too smiled, laughed and sang with the fullness of their joy and happiness in this secret paradise.

CHAPTER FIFTEEN

South of the Clouds

> China may be regarded as
> an artist nation, with the virtues
> and vices to be expected of the artist:
> virtues chiefly useful to others,
> vices chiefly harmful to oneself.
> —BERTRAND RUSSELL

Flying northeastward from Hong Kong on October 20, 1987, we peered into the clouds to catch sight of our goal, the western province of Yunnan. Yunnan means "South of the Clouds," but today the land lay beneath them. Only as we began our approach to Kunming did we see the earth below: a large river red with mud, red earth, Red China. The countryside was so tidy it looked like a storybook. Orange brick buildings with tile roofs stood in tight clusters amid a green patchwork of fields and harvested rice paddies. With the rousing strains of Tchaikovsky piped in over the aircraft's speakers, we landed amidst Slavic fanfares and crescendos in the People's Republic of China.

Despite Kunming's position as the provincial capital, the airport is modest, and the prevalence of soldiers in loose green uniforms sporting pistols in worn leather holsters gave me the feeling of having landed in a World War II movie. Perhaps the feeling was a residue of the not so distant past, when Kunming was an important access point to interior China following the Japanese takeover of the coast. Here, at this same airport, were based the famed Flying Tigers—the American Volunteer Group, aviators under the command of "Old Leatherface," General C. L. Chennault, who fought for Free China against the Japanese even before Pearl Harbor. One could almost see leather-jacketed John Wayne descend from his cat-faced aircraft, glance at a fuselage peppered with bullet holes, and shrug it off with the laconic "Termites."

Jim Slade, SOBEK's point man in Kunming for the previous week, met us as we entered the customs area, and helped gather our cargo into one enormous pile: suitcases, backpacks, duffels, aluminum camera cases, a red C-1, and a yellow kayak. The sheer volume of our cargo failed to intimidate the Chinese customs agents, who blandly insisted upon fully documenting the load even though they made no effort to search a single bag. We counted nineteen heads: all present and accounted for, with a single exception. Our expedition doctor, Jack Tolliver, didn't answer the roll call. Had he been Shanghaied? No, John Yost announced, he had called the Angels Camp office moments before our own takeoff to admit he couldn't catch his flight out of Charleston, West Virginia, because of a cold fog.

With that news, some of us winked and bet on cold feet. But nobody blamed him: with all the trials and tribulations that had been suffered on the Yangtze the year before, everyone was carrying a duffel full of fear. We were now without a designated trip doctor, but immediately heart surgeon Dick Moersch—a veteran of several SOBEK expeditions, and an Olympic-class high hurdler in 1948—volunteered to act as a replacement. Then Jon Ingleman, a quiet, bearded orthodontist from Fort Wayne, Indiana, also volunteered to help out. "Great," said Christian. "Now we're covered if our hearts go into our mouths."

On the twenty-minute drive from the airport to the stately Kunming Hotel on the west side of town, Slade filled us in on what he had learned during his week in Kunming. He had flown in ahead of the group to assure that our equipment safely entered the country from Hong Kong, and to make final purchases of food, kerosene, and other items. He had found the two-million-strong city surprisingly easy to find his way in, and had even ventured into the nearby hills on one of the ubiquitous one-speed bicycles that clotted the city's avenues. Wide streets, busy industrial districts, and modern office buildings gave Kunming the atmosphere of a progressive city, but it had not always been thus.

Over two thousand years before, the pleasant and fertile plain surrounding Dian Chi (Lake Dian, formerly Tien Chi) had been the encampment for a Chu Dynasty army, according to ancient historical records. More recently, archeological excavations near the lake have unearthed weapons, drums, and jewelry of silver, jade, and turquoise, dating back to the quiet years before the eighth century. Then, the ascendant Nanzhou Kingdom centered in Dali captured the Tang lakeside dynastic outpost, and made the town its eastern capital. When Kublai Khan expanded the Mongolian Empire to conquer China in the thirteenth century, one of his first major victories was over the Nanzhou Kingdom, in 1253; six years later, Khan completed the conquest of China by founding the Yuan Dynasty. Kunming—then called Yachi— had become a vital and energetic trading town, described by the peripatetic Marco Polo as being filled with "merchants and artisans, and a mixed population consisting of idolaters, Nestorian Christians and Saracens or Mohametans."

Once the imperial power of the Khans began to erode, however, Kunming—known until less than fifty years ago as Yunnanfu—suffered under the administration of a succession of warlords. During the nineteenth century, the city was several times attacked by the rebel Moslem leader, Du Wenziu or "the Sultan of Dali," whose rebellion lasted for nearly twenty years, ending only in 1873. As the Western powers made their presence more strongly felt in China during the waning years of the Qing Dynasty (the Manchus), Yunnan was exploited for copper, tin, and lumber by the French. The Europeans built the Indo-China Railroad to exploit the riches of Yunnan, and it reached Kunming in 1910, thus opening up southwestern China to sea trade via the port of Haiphong.

Aware of Yunnan's growing economic power in the world, and of the developing governmental chaos in Peking, a former military governor named Ts'ai Ao declared Yunnan's independence from the Republic of China on December 25, 1915, thus precipitating the downfall of Yuan Shih-k'ai, first president of the Republic. A succession of governors and bandits ruled the region until 1927, when Kunming fell under the control of Lung Yun, a warlord from the Yi tribe of northwestern Yunnan. Lung Yun—his name means Dragon Cloud—made a personal fortune in protection money and opium, but did manage to keep some semblance of order in Kunming throughout the turbulent war years.

But it was the Sino-Japanese War, more than anything else, that initiated Kunming into the modern world. When the Nationalist government fled Nanjing for its inland capital of Chongqing in 1937, hundreds of thousands of Chinese refugees fled from the coastal cities, and many of them reached Kunming. Furthermore, because of the war effort and the establishment of factories to make use of Yunnan's mineral resources, thousands of peasants and tribespeople from surrounding regions came to Kunming to find work. The presence of American and

British troops did still more to break the isolation of Kunming. By the time the Chinese Communists made their final assault on Chiang Kai-shek's government in the years following World War II, Kunming had been propelled into the future.

Our very modern jet lag propelled most of us into our rooms for an afternoon nap, but some of us greased the gears with green tea and rolled out into the streets for sightseeing. Free citizens of the world's greatest democracy, we looked closely at these comrades of the world's most populous Communist country. Perhaps we expected to see a certain stiff formality, a rigidity of behavior, or a cursory contempt for us running dogs of imperialism, or at least the behavioral scars of a century of trial. Instead, we saw posters advertising Mitsubishi cars, toothpaste, the new Superman movie now showing at the cinema. The Chinese themselves were relaxed and spontaneous, full of shrugs and ready smiles, and openly curious about their lanky, relatively youthful visitors: most American tourists in China are senior citizens even now, passengers on package tours to the mysterious cities of the Orient.

That evening the group gathered in a large tea room at the hotel for a formal logistics meeting. John Yost took the role of discussion leader, and started right off with the bad news: the maps he had studied showed several sections of very steep drop, the severity of which would depend on the water level. A drop of fifteen feet per mile might be insignificant on a small-volume river, but on a river the size of the Yangtze—which might be running anywhere from 30,000 to 50,000 cubic feet per second through the Great Bend, according to our best guesses from past years—it could be perilous.

But fifteen feet per mile, according to Yost's figures, would be our flat-water stretches. The Great Bend seemed to have two major sections of drop: Tiger's Leap Gorge, with a drop of about twenty-five feet per mile for some twelve miles; and an unnamed section around the top of the Great Bend, which showed a gradient of some fifty feet per mile for fifteen miles. That was an astounding figure, and accordingly, Yost assured us, he had every reason to doubt it.

The maps also showed that in several regions the surrounding mountains were more than 12,000 feet high, with no nearby roads and few villages. The possibility of emergency evacuation in case of serious injury was remote, if not impossible. SOBEK is, we kept reminding ourselves, the world's most experienced river outfitter, and we had close to a century of collective experience among the guides in the room. But should a section of the river become unrunnable and unportageable, there was a reasonable possibility we would be facing a lengthy hike over high mountain passes to distant villages, and the abandonment of all the expedition gear and most of our personal equipment in the gorges of the Yangtze.

The white porcelain pots of green tea remained untouched, ignored. This was the fate that had befallen the Ken Warren expedition a little over a year earlier, and it was a trial that no one wanted to experience for himself. Each of us took some moments to consider his own mortality and commitment to adventure. After all, many of the group —New York clothier Ken Jarkow, San Diego investment counselor Larry Krasnow, Marin County real-estate entrepreneur Julia Amaral— were in business, not adventurers by trade. Then there were our two senior members, sixty-seven-year-old Washington farmer Gerrit Schilperoort, and seventy-four-year-old Ray Hubbard, an industrial machines manufacturer from Stockton, California. They had proved to be tough as nails on earlier expeditions with SOBEK, Gerrit in Ecuador and Sumatra, and Hubbard in Pakistan and Ethiopia; but they had not been called upon to make a lengthy hike over 12,000-foot passes. And in the past year, both had endured health traumas that would have felled lesser men: Gerrit had been in an auto accident that broke eight ribs and collapsed a lung, and Hubbard had undergone prostate surgery.

Yost continued with the business of the meeting, deciding which tents would come with us, outlining the route we would take over the next two days to reach our put-in, and suggesting which items of personal gear should be left behind as nonessential. Yost decreed that hiking boots fit this category—although they might be handy for an emergency evacuation, they were too heavy and bulky for the more likely scenario of portaging around unrunnable rapids. It was a judgment call that would come back to haunt us in less than a week.

At one point Jacques Vroom, a towering, big-boned computer consultant from Dallas, asked if any of the Chinese from CIST would accompany us down the river. "After dropping hints and invitations, I finally asked them point-blank if they would come," Yost said. "They all refused, saying that none of them have had the special training." Everyone laughed; though it was probably a reference to the three Chinese Ken Warren had trained in Oregon, who *has* had the "special training" for big drops, certain portages, steep and impenetrable terrain, and the unknown and potentially dangerous nature of rafting the Yangtze?

After the meeting, we adjourned to a nearby restaurant for a banquet.

Wave after wave of dishes were brought to our table—a variety of meats in ginger, pickled vegetables, barbecued chicks with heads still on their scrawny necks, a gristly dish called "elephant nose" in gravy, stuffed biscuits, cabbage soup, and finally white rice, just in case anyone was hungry. Of course, it was all accompanied by toast after toast of the bitter rice liquor called *mao-tai*.

"*Ganbei!*" we toasted CIST. "*Ganbei!*" they toasted SOBEK. We all toasted the Yangtze, Ken Warren, the food, international friendship, the flowers on the table. Someone tried to teach us how to count to five in Chinese, but it seemed impossible—learning Chinese, with its subtle consonants and intonations, is like learning to speak Wind Chime. And the liquor didn't make it any easier. Then we staggered back to the Kunming Hotel, and tried to remember what we were supposed to pack in our waterproof bags and what to leave behind.

Unspeakably early the next morning, we loaded most of our gear into a large truck, which took off ahead of us with equipment manager John Kramer duly riding shotgun; then we each took a seat in the soon-to-become-familiar yellow minibus. Our route was to take us nearly six hundred miles across Yunnan to Shigu, the projected put-in point on the Yangtze. If being a passenger in a rattling minibus is nothing to brag about, neither is it easy to forget: we squirmed in narrow, uncomfortable seats, swaying side to side as the road rose out of the flat lake valley of Dian Chi, passing for hour after hour along the two-lane highway through mud-brick villages and the rice fields of Yunnan.

From Kunming to Dali, about two-thirds of our total route, the main highway followed the historic Burma Road, first constructed by a workforce of 160,000 Chinese between 1936 and 1937, using tools that ranged in sophistication from hoes to teaspoons. Although the route had long been used for trade between Yunnan and Burma, the loss of coastal China to the Japanese in the Sino-Japanese War had meant that traditional contact with the outside world could no longer pass through the port cities of Shanghai and Canton (as Guangzhou was then known). Chiang Kai-shek had set up his government in Chongqing in Sichuan, which necessitated the building of a paved road, suitable for trucks, to link interior China with the outside world. Supplies could be shipped to Rangoon by sea, and thence by rail to Lashio in northeastern Burma, where the Burma Road began.

In April 1942, the Japanese overran Burma, driving out General Joseph Stilwell and forcing his army's march along a 140-mile jungle trek into India. While all of Stilwell's party arrived in Assam safely, the British-Indian army occupying Burma fared less well. Some 42,000 strong before the Japanese invasion, they numbered only about 12,000 upon their arrival in India. Stilwell, furious at the loss of Burma, had Allied forces build a new road from Assam to Ledo in northern Burma, thus reopening the Burma Road to inland China. The cost in human terms was high: Japanese snipers killed 130 workers and engineers, hundreds more died due to accident and illness (the route cut through malarial swamplands, down steep gorges and over swift-flowing rivers), and the road became known as "Man-a-Mile Road."

During the two years the Ledo Road (also called the Stilwell Road) was under construction, supplies were flown into Kunming from Assam five hundred miles away, a route that crossed over the "hump" of the Himalaya Range with its 20,000-foot peaks, as well as the jungle-covered gorges of the Irrawaddy, Salween, and Mekong rivers. It too was a costly link, as about one thousand men and six hundred planes were lost while flying 650,000 tons of cargo to China. One previously unnamed mountain along the route claimed so many flights that it earned the nickname "Aluminum Plated Mountain."

Our passage along the Burma Road took us past rice fields lined with sycamore trees and beehive kilns, the last fired and worked by peasant women in red tunics and blue aprons who produced mounds of roof tile and clay piping. In the big truck carrying the bulk of our expedition gear, John Kramer ran into an impenetrable language barrier when he tried to talk with the driver. So he turned his attention to the road, and watched the work that went into its improvement—work done almost entirely by hand. The workers were filling ditches, digging out stumps and embankments, and chipping rocks of varying sizes, then fitting them like the pieces of a Chinese puzzle into the roadbed. The final surfacing was gravel and sand covered with hot tar; retaining walls of stone were built slowly with stout and craftsmanlike masonry.

The countryside was a beehive of farming activity, with harvesting and planting everywhere. At one rest stop, when we all piled out of the Toyota minibus for roadside relief, Gerrit Schilperoort, the consummate farmer, moseyed over to a fellow tradesman hard at work behind a stolid water buffalo. Gerrit grabbed the man's plow and tilled a couple of rows, passing on pointers to a perplexed and uncomprehending peasant.

For twelve hours we bounced through the bucolic countryside. The narrow road was barely wider than two vehicles, and it was never free of horsecarts stacked with hay or coal, bicycles, pedestrians, and tractors that looked like slant-six engines mounted behind a go-cart on risers. We whizzed around mountain twists and tree-blind turns with abandon. The techniques of Chinese driving, possibly the result of ancient ideologies applied to modern technologies, seemed to compel a fearless claim to road space: vehicles straddled the middle of the road until the last possible second when meeting oncoming traffic; then both contestants blasted their horns and swerved to opposite sides, like blustering schoolyard antagonists.

After the sun set, this game of chicken rose to a new level. Chinese drivers prefer to drive without benefit of headlights. Rather, they negotiate the potted, dark highways with their parking lights dimly aglow. When they see an oncoming set of parking lights, they blink their headlights on, then shut them off. The drivers then continue to career towards each other in darkness, still in the middle of the road. At a distance of a hundred feet or so, they blink again: Still there? Then, when finally close enough to blind one another, they flash the lights on for an alarming few seconds, and the two vehicles pass in a white-hot roar. This practice evidently helps keep the drivers awake and alert; it certainly works for the passengers.

Our first night was spent in Xiaguan, a city on the banks of the river that flows into Erh Hai, also known as Dali Lake. Although it had been a long and uncomfortable day, it was only a single day—for the merchants and travelers of past centuries, it had been a thirteen-stage trip from Kunming. Although there is much to be said for speed, many of us wished we could spend more time seeing China other than through the windows of a minibus. That evening, the group's youngest member, twenty-five-year-old Bronx-born Sonny Falack, and the two senior citizens Gerrit Schilperoort and Ray Hubbard purposely "got lost," and ate dinner in a small shop outside the hotel walls while the rest of us dutifully dined within.

The next morning, we again rose early to begin the second stage of our two-day journey to Shigu; but on the strength of Sam Moore's description of nearby Dali as "something of the Old China," we lobbied for and won a stopover in the historic town. Its links with the past have been preserved in part by its isolation—the 260-mile ride from Kunming takes the tourist well off the beaten path—and in part by its situation in what was once called "the Forbidden Zone," isolated regions of China closed to outside visitors for reasons of political instability. In any case, when we pulled up to its imposing south gate—Wu Hua Lou, or the Tower of Five Glories, originally built in 856—for a walk through the streets of the old town, we could tell at once that we had only to step beneath the stone arch to enter Old China.

Dali, formerly known as Ta-Li (frequently translated as "great principle"), rests at 6,400 feet, between the base of the 12,000-foot Changshan mountains and the four-hundred-square-mile Erh Hai lake, stretching emerald beneath the clouds. Three ancient pagodas dating from 632 A.D.—one of them leaning like an Asiatic Tower of Pisa—watch over the walled city from the nearby foothills; red-tiled temples reach towards the skies; the narrow cobbled streets are filled with horsecarts, strolling soldiers, and laughing Bai women trading vegetables and wares. The Bai are one of several minority groups centered around Dali, each recognizable by their clothing. The red-aproned Bai, the blue-vested Naxi, and the white-capped Hui are the most prominent. For some reason, the women were more readily distinguishable by their clothing; most men were dressed in the simple green or blue coat and cap of "the people," the "Mao suit" fashion still most prevalent throughout China.

The Bai, most visible of Dali's minorities, have lived along Erh Hai for nearly three thousand years, according to their legends. Today they number over a million, and their birth rate, like that of many of China's minorities, surpasses the national average. The Bai are known throughout China for their singing, and the lilting voices of the women can often be heard exchanging gossip, retelling folktales, or welcoming visitors as the Bai work in their fields. At seasonal festivals such as San Yue Kai, the "Third Moon Feast" held in March, traders come to Dali from all over Yunnan to join a pan-tribal market, an ancient tradition that has led to the spread of fine marble carvings from Dali into the imperial courts of Nanjing and Beijing.

The Bai pride themselves on their illustrious history, and eagerly recall the glorious era of the Nanzhou. But the Nanzhou (formerly Nanchao) were probably not Bai, nor any other group of the local Minchia ("common people," the Han Chinese name for the region's inhabitants). Historians believe the Nanzhou Kingdom originated not in Dali, where it came to be centered, but in the south, through the unification of two rival kingdoms of the Shan culture most dominant in Siam (Thailand) and Burma. The "Great Meng Kingdom"—which became known as the Nanzhou or Southern Kingdom—lasted for over six hundred years, and at its peak stretched into eastern Tibet, north across the Yangtze, and eastward to Kunming, a territory that became, in time, Yunnan Province.

Although the Nanzhou were able to withstand attacks by the Tufan (Tibetans) in the tenth century, and preserved their independence from dynastic China for over half a millennium, they were unable to hold out against the Mongolians. In 1253, Kublai Khan entered the Nanzhou Kingdom by defeating their warriors at the banks of the Yangtze between Shigu and Tiger's Leap Gorge; the downfall of Dali was only a matter of time.

The Chinese never had to "civilize" the Erh Hai region in the way they did the mountain territories where the "barbarians" lived, for the Bai have been an agricultural people for millennia. When the Chinese came, with their unified creed of Taoism, Confucianism, and Buddhism, the Bai were more than willing to assimilate these religions into their local cults. Still, according to anthropologist C. P. Fitzgerald, the Bai also held to their more primitive gods, including Sai Sur, a mountain god who lived in the caves of Changshan; Lur Wa, a dragon king who dwelled in the huge lake; and a wind goddess known as Tai Po, or the great mother. The Bai also took bits and pieces of other beliefs, accepting spirit possession, poltergeists, and the germ theory of disease with equanimity. Christian missionaries, perhaps not coincidentally, have had little success in Yunnan, or in China as a whole. "The idea of an exclusive creed, the one true way distinct from all others which are false," wrote Fitzgerald of the Minchia of Yunnan, "is so unfamiliar to their mental habits as to be barely comprehensible."

But not all has been easy for the "common people" of Dali in the past few centuries. A combination of natural and political disasters swept the land, spearheaded by the Moslem uprising that nearly toppled the Yunnan provincial government in Kunming. In eliminating this threat, one-third of the population of Dali—at least ten thousand inhabitants— was executed in 1874. Fifty years later, in 1925, a severe earthquake nearly destroyed the town, killing thousands and felling a great many buildings—though all three pagodas and three of the four main city gates survived the shock. So although our promenade through Dali seemed to offer a glimpse of Old China, the buildings whose tile roofs swept towards the blue skies were nearly all younger than Ray Hubbard or Gerrit Schilperoort.

Our brief visit to Dali provided a glimpse of the New China as well. A bus schedule near the station was written in English as well as Chinese, as were many other signs in the town; one of them read HOT BATH MASSAGE HOUSE. Several of us took refuge from the brightness of midmorning in a small restaurant, where a menu printed in French and

English as well as Chinese offered cakes, cookies, and coffee. To loiter on these ancient streets, buy red-starred Mao caps and beaded bags from attractive, brightly clothed Yi women, sip French coffee and nibble almond cookies after a hot bath and a massage—well, that seemed like a tantalizing prospect. What good, after all, was it to run a river? But the yellow minibus awaited, and at last we climbed reluctantly aboard to make the final haul to the north, and the Great Bend.

The landscape seemed to expand around us as we headed north, and soon the snow-covered peaks of Yulong Shan—Jade Dragon Peak—loomed in the distance. The broad rice fields of central Yunnan gave way to small cultivated fields in remote valleys, and golden grain draped the steepening terraces. Spur roads branched off the main highway and disappeared into dusty canyons; we passed slow-moving trucks burdened with stone, raw ore from copper and tin mines. With its favorable climate and mineral wealth, Yunnan plays an important role in the economic health of the People's Republic. Oddly enough, its past economic importance was far greater, though for very different reasons. Fifty years ago, Yunnan was one of the richest opium-growing regions in the world.

China and opium seem as firmly connected as American Indians and corn, but it was not always so. Although the resin from the poppy seed pod had been used as an internal medicine in China for centuries, the practice of smoking opium apparently did not begin until the seventeenth century. Originally the resin was mixed with tobacco; later, sources mention a combination of opium, tobacco, and cannabis, a blend that was revived among young American and Dutch smokers three centuries later. The well-known antisocial effects of opium smoking—lassitude and the eventual shedding of other social concerns—became immediately apparent, and the smoking of opium was first proscribed in 1641; its sale was forbidden by imperial decree in 1729 under the Qing emperor Yung-cheng. When these steps proved ineffective, the importation of opium was prohibited in 1800. The efforts of the Manchus to halt the spread of opium consumption ran head-on into the interests of British businessmen, who were making their fortunes in opium and other trade items. The result was a Sino-British conflict over free trade known as the Opium War.

The war was touched off by the 1839 burning of a huge opium consignment in Canton (Guangzhou)—unfortunately, though perhaps not coincidentally, a British-owned consignment. The British had been looking for a pretext to establish more advantageous trade policies within the rich Asian market, and this attack on their goods struck them as a good excuse to go to war. With their superior technology and training, the British won easily; the result was the 1842 Treaty of Nanking, and the opening up of previously "closed" ports in Canton, Shanghai, Amoy (Xiamen), and elsewhere, as well as the ceding of Hong Kong to Britain. A second Opium War in 1856 ended with the 1858 treaties of Tientsin, and the opening of ports from the Yangtze north to Manchuria.

In 1911, however, a repentant Parliament forbade the shipment of opium into China, and millions of addicted Chinese were faced with the problem of procuring the drug. Until this time, most of the opium found in China was traded in from India, Burma, or Thailand—the so-called Golden Triangle region. Into the economic vacuum stepped Chinese businessmen, who oversaw the cultivation of poppies in remote and underutilized regions of China, primarily the western provinces. Although the sale of opium and its consumption were still technically illegal, its cultivation was not; and cleverly corrupt civil and military officials approved its cultivation as a source of revenue. Agricultural land could be taxed, and land used to grow poppies could be taxed at a rate higher than any other.

The result was that small farmers in the west—especially Yunnan, Sichuan, Gansu, and Guizhou—were virtually forced to grow poppies in order to pay the taxes that were levied upon them. Tribal farmers who had been growing produce shifted over to the cultivation of opium; the drug found its way into their life-style, and soon opium addiction became a serious problem in the ancient traditional tribal areas of these western provinces. As the cultivation of opium became more widespread, the economic motivations for using it became compelling—in Yunnan, opium was cheaper than tobacco, and by the mid-1920s the situation was devastating.

"Yunnanfu smelled of opium everywhere; pipes and lamps were sold in all the markets; the drug was as easy to buy as rice. On the streets you could see mothers give their tiny children sugar cane smeared with opium in lieu of a pacifier. Demoralization and impoverishment were especially apparent in the abuse of children, who were exploited all over China but nowhere quite so unconscionably as in Yunnan." Edgar Snow's recollections of Kunming in 1930 are horrifying; other observers bear out his notes. Geographer George B. Cressy estimated that by 1923, the poppy was cultivated in two-thirds of Yunnan's arable land, a situation that naturally produced serious shortages of food. He also reported that 90 percent of the men and 60 percent of the women in Kunming were

addicted to opium smoking—a figure so appalling that it must be doubted. Nonetheless, a friend of Joseph Rock who worked at a mission home in Kunming told him that 80 percent of the expectant mothers had to be supplied with opium during their stay at the mission's maternity ward.

Certainly there were other factors leading to the collapse of imperial China at the outset of the twentieth century—trade wars with European powers, a corrupt officialdom, the breakdown of irrigation systems, earthquakes and floods, as well as decadence within the Forbidden City itself. But if the figures given above are anywhere near accurate, it is little wonder that no real change could come to China until a government came to power that could attack its population's demoralization and decay at the source. Neither the first Republic of China nor the Kuomintang government of Chiang Kai-shek made a significant dent in these problems, or in the debilitating effects of opium production and use.

The first strong indigenous revolt against the powerful hold that opium held on the Chinese people had come in the nineteenth century, in the Taiping Rebellion roughly coincident with the years of the Opium Wars. Led by Hung Hsiu-chuan, a scholar converted to Christianity who came to characterize himself as the younger brother of Jesus, the Taiping attained their greatest success when they captured Nanjing, southern capital of the Qing Dynasty, in 1853. The motivation for the revolt was to establish a "heavenly kingdom of great peace"—tai-ping tien-kito—a kingdom which forbade the use of opium. Fearful of losing their empire, the Manchus found themselves forced to turn to the British for assistance, a move that was to ally them even more firmly with the pro-opium trade policy of the Europeans. The Taiping Rebellion was put down by combined British and Chinese forces under General Charles George Gordon, who thenceforth became known as "Chinese Gordon"; Nanjing was recaptured in 1862, and Hung committed suicide.

The unsuccessful revolt did, however, become the inspiration for a later generation of more successful revolutionaries. Edgar Snow, the first Western journalist to be granted interviews with the leaders of the Red Army, identified this inspiration, and drew an insightful conclusion. "Its martyrs were childhood heroes of Chuy Teh, P'eng Teh-huai, Mao Tse-tung and Chou En-lai; the enemies of the Taipings became their enemies, and in place of a Christianity discredited by Christian interventionists they were to seize upon and glorify a new 'universal faith' of the West called Marxist Communism."

The cultivation and use of opium was but one of many causes of the Communist revolution in China. Clearly, the country was due for change. Nearly forty years after Yunnan itself joined the new People's Republic, the road we traveled passed through a landscape of peace. At last it crested a ridge, wove along a small stream, and entered the town of Shigu, poised on a bluff above the start of the Great Bend.

CHAPTER SIXTEEN

To the Gates
of the Gorge

What a panorama! After the sun
disappeared, magnificent rays
streamed above the mountain
battlements. The snow range assumed
that aspect of an icy dragon floating
in mid-air, for the deep valley
was filled with smoke-blue mist,
and only the peaks and ice fields
reflected the silvery light of the
full moon.
—JOSEPH ROCK

Our first glimpse of the Yangtze showed a wide, bent band that
shimmered like liquid pewter, laid upon a folded tapestry of dun and
sienna. It reminded me of the Indus River flowing through the Skardu
Valley, only this was bigger, steelier, commanding. From the left entered
a friendly trickle of a stream in a broad fertile valley, the Hsi-Ma River;
to the right the broad current of the Jinsha Jiang forced its way through
the landscape towards the snowy crest of Yulong Shan. Between the two
stood Shigu, "Stone Drum," its richly carved wooden buildings and
glistening roofs of blue and yellow tile hanging over the river in an
architecture of fantasy.

We stopped in Shigu to look for a place to set up camp. Down a steep
stairway, just above the clear, turquoise Hsi-Ma tributary that gurgled
into the mother Yangtze, I stopped at an open temple on a pedestal. I

climbed the steps and found a huge marble gong, over six feet in diameter, engraved with hundreds of Chinese characters. This was the famous Stone Drum, a memorial honoring the Sino-Naxi victory over a Tibetan army in the summer of 1548, a relatively recent event in Chinese time. Some people, however, told us that the drum celebrated a more recent event, the famed Long March. The Second Front Army of the Chinese Workers' and Peasants' Red Army, led by General He Long, began their long march in November 1935. In April 1936, a year after Mao Zedong's First Front Army made their epic journey, He Long led his troops across the Yangtze at Shigu. As is so often the case in China, history was so thick it almost obscured the view.

The steep streets of Shigu were too precipitous for a proper rigging and put-in, so we bused upriver towards Chu Tien, and at last found a soccer field near the hissing waters of the Yangtze. It was here, at 6,200 feet by our altimeter, that we first touched the Yangtze. It was enormous, almost a half mile wide, and rushing by at perhaps ten miles an hour. It was frightening. This was supposed to be a low water season, yet the river here, in a quiet mood, was perhaps ten times the size of the Colorado through the Grand Canyon, and it crackled with power. When Marco Polo first saw the Yangtze seven hundred years ago, he wrote, "It seems, indeed, more like a sea than a river." I couldn't agree more. What were we doing here, I wondered. I thought of the haiku of the Zen poet Issa: "Closer, closer to paradise. How cold!" This could very well be a suicide run.

Ignoring as much as possible the flexing of the river, we slipped into uneasy sleep, and early the next morning went about rigging our boats: three self-bailing Avon Pros and one Achilles HVD 16, a heavier boat with a solid floor, a throwback to an earlier era of river running. Self-bailing boats were first introduced in the early 1980s, and within five years they had become the standard for whitewater rafting. The design is so simple it took years to conceive—the floor itself is inflatable, so it floats on top of the water, rather than being supported by the lift of the tubes. Since the floor is laced, not sealed, into the bottom of the boat, large grommets allow whatever water splashes in to flow back out, so no one has to expend time or effort bailing a swamped boat—the design does the job in about ten seconds.

Ken Warren hadn't used self-bailing rafts on his expedition. Because they are light, he reasoned, they are more likely to capsize in big water than closed-bottomed rafts. The Oregon hunter-turned-boatman believed the old-style bilge rafts would better serve his needs in the high volume of the Yangtze, and he may have been right; but a bilge boat can become so heavy it is extremely difficult, if not impossible, to control until bailed. When four of these bilge rafts were attached in the ill-fated diamond rig, and all filled with water, it must have been like trying to row the *Titanic*. Later, when Christian spoke with Chu Siming in Beijing, the Chinese boatman expressed curiosity about self-bailers, a curiosity that soon turned to longing.

We also had two one-man boats—one of them not a kayak at all but a red C-1 Gyramax closed canoe, piloted by Sam Moore of Kentucky. I was curious to know why anyone would prefer a canoe to a kayak, since the latter craft seems so much more stable.

"You sit higher out of the water," I pointed out, "so your center of gravity has got to be higher, so you're more likely to tip over. Yet you paddle it with a canoe paddle, which has only one blade—isn't that a handicap once you're in a rapid?"

"Half the paddle, twice the man," he countered, and the brash rebel grinned.

The other one-man boat was a brand-new yellow Perception Dancer kayak that had not even gotten wet yet. Seeing the spry yellow kayak made my stomach tighten, as it did every time I thought of Joel Fogel. As we continued to unload our gear on the soccer field north of Shigu, Fogel, wearing peacock-bright underwear, started doing isometrics against a side panel of the Mitsubishi truck. Then he ran circles around our camp, hyperventilated, then dropped down in the grass for a series of push-ups. "What's he doing?" Breck O'Neill asked. There didn't seem to be an easy answer.

Sam leaned over to ask if I had received Joel's press kit before the trip. "No," I looked back, my eyes asking for more.

"Yeah," Sam continued. "He sent a press kit to all the members of the expedition. A veritable catalogue of his exploits. Like when he led an expedition to Suriname last year, and was captured by guerrillas. They finally let him go, once he traded them his Explorers Club flag. Then just last Christmas Eve he jumped into an icy river and pulled a drowning woman from a crashed car. He got a letter of praise from Ronald Reagan for that one. He's a real hero."

I looked over at Joel, who by now had gathered a crowd of baffled locals. Same old Joel, I thought; then in the next breath: God, I hope not.

Amidst knots of curious villagers, we sorted and packed our gear for the coming adventure. John Kramer had packed the equipment and food in two large wood boxes back in Angels Camp, and shipped them on to

Hong Kong months earlier. When we unpacked there were some surprises—no instant milk or coffee, for instance, but an abundance of pancake mix. Most of the food was freeze-dried AlpineAire packages, huge expedition-sized envelopes that had been provided to SOBEK a year earlier for our revoked 1986 permit. Oddly enough, here we were in China with neither a grain of rice nor a Chinese noodle included in the food supplies.

But Kramer had done some things right: when the big wooden boxes were dismantled, and holes drilled in them for tying rope loops, they became the decks for the rafts. The big square rowing frames, from which the decks hang and oarlocks are mounted, were made of lightweight tubular steel; they too had been broken down for shipping, and could be reassembled on the spot in seconds. Large plastic boxes with foam seals lining their lids provided storage space for the food; they dropped neatly within the frame structure, doubling as seats for the boatmen. The total weight shipped overseas came to only 1,120 pounds—far less than a ton, about a fifteenth of Ken Warren's load.

At midday we finally tightened the straps holding the frames to the inflated boats, and started to carry the rafts down to the water's edge. Breck O'Neill, our unofficial videographer, taped the action with a JVC home video camera, one of three on the expedition. At that point Luo Sixiang, the thirty-four-year-old CIST representative assigned to field-supervise our activities, called John Yost over for a huddle. Through the official CIST translator, Cao Huiying, Luo explained that since we had not paid the $10,000 film fee, Breck must stop shooting immediately.

John protested, saying it was just a home video—not for broadcast, just something to show the folks back home what we had done. But Luo persisted, saying that if we chose to video, we could pay him the $10,000 right there and everything would be fine. Exasperated, John called me into the fray.

After listening to the protests, an idea popped into my head. "Mr. Luo," I suggested, "This video camera is not for making films, but strictly for safety. We can videotape a dangerous rapid with this camera, then play it back through the viewfinder to help us determine the safest run. If you took this camera from us, you would jeopardize our safety."

To demonstrate, I took Luo and Cao over to the riverside and asked Breck to shoot a slow pan of the river. With Haskell Wexler steadiness, Breck panned the scene, then played it back on the viewfinder to Luo. He nodded with approval, and said, Okay, we could bring the cameras, just so long as we promised not to make a television special. We shook hands and stepped down to the rafts.

Over one hundred villagers crowded the water's edge as we tied down the last of the gear. Skip Horner and Jim Slade would row two of the Avon self-bailers. John Yost, though usually confined to a desk, eagerly accepted the oars of the other Avon. While we had planned on John Kramer's rowing the fourth boat, his back problem had flared up badly on the long flight over from San Francisco. Reluctantly, I agreed to row the orange Achilles, though I felt I was out of shape for the task. It was a heavy boat anyway, and its bilge would fill up with water in any rapids. But with photographer Dave Edwards and videographer Breck O'Neill riding along with me, I had two good oarsmen to fall back on. The combination of crew, however, gave the raft an immediate nickname— "the Media Boat."

Joel Fogel pulled out an official Explorers Club flag, Number 134, and had several people take still and video shots, with his own cameras, of him proudly posing. The flags are awarded by the famous New York– headquartered club to members who convince a committee that an expedition has true scientific or exploration value. An awarded flag must be returned with a full report of the expedition, so each flag consequently has a distinguished history. Joel announced that this particular flag had been with Neil Armstrong on his Apollo mission to the moon. This impressed everyone, especially Luo, who mistook the boasting to mean that Joel was in fact Neil Armstrong, and had personally carried the red, white, and blue cloth to the moon.

Months later, when visiting the Explorers Club, I found that Neil Armstrong did indeed carry an Explorers Club flag to the moon, but it was a special unmarked issue. Flag Number 134 had traveled with Prince Peter of Greece in 1948 to Afghanistan, and with later explorers to Venezuela, Ecuador, New Guinea, and Poland. But the closest it had ever come to the moon was a 1986 mountain biking expedition to Tibet.

After Joel's show, we unfurled a banner presented to us just a few days before at Berkeley's Yangtze River Inn by photographer Pam Roberson. It said, BRING BACK THE YANG FROM THE YANGTZE: SOBEK CHINA 1987. Julia Amaral, the sole woman on the expedition, protested a bit that the yin wasn't cited, but smiled for the cameras all the same. Moments later, beneath a brilliant blue sky, to the whispers of Tibetan prayers and the murmurs of the river, we shoved into the brawny currents of the Yangtze, and sailed into "the land of stars and horses."

We drifted down the pulsing current of the Jinsha Jiang towards Shigu, and as our way of bidding adieu, rowed the rafts a couple of hundred yards back up the Hsi-Ma Ho, the clear tributary that babbled past the Stone Drum. As we reached a swinging bridge at the base of the village, a troop of about one hundred uniformed schoolchildren paraded across, carrying a score of crimson Chinese flags and singing high-timbred inspirational songs. Once across the bridge, they formed a circle in a parklike clearing near the village for a lengthy songfest. We suspected the inspired youth were the local Red Guard, and uneasily wondered if they would break into a hunt for the nearest running dogs of imperialism. If so, they didn't have far to look.

We were almost right. Luo Sixiang—who had elected to come with us for the first two days of floating, to the entrance to Tiger's Leap Gorge—told us they were Young Pioneers, a kind of Communist scouting organization. This was somewhat reassuring, and we treated the spectacle as a photo opportunity instead of a cultural threat. They sang more songs and waved their flags, and we waved back, then headed back down to the main current of the River of Golden Sands.

We rounded the nadir of the Great Bend, and passed a small diesel-powered ferry boat, chugging importantly across the river. The swollen current tugged us northward. Within minutes we were presented with the breath-grabbing view of the snow-covered spires of Yulong Shan, Jade Dragon Peak. For half a century Yulong Shan, the 18,899-foot mountain that practically leans over the Yangtze, denied every attempt to climb its summit. Although a team from the Beijing Geological College had climbed to the summit on May 15, 1963, subsequent attempts by teams from Britain, New Zealand, Japan, and the United States all had failed. Only the year previous to our expedition, however, Californian Eric Perlman reached the top on his second try in as many years. The summit was snowbound, its several peaks sharp as the armored spine of a dragon. It was between the Zhongdian Mountains, with their summit peak, Haba Shan, 15,420 feet high, and Yulong Shan that the Yangtze cut its closefisted course through the gorge called Hutiaoxia, "Tiger's Leap."

For hours we floated towards this magnificent vista as though into a fantasy. The peaks seemed to stretch higher, the sky seemed to stain a richer blue as we glided northward. At one point we passed a pretty hundred-foot-high tributary waterfall spilling what seemed to be a million brilliant gems down an eastern travertine wall. We finally set up camp on a long, broad, fine-sand beach that would have been covered in high water during the summer monsoon months. We pitched our tents with the doors facing Jade Dragon Peak, which was topped by a screen of clouds that sometimes thickened, sometimes parted, sometimes drifted across to register the mountain's changing moods.

At twilight we collected at water's edge for swigs of a bottle of twelve-year-old single-malt Cardhu Scotch. A few moments later a small fireworks display erupted just outside the campfire ring, courtesy of Jim Slade, who had picked up the firecrackers in Kunming. October was a good month for celebration in China: the Nationalist regime was founded in October, the Long March began in October and ended the next October, the Communist victory was finally achieved on October 1, 1949. It was Friday, October 23, and SOBEK was finally on the Yangtze.

Despite the Cardhu, sleep was slow in coming that first night on the river. Several of the crew were discovered to have world-class snores, and the tent-sharing arrangements were destined to undergo a revision the next day. One particularly odd pairing was revealed: seventy-four-year old Ray Hubbard was tenting with the Peter Pan of adventure, Joel Fogel.

The following morning I pulled back the dew-soaked tent flap to see Christian down by the river practicing t'ai chi ch'uan, and in the distance Luo jogging—an odd inversion of cultural morning exercises. John Yost, as usual, had been among the first up, and was hovering over the campfire flipping wheat-germ pancakes, mixing freeze-dried apples, and stirring the thick morning coffee. Without bothering to change from my bright red Patagonia capilene long underwear (one of ten sets donated to the expedition in hopes of seeing the product in print), I staggered through the sand to the campfire, arriving simultaneously with eight others.

At once the expedition's first crisis presented itself. We were short of cups, and a minor verbal scrap ensued as we tried to determine who deserved the first jolt of java. As our fracas reached a fever pitch, it was interrupted by the sound of a splash and a shrill cry of "Help!" from the river.

We all spun around, and there was Joel, snug in his full-body Spiderman fluorescent wet suit and yellow helmet, drifting past us in the main current. "Help me," he implored again. Had he somehow fallen in? The water was bitter cold, enough to give a naked swimmer near-immediate hypothermia, but Joel was snugly wrapped in a one-eighth-inch-thick double-sided neoprene surfer's wet suit, which would keep a rattlesnake warm in the Arctic Ocean. The Yangtze current might be strong, but the water here was flat, and Joel was only a few yards from shore.

Several of us almost snapped into action, getting ready for a rescue, but the scene didn't make sense, so we all stood there, exchanging puzzled looks as Joel continued to scream and float by. "What a cry-wolf jerk," Breck said, and turned back to the fire to flip a flapjack.

Everyone followed suit, and Joel, flummoxed in his perverse effort to find some early-morning attention, gave up and paddled to shore, changed clothes, and wandered down to join us for breakfast.

Pancakes apparently didn't sit well with Luo, so he produced from his kit two flat cans of processed meat. At first curious about this exotic food, we were alternately relieved and disappointed to recognize the smell as he fried it up in a Teflon pan—Spam, by whatever name it had in the Celestial Empire. Luo shared pieces with those interested, and it turned out to be the best of our first breakfast on the Yangtze.

The day's floating was even more spectacular than the one before, as we were swept towards the gate at the base of Yulong Shan, the gate that swings into the narrowest, steepest gorge holding any major river. The quiet of the float gave no hint of the tumult ahead. We passed pumpkin fields, groves of birch, pomegranate, and walnut, skinny barking dogs, patches of marijuana plants—grown for hemp and bird seed, we were told—and a crockery factory where clay was fired into roof tiles and conduit pipe. Then we approached an anomaly: a sunbather in bikini briefs perched on a black rock. Looking closer, we saw it was Joel Fogel, who had paddled ahead of the rest of the flotilla so he could enjoy some leisure time.

High up on the cliff above us, we saw what appeared to be bore holes, the pockmark scars left by geologists sampling rock core and strength, usually a first step when considering a dam site. The Yangtze gorges have long been brimming with hydroelectric promise and flood control possibilities, but we were surprised to see that geologists had made it this far into western China. We were, however, well aware of one major dam project far downstream, at the end of the famous Three Gorges in Hubei Province. The Three Gorges area between Chongqing and Yichang has long been one of the most famous river regions in the world, notorious for its impediments to safe travel and the dedicated and skilled junkmen who plied its waters nonetheless (*see* chapter 1). Today's traveler, however, can safely ignore many of the dangerous whirlpools and rapids of the past, because they no longer exist: the final reaches of the Three Gorges are tame and passive, calmed by the turgid waters behind Gezhouba Dam.

On Mao's birthday, September 26, in 1970, construction began on 130-foot Gezhouba, a 2.7-megawatt hydroelectric dam situated at the entrance to the Three Gorges near Yichang. Though initiated by the Soviets, Gezhouba eventually was built entirely with Chinese labor and materials; among its benefits must be counted the experience for subsequent large-scale engineering projects, as well as hydroelectric power for four provinces and the clearing up of many of the navigational difficulties in the Three Gorges.

But Gezhouba is only the first stage in a two-part effort to dam the waters of the Yangtze at the Three Gorges. The second part is by far the more ambitious: the biggest hydroelectric dam in the world, Sandouping or Three Gorges Dam. This gigantic plug is designed to be 550 feet high and a mile and a quarter long, and it will raise the river behind it nearly 500 feet. In so doing, it will create a reservoir eight hundred miles long, increasing shipping to Chongqing tenfold but essentially flooding the historic Three Gorges section of the river. The project would generate 13,000 megawatts of power—400 megawatts more than the largest -current hydroelectric dam, Brazil's Itaipu, and roughly ten times that of a conventional nuclear power station. But it would have the corresponding effect of displacing at least half a million people, perhaps double or three times that many; and of submerging towns, villages, and landmarks of tremendous historic importance to China.

There are grave doubts within China about such a massive undertaking: the economics of big dam building make the Three Gorges Dam daunting, to say the least, and a loan of at least $18 billion from the World Bank would be necessary to embark on the thirty-year project. In addition, environmental groups such as the World Wilderness Congress, World Rivers, and the Environmental Policy Institute point out a number of objections, both economic and ecological. For one, the tremendous sediment load of the Yangtze could lead to downcutting below the dam, an effect whereby the loaded reservoir would overflow and erode around the impeding plug, endangering the 300 million people who live in the flood plains below Yichang. Other environmental effects are also projected—the intrusion of salt water up the river's estuary would endanger Shanghai's water supply, coastal erosion would change dramatically, and floods would not necessarily be eliminated despite the enormity of the project. Other risks, such as earthquakes in the flooded gorges and the eventual collapse of any large structure, have also been predicted. Currently, however, indications are that China's leaders, acting on the advice of the US Bureau of Reclamation and the Bechtel

Corporation, do plan on building the dam, whatever their motivations and whatever its cost.

Salinity, siltation, and the Bechtel Corporation aside, we river runners tend to be concerned with two more direct victims of such big dams: people and fish. Of the latter, consider the Dabry sturgeon. In Chinese lore, this half-ton river fish was often called "the water dragon," and his impressive size made him the focus of rumors about land-walking monsters that ate children. Despite his size, the sturgeon has also been considered a delicacy by connoisseurs, and has graced the table at many an emperor's feast. The twelve-foot-long oceangoing fish has spawned for millennia in the waters of the Upper Yangtze—five hundred miles beyond the proposed site of Three Gorges Dam, above the new Gezhouba Dam. Fish ladders were never built, and efforts to catch the fish and carry them over the dam to spawn have proved inadequate (only forty sturgeon were caught in 1984). Currently, the only option is artificial spawning ponds, a sad end for a legendary beast indeed.

Then there's the half million or so people who will be displaced by the enormous reservoir. Count among them the simple, poor farmers who are—ideologically at least—the backbone of Mao's China; count too the thousands of laborers who for a hundred generations have served as trackers, hauling freight-laden junks up the historic rapids, living within the rock walls of the legendary gorge. Among the landmarks to be drowned are the famous battlegrounds of the Three Kingdoms period 1,800 years ago; ancient towers and pagodas built to worship the gods and goddesses of the river; the hanging coffins of the mysterious Bo people, who disappeared 600 years ago, and the still more ancient pictographs and petroglyphs that decorate the ancient river channel; and the rocks, shoals, and shelves that have served as signposts for river pilots for 2,000 years, each one named, each one steeped in lore.

One of the historic villages to be lost to the rising waters of the Three Gorges Reservoir is Fengdu. In the Old China that will never return, Fengdu was thought to be the gateway to the underworld, and traders would sell "express passes" to believers who wanted a quick and less painful transition to the afterlife, passes that would take them directly to Fengdu at death. Although such passes may be no more than talismans of primitive belief, Fengdu—located halfway down the Long River, in the geographical center of China—may be, more than just a symbol of superstition, the mythic heart of an ancient land of mystery.

No doubt the Yangtze that carried our rafts in Yunnan, as with virtually every great stretch of wild river in the world, was also being seriously considered as the site of a hydroelectric dam. Voices of river enthusiasts raised in protest have shelved these plans in a few instances, and salvaged bits of free-flowing rivers from death by drowning. Even the Colorado through the Grand Canyon was once threatened, but saved by a chorus of river runners and canyon hikers. Perhaps, with our little float, we might be the vanguard for such a chorus; but we knew that politicians and engineers could drown our faint song of praise in their tuneless symphony of statistics.

At 3:42 P.M., just above the Xiaozhongdian tributary, we passed beneath a double-arched metal bridge that appeared on none of our maps. The banks began to close in on one another, and the current began to pick up speed, as though eager to carry us to an important engagement. At 4:30 we pulled into a narrow, steeply sloped beach on the west bank, in Zhongdian County, near the village of Loyu. Our CIST crew, who had driven ahead with the gear truck, was waiting with a case of warm San Miguel beer. This was the last port before the storm. Just around the bend was Tiger's Leap Gorge, the magical and mysterious landscape we had come halfway around the world to challenge.

CHAPTER SEVENTEEN

"A Headache for the Monkeys"

"A journey of ten thousand *li*
begins with a single step."
—MAO ZEDONG

The bold afternoon light was still strong when we reached the town of Loyu at the gate of Tiger's Leap Gorge. In many ways this was our goal—the infamous gorge that had inspired poets and explorers, and that had claimed the lives of three Chinese just the previous year, the gorge we hoped to conquer. The adrenaline was pumping.

Sam Moore, our Kentucky kayaker, was the only one of our group to have seen the gorge before, on his informal scout of the area a year earlier. Hiking along the trail, he had sighted seven major rapids, five of which he deemed runnable and two portageable. That sounded good to us—the ratio was far better than we had experienced on the Indus, where some days we had managed only two miles on the river. Then again, we all had been younger then.

Now he assured us that the first rapid—the one the Chinese had sent a dog over, then run in a rebuilt capsule—was only about a mile downstream. The late hour notwithstanding, the group broke up into twos and threes, and started hiking down the ancient trail to see the first rapids. Whether or not we would run the river depended almost entirely on what we would see that afternoon: if the first rapid was unrunnable, which we had every reason to believe it would be, then we would have to portage it. If, however, it could not be portaged, we would have little choice but to pack up the boats in the truck and put in on the river farther downstream. Nobody wanted to shy away from the challenge; but nobody wanted to drown either.

In the languishing light of the late afternoon we stepped along the path into the dark wedge that was Tiger's Leap Gorge. We passed a group of convicts ending their workday of widening the path by chiseling the marble cliffs with handpicks and hammers. What could they have done, I wondered, to deserve such a sentence, chipping at rocks twenty minutes this side of hell itself? Then, as I looked downstream and saw the shimmering crowns of Black Water Snow, White Snow, and Cloud Snow peaks, all over 12,000 feet, spectacularly poised on the northwest side of the Yangtze, I thought this perhaps wouldn't be such a bad place to do time after all.

We next passed through the outpost of Bendiwan, three large mud-and-timber buildings, and several freshwater springs bursting from the cliffs. Across the gorge, the north face of Yulong Shan spilled down to the river, a fissured wall of granite soaring almost ten thousand feet above us. We passed a marble quarry, then an electrified sawmill, then the trail narrowed as it wound upward. At a high 90-degree switchback known as Dayanfang, we rounded the corner and came face-to-face with two tigers—marble tigers, male and female, anatomically accurate, carved in a crouched position, aimed as though ready to make a great leap forward across the gorge.

Scrambling up and over recent rock slides, we kept looking down at an ominously accelerating river. It seemed farther than the mile that Sam had guessed, but we thought little of the discrepancy. Downstream the canyon walls were so close they seemed to touch. It was easy to believe we were trekking through a canyon lost in time, a primeval landscape yet to be tarnished by human habitation, a true wilderness somehow surviving within a country that held over a billion people. The illusion was quickly shattered as we turned another corner and met a band of Chinese tourists from nearby Lijiang, one carrying a guitar, another a ghetto blaster tuned to high volume. They were returning from a day's picnic at the first rapid, their version of visiting Victoria, Virginia, Yellowstone, or Yosemite falls.

We were over five hundred feet above the river at this point, and after we passed the picnickers, a low roar seemed to waft up the canyon and the trail seemed to shiver. This was the area, I had read, where seven spirits are said to haunt, moaning to signal the approach of storms or other dangers. Were we being warned? With a few more steps the cause of the commotion came into view: the horrendous first rapid.

Even from our aerie, where size and distance were distorted, it was evident this rapid was a potential killer. The entire river, which was over half a mile wide just a few miles upstream, funneled into a chasm just twenty yards across, then made a white leap into a bottomless maw. The river reared its back like a whale surfacing, and slammed into a huge rock the shape of the Cheops Pyramid of Gizeh, split to either side, and fell again and again, and once again. It was awesome. This was Shanghutiao, Upper Tiger's Leap, the rapid that Lei Jiansheng and Li Qingjian had dropped through a little over a year before in their spaceshiplike rubberized capsule.

The river was lower now in late October than it had been the previous September, but it was still a horrifying piece of whitewater. Because the sight of the two Chinese rocketing through this white galaxy with absolutely no control was burned into my consciousness from repeated viewings of the John Wilcox film, and because it so reminded me of the circumstance of the original Mercury astronauts as described in Tom Wolfe's *The Right Stuff*, I proposed we called this rapid "Spam-in-a-Can." At least for our expedition, it stuck.

Skip Horner and John Yost decided to bushwack down the steep canyon wall for a closer look at the drop before the daylight faded entirely. Meanwhile Jim Slade and I hiked a bit farther down the path to see what we could see. We made another half mile, and in the dusk could make out two more major rapids, both of which looked unrunnable, even unportageable at river level. We turned, and as the veil of darkness fell, headed back to the boats to huddle and commiserate.

Skip and John had arrived back in camp first and were struggling to ignite our multifuel stoves and pressure lamps. John, in a frantic state of mind, had spilled kerosene on the lamp, and when he tried to light the mantle the whole unit seemed to go up in flames as the kerosene burned off, for a few brilliant seconds illuminating the entire camp, the Yangtze, and the canyon wall across the river.

"Shit happens," Ken Jarkow shrugged, expounding a bit of midtown philosophy.

"I've never seen a rapid like that, ever," Skip offered in a somber tone to match the darkness of the surrounding walls. He estimated the river dropped sixty-five feet in three tiers within the first rapid alone, the only one he and John Yost had seen up close. They described the power of the rapid as being practically nuclear. The walls were sheer on both sides, making portaging an impossibility. Unless we were willing to attempt a Chinese-style do-or-die run, it was an impasse. Still, no one was willing to give up quite yet. We had come half-way around the world to try our skills at Tiger's Leap Gorge, and something within us would not give up so soon, on the basis of a short afternoon hike.

After a practically inedible dinner of freeze-dried beef and noodles that conspired to incite several stomachs to revolution, the senior guides retreated into the shadows for a powwow. It seemed clear from our little survey that the first three rapids, the ones we had been able to see before darkness fell, were undoable, at least for our crew, in our boats, at that water level. Perhaps a crack team of kayakers at lower water . . . but not us, not then. Briefly the notion of a paddle boat was entertained, crewed by the most experienced guides, in a "guerrilla-style" attack on the gorge, supported by a land crew hiking along the trail with food, extra gear, clothing, medical supplies . . . It all got too complicated too fast, too time-consuming, and, ultimately, too risky.

Our options included hiring mules and horses to carry our gear through the gorge on the high trail to a navigable point below these rapids, and then lowering everything down to the river; or trucking the gear around the entire gorge to rendezvous with the crew, who would hike through. Because we were pretty certain from the Chinese accounts that the middle section was even worse than what we had seen, the latter option seemed the most prudent, and so it was accepted. We had no driving stake in running the gorge—neither nationalism nor macho pride compelled us to risk it all for a few miles of whitewater.

Then another dilemma reared its horns. Poring over our maps, we saw that the gradient below Tiger's Leap could be even worse than what we were going to truck around, and downstream there were no roads for such a luxury as vehicle portaging. We discussed the possibility of dividing the expedition below Tiger's Leap, leaving a core of the most experienced rafters to attempt the unknown section of the Great Bend with a minimum of gear and food and a maximum of climbing gear, so that an escape could be managed if necessary. The other members of the expedition would truck around to an access bridge at Sidu, about two hundred miles downstream; they would raft the final section of our route, which by our maps had a reasonable gradient and was never far from villages or a road.

Such an operation would be difficult to execute—dividing up our commissary, our tents, and our safety gear, then choosing who would tackle the tough unknown section and who would ride in the back of a truck for three days to raft a section that probably would be less challenging than the Colorado. We also didn't know if the Chinese would allow such a split, as it wasn't in our permit, and they seemed to

members thought he came perilously close to dying. His recent prostate surgery was another strike against his immortality, but he looked upon a ten-mile hike as just another day in the life, as long as he got an early start.

The first hour brought us back to Spam-in-a-Can, and several of us negotiated a steep, angular path down to a rumbling vantage at rapid's edge. There we met a score of bag-lunch-carrying Chinese tourists posing in front of the great white whale of water. Over the roar, a Chinese teenager asked if I would take his photo with my camera; once I did, he scribbled his address in Chinese and indicated I should mail him the results. We Americans did the same—mugging, trading cameras, and smiling as though smugly posing in front of a caged beast. Almost within reaching distance a monstrous wave opened and closed its jaws as though chomping boulders for breakfast.

In a pothole adjacent to the rapid, the disfigured, rotting carcass of a calf, neck broken and dark eyes frozen in fright, looked up at me as though asking for help. The poor creature had probably slipped and fallen into the river not far upstream, and was swept over Spam-in-a-Can to this ignominious final resting spot. Its face looked almost human, and I couldn't help thinking that its fate might easily have been ours.

After a humbling hour, we climbed back up to the trail, and began the trek to Daqu. Skip and John Yost, who had finished up the packing of the truck, passed us at a hurried clip, reluctant to pause even for a moment's appreciation of the scenery. Most of the others, however, took a medium pace, keeping cameras at the ready. I hung back with Breck O'Neill, Jacques Vroom, Julia Amaral, and Dave Edwards, our expedition photographer. John Kramer brought up the rear, taking long stops to sketch geological features in his notebook.

It was a hike as impressive as the rapid, through a landscape of distorted size and scope. Little dots of scrub on the wall just a few minutes downstream turned out to be hundred-foot pines and miles away. The trail was a balancing beam chipped from the cliff face, often covered with debris from recent landslides. A false move could effect a half-mile fall into the boiling waters below, which looked like the vat of acid in some hyperkinetic Hollywood adventure flick. But not even a Spielbergian fantasy could cook up a river like the one cooking below. Every bend in the trail revealed new rapids. Some looked runnable; most were nightmares; a few were so ugly that if you stared too long you'd turn to stone. The Chinese had counted three major sections of drop; Sam Moore had said there were seven rapids. Many of us lost count somewhere over thirty.

Lifting our eyes from the river, slowly panning up the opposite canyon wall, we saw a geologic frenzy as troubled as the waters. Amidst the metamorphic rocks were olive limestones and pink marbles with saffron tints. Sometimes an entire wall was spectacularly creased, like a giant rug that had been folded together. We were hiking through the great fault of the Yangtze, a cataclysmic piece of geology that had picked up one of the world's major riverbeds, twisted it like a piece of taffy, and turned it back upon itself. Continuing the pan upward, we craned our necks to see beyond the lip of the canyon, up into the granite flanks of Jade Dragon Peak; then up farther into snow line, to the ice tongues of the southernmost glacial system in Asia; and finally to the shimmering spires and crags of the summit, stabbing the impossibly distant blue sky. Not even a 17-millimeter fish-eye lens could take in the entire panorama. Thank God we weren't paddling, but hiking through the most spectacular canyon I had ever seen. A local ballad expresses the feeling one has hiking in Hutiaoxia, and had we known the melody we would have whistled our way down the trail.

> *A thread of blue over your head,*
> *An abyss down at your feet.*
> *A headache for the monkeys,*
> *An impasse for the eagles.*

By early afternoon we were into what the Chinese had called the second section. Far down below us we could see rapid number nine, where the entire river slammed into a warehouse-sized boulder, then crashed down either side. The boulder, we later learned, was the stepping stone the legendary escaping tiger had used when leaping across the river. It almost looked possible.

Up one side canyon, where a rainbowed waterfall burst from a high wall, then ran beneath a feeble wooden bridge, we met another group of young Chinese hikers who had stopped for lunch. We shared a cross-cultural snack, trading bites of our candy bars, gorp, and apricot fruit leather for wok-heated beef, peppers, pork rind chips, and crispy fried noodles. Then, after gracious nods and smiles, as we loaded up to take off in our separate directions, another cultural difference presented itself. While we stashed all our litter, the Chinese scattered theirs.

The trail reached far up into many tributary canyons to a point of crossing, then returned to the Yangtze proper, making our hike about double the distance the river itself was traveling. Because the vistas were so spectacular, it was impossible not to stop to absorb the sights, from the wild orange marigolds and little flower clusters that looked like Texas blue bonnets to the El Capitan–type walls fragmented into dark stone pinnacles, such as Black Wind Embankment (Heifengtang), and the utterly grand scope of the river, its rapids, and the dazzling peaks above us. It was a spectacular hike—but slowly the realization dawned that it was no ten-mile walk, and that some of us would have a hard time making the six-o'clock ferry across the river to Daqu.

By late afternoon Breck was limping with blisters from his brand-new Sierra sneakers. Young Naxi boys leading goats with tiny bells slung from their necks would pass us. At one turn, we recoiled at the sight of a thin snake in the middle of the trail; in response to our intrusion, the snake seemed not to slither off, but to deliquesce into the scree. We'd stop every couple of hundred yards for a rest and a look about—we were in the heart of the Celestial Empire, in a canyon seen by few Westerners throughout time, even forbidden to outsiders since 1949. It had cost us a pretty penny, but it was a special place, and we felt privileged.

Still, it had occurred to several in our party that if the Yangtze below Tiger's Leap Gorge were not raftable, collectively we might have paid for the world's most expensive hike. Then we turned the next bend and saw two fair-haired, round-eyed young men tossing a Frisbee. We walked up to the incongruous sight with mouths agape, and shook hands with Colorado-based John Fayhee and Norbert Bame, free-lance writer and photographer respectively, on assignment for *Backpacker* magazine. We had met the pair in Kunming several days before, but since they had no official permit and had not paid outrageous sums, we had given them little chance of making it into the Forbidden Zone, into Tiger's Leap Gorge. Now the two Yankees, armed with backpacks and chutzpa, were standing in no-Western-man's land, grinning broadly and offering us grape Kool-Aid generously mixed with 151-proof rum. When asked how much Fayhee and Bame had spent to get to this point from Kunming, they claimed it was all of 6 yuan, about a dollar each, which they paid the driver of a twin-axle flatbed to carry them to Daqu. The authorities had no idea they were even in the precious Tiger's Leap Gorge—they'd snuck in the stage door to the opera, and had taken the best seats.

After the boys from *Backpacker* helped bandage up Breck's popped blisters while we nibbled on some of their trail mix, we headed on down the trail, Breck hobbling like the hunchback of Notre Dame. Not a hundred yards farther, we bumped into another American couple smoothing out their sleeping bags next to the path. They looked up in greeting as though we were meeting on the Appalachian Trail. Our latest encounters were Bruce Berkman and Wendy Fulton, both from Los Angeles. Bruce had spent the last nine months in China studying soil erosion on an educational friendship grant from the Durfee Foundation, and now he wanted to travel through Tiger's Leap Gorge en route to Tibet with his girlfriend. They had hopped the local bus from Lijiang to Daqu. The fare: $2 for the two of them. Dividing the nearly $200,000 we had spent for the purchase of food, equipment-shipping, airfares, and the kicker, our permit, the per-person cost for the nineteen members of the SOBEK expedition to reach this little perch on the Yangtze came to over $10,500. But then, we had a private bus with cushioned seats.

Bruce, it turned out, was a part-time river rafter, and knew several SOBEK guides back in the States. He, too, had been negotiating to run a river in China, the Brahmaputra or Tsangpo, which glides past Lhasa in Tibet, then slices through the Himalayas into India and Bangladesh, where it issues into the Bay of Bengal. The rafting-permit fee CIST had offered to Bruce: $1 million plus a one-time $10,000 tag to take a look. Suddenly, our deal didn't look all that bad.

The sun was now on its final approach to nightfall, but Bruce estimated we still had another two and a half hours walking to Daqu, so we bade goodbye and hustled down the trail on what was turning out to be our own Long March. We knew we were woefully behind schedule and would probably not make it through the canyon before dark. We might even have to bivouac in this isolated wilderness. We passed through a small village stepping up the canyonside in tiers. Known to the Naxi as Ngyiperla, its name translated as "Walnut Garden," and it was said to be founded by squatters from Sichuan Province. Fleetingly, we considered stopping here for the night but thought it would only panic those who had gone on ahead. So we collected water from one of their springs and continued down the trail as the shadows quickly lengthened on a dramatic cliff face across the river called Cock's Comb Ridge (Jiguanliang). As we walked, the distant mountains turned purple, their folds an angry blue. The world seemed to bend towards us, and it was not a gesture of welcome.

✻   ✻   ✻

Far ahead, John Yost and Skip Horner had finally reached the end of
the trail, a village called Kou Ka on a windswept plateau above the last
rapid. It was nearly five P.M., and darkness was not far away. Racing
down the trail towards the ferry, they were surprised by a Chinese girl
coming in the opposite direction who greeted them in English. She was
a Hong Kong native who had just hiked the full length of the canyon,
as they had, only to find that the last ferry across the river to Daqu had
left two hours before. Disappointed, the two senior guides joined the girl
as she walked door-to-door in the village, asking for a place to stay for
the night. Perhaps the combination of two sweaty Americans in shorts
and a prim Hong Kong student was too much for the Naxi natives, for
it was some time before the group found a farmer willing to let them stay
in his family's manger for 5 yuan. That worked out to about 50 cents
each, and they accepted.

Just before dark, Jim Slade reached Kou Ka and realized he had
found it almost by accident, by exploring a trail that took off from an old
road cut. He decided to go on and try to stop the ferry, if it were still
there; but as the darkness descended, and the trail began to wind down
a steep cliff, Slade decided to head back to the village. After trying for
over an hour to find a place to stay, he was finally led into a room where
he found three other red-faced round-eyes: John Yost, Skip Horner, and
Larry Krasnow, who had found the village shortly after Slade. The four
men were happy to be reunited; the Hong Kong girl sat silently by,
looking on, curious.

Back up the trail, Christian was steadily gaining ground on the three
hikers ahead of him. He could see them across the great chasms of
tributaries, when the trail wound deep into the mountainside to cross a
stream, then swung back out along the ridge towards the Yangtze. He
thought he could recognize Luo Sixiang, the CIST liaison, but it was at
least half a mile or more across the gulf between them, and he could not
be sure. Still, at this point, he thought, any company would be welcome.
He had been hiking with Jim Slade until midafternoon, when the
boatman decided he better "make some miles" and took off like a shot.
Now, as darkness began to fall, Christian realized that being alone in a
place like this was not his idea of a good time.

To occupy his mind, he tried to figure out who he had passed and
who had left before him, so he would know who was behind him on the
trail. He thought that Jacques, Joel, and maybe John Kramer were

behind—of course John Kramer would be bringing up the rear, drifting steadily on in some sort of geologist's ecstasy. And Julia—he worried that her self-confessed acrophobia might be a problem, especially at the last dangerous rock slide he had just passed over. Then he remembered the village, and thought, Oh, they'll just stay there. That's the sensible course—nobody would dare hike further than that village, especially this late in the day.

By now it was dark enough for a flashlight, and Christian could see, still far ahead, the three dim beams of Luo and his companions. Almost running now, he stumbled along the trail, noticing in the last light of day that the canyon seemed to be opening up.

It was completely dark by the time he caught up with the three Chinese, and virtually impossible to see the trail. As it happened, they had reached the point where the trail forked, and the footpath climbed up over the ridge to the village, while the old roadbed continued along a final long bend in the river. They took the low road, and followed it past a horse corral, down side trails towards the canyon, and back up to the increasingly overgrown tire tracks. After about an hour they finally realized that this had to be the wrong way—although they were unable to communicate their thoughts to each other because of the language barrier—and backtracked to the split in the trail. Looking in the darkness back up the canyon, they could see the tiny, tired beams of flashlights— three, four, five of them, still far away up the gorge trail.

The Chinese hollered up the hill, and were answered by high voices from above. Grinning in the darkness, they began to hike up over the ridge, on the right trail at last. Christian sat down to wait for the distant flashlight beams to come closer.

Jacques Vroom thought they might be the last ones on the trail. He had been hiking with Julia Amaral, and as the day waned, Julia tried to squelch her feelings of panic by trading stories with Jacques about their respective love lives. Then, as she hiked out in front with a penlight, somehow they got separated, and Jacques found himself alone in the darkness.

A sense of panic started to well up in him. In the blackness, it seemed the canyon was closing in on him. He didn't know exactly where he was to go, what he should do. He couldn't stop thinking about the fact that he was 14,000 miles from home, in an alien land, on a treacherous path, by himself. He felt as alone as he had ever been. Suddenly, like Alice when she was hopelessly lost in the rabbit hole, he needed to sit down.

He was frightened. When Julia retraced her steps and found Jacques, he could see she was scared too.

They sat together in the darkness, alone with each other and their unspoken fears. They hadn't been sitting long when they heard music floating through the darkness. Was that a harmonica? Playing an American tune? Jacques, who had attended Williams College, recognized the fight song of arch-rival Amherst. The musician was John Kramer, who had studied at Amherst. The lanky boatman was plodding along in his old sandals, happy as could be.

Jacques was sure Kramer would immediately see he had lost his nerve, would realize that a full-grown man was scared of the dark. Instead, Kramer plopped down, gestured towards the night sky, and said, "Isn't this fabulous? Feel that warm breeze? God, I love this!"

It was one of those moments, Vroom would later report to Joe Rhodes of *Dallas Life* magazine, when the universe seems to come together in an instant. In the time it took for Kramer to say those words, all of Vroom's anxieties disappeared.

"It occurred to me, with an intensity that is hard to convey, that he was absolutely right. This wasn't a problem. This was great. The unknown isn't something to be afraid of, it's something to be thankful for. We are out here in this extraordinarily beautiful place about to do something great. We don't know what it is yet, but whatever it is, it'll be something we haven't done before.

"That moment burned into my synapses in a way that all those people who would tell me, 'Jacques, when you're distressed about something, you just need to think positive,' never had. Somehow, seeing all those Norman Vincent Peale book covers never prompted me to open them up or make me believe it. But this guy, playing the Amherst fight song in the middle of China, just struck something in me."

Jacques, Julia, and John Kramer walked together until they met up with Dave Edwards and Joel. It was the dead of darkness when the five of them finally caught up with Breck and me, by which time the trek had turned into a stumble. A few of us had brought flashlights, but it was still frightening to be edging along a razor-edge path knowing that a wrong step could bring a quarter-mile fall. We could hear the river bellowing below—at last light we had counted twenty-five of the thirty-four rapids said to be contained in these walls—and occasionally the pings of loosened rocks kicking down the path and over the precipice into the roaring nothingness. Breck's blisters were so bad he had to cut open the sides of his shoes to continue. We were all suffering form varying degrees of exhaustion. Still we continued, our weakening flashlights burning dim holes in the night. At one point the trail split, and we tripped to a dead end, right at the edge of the canyon. Youthful Folly, indeed.

Sometime around nine P.M. Christian came back down the trail towards us, with the good news that the trek was almost over. Our much-in-pain party started up a steep switchback towards a plateau. Near the top, we heard the tinkling of goat bells and a cascade of children's laughter. It seemed like a hallucination. At the ridge top we came upon a group of teenage Chinese boys camping out, and they seemed strangely amused by our unexpected stumble into their camp. They were clearly having a jolly good time in a situation that seemed life-threatening to us.

Three of the boys volunteered to lead us on, and we took off through a byzantine network of trails that wound between village walls, alleys, and crooked corridors. We never could have figured out on our own how to find our way in the village of Kou Ka, but soon our guides led us into a mud-plastered woven reed hut. Three dead goats hung from the ceiling; in the corner we spied the smiling face of Luo Sixiang. Luo had arrived some time before us and had arranged for us to sleep in this homestead, but he knew nothing of our other team members. We assumed, since we brought up the rear, that some if not all of them had made the ferry, and were comfortably ensconced in Daqu. Either that or they had walked over the canyon lip.

The floor of the hut was packed earth, and as we circled for a position, Julia announced, "You know, I have this thing about dirt. I detest it!" Kramer let out a howl, as if to say, "Then why did you join this expedition?" But everyone else kept their thoughts private. We were all tired, not at our best.

We crouched around a bed of coals in the smoky hut and accepted porcelain bowls filled with a clear liquor that had been poured from a plastic jerry can. It tasted like a cross between fermented pear-apples and paint stripper, and had us reeling within minutes. A wrinkled woman in the back of the hut steadily stirred her giant wok, and by eleven P.M. served up her specialty: goat's innards stew mixed with homemade noodles and chives. Even as exhausted and hungry and drunk as I was, I couldn't stomach goat's innards stew. I begged for a bed, and thirty minutes later we were led outside, up a crude ladder, and into a corn crib packed with thousands of husks. It felt therapeutic, and within seconds we were deep into sleep.

CHAPTER EIGHTEEN

Into the Great Bend

The air was like champagne;
the weather, warm but with a tinge
of freshness that came from the great
Snow Range dominating the valley.
—PETER GOULLART

The morning brought stiff necks, sore backs, the discovery of unknown blisters, and sunshine showering the plains before us. The first sign of movement was a dark figure limping towards our corn crib—Larry Krasnow. Larry reported that he had spent the night in a nearby manger with Slade, Yost, Skip, and the Chinese girl from Hong Kong. She had already left to hike the twenty-mile trail again, back through the gorge to Loyu. We all wondered what sort of shoes she had, and where to get some.

With the eight of us who had struggled in after nine at night—Jacques and Julia, John Kramer, Dave Edwards, Joel Fogel, Breck O'Neill, Christian, and myself—that brought our total to twelve. Still missing were our trip doctors, Dick Moersch and Jon Ingleman, and our two seniors, Ray Hubbard and Gerrit Schilperoort, as well as the New York contingent composed of Ken Jarkow and Sonny Falack. That made eighteen: odd man out was Sam Moore, the confident rebel kayaker who had coolly told us we could hike the ten-mile trail in time for the six-o'clock ferry. We all wanted to speak with Sam Moore.

After our hostess fixed us a quick breakfast of fresh cornbread and fried bamboo shoots mixed with peppers and onions, we set out towards the river and the ferry to Daqu. A few hundred yards on, in the lower section of the village, we saw a flash of red parka through a jalousied window. We rushed over, and inside was another SOBEK group: Gerrit, Dick, and Jon

Ingleman, as well as the two New Yorkers, Ken and Sonny. After heartfelt greetings, the two doctors told us they had been hiking together as darkness approached, and had discovered the nearly insentient Gerrit staggering, foot by heavy foot, back up the path from a side trail that led to a precipice, muttering that he just wanted to lie down and get some sleep. Dick Moersch insisted he keep moving, since it might get cold enough for hypothermia after darkness fell. So Gerrit hooked his hand—on which he had written the word *Daichi* in blue pen, to remember his destination—to the back of Jon's belt, and was literally dragged up the trail into the village.

Ken Jarkow and Sonny Falack had reached Kou Ka at the same time as the two doctors and their charge. Sonny, who looked enough like a pirate to begin with, was now sporting a saber-sized black anodized Tekna diving knife strapped to his right thigh. When they first stumbled into the village, a pack of barking dogs had run out to check on the intruders. Instinctively, or perhaps nervously, Sonny had whipped out his knife, silver blade flashing in the starlight, and crouched in commando position. Nearby villagers watched the Western barbarian, confirmation of their worst fears, and shut their gates and locked their doors. The incident made it difficult for them to find lodging, and after an hour of knocking on unresponsive doors, they finally found a corn crib and wearily collapsed. As Gerrit started to let loose his distinctive snore, a pig came squealing out of his corn-cob bed, startling them all. They decided to look for a better bunk. They had no money, but finally, when Ken and Jon traded their wristwatches, they secured cozy accommodations under a tiled roof on a clay floor.

Counting heads, we were now just two short: Sam Moore and Ray Hubbard, the seventy-four-year-old peregrine-eyed patriarch of the trip. A few weeks previous, Ray had undergone prostate surgery, and his acceptance on the trip had been reluctant. Now, we feared we might have made a fatal mistake in judgment.

At a fraction of the bounding pace at which we had originally started into Tiger's Leap Gorge, we plowed down the final pitch to the river. There, at last, we found the remainder of our team. Sam and Ray had arrived at river's edge around eight P.M., and had found the ferry tied up at its cove. With no prospect of crossing the surging current alone, they had climbed into a cave and snuggled under Sam's lightweight survival "space blanket," with the greasy blanket that covered the ferry's engine on top for extra warmth. Since we already knew what a crusty and outspoken codger Ray Hubbard was, we decided to lay off on our comments to Sam Moore. We were sure he had got an earful the previous night.

It took two overloads in the rusted, leaky, twenty-five-foot-long diesel ferry to get us all across the river to the outskirts of Daqu. We were so heavy that water spilled in over the transom, and several of us frantically bailed the bilge water with our Sierra Club cups. Even the most experienced boaters looked around nervously, unused to being an open water without a life jacket. A mustache of sweat formed on the boatman's mouth as he steered his palsied craft upstream through whirlpools and tricky currents.

Our resupply truck was waiting, along with a welcome case of San Miguel beer. While we regrouped, Cao Huiying and some other CIST regulars started cooking a much-needed brunch of noodles, soup, stir-fried vegetables, and (what else?) Spam. It promised to be a happy reunion, but then all hell broke loose.

Though SOBEK rarely designated a leader on an exploratory trip, since there were usually too many qualified leaders participating to select just one, John Yost had assumed the role this time, largely because he had spent the most time organizing the undertaking. Now, as John, wearing his signature Yankees baseball cap and a dirty SOBEK Zambezi T-shirt, called a meeting to discuss the upcoming section of river—an extremely isolated passage of 110 miles without road access—several members let loose their volleys of complaint. Larry Krasnow, Ken Jarkow, Joel Fogel, and Julia Amaral complained bitterly, and probably justifiably, about the organization of the hike. It had taken longer than expected; they had been advised not to bring hiking boots; nobody had been prepared to bivouac; individuals were left without direction to wander down perilous trails. Their protests pointed up the division between the two types of explorers on this trip: the died-in-the-wool SOBEK squad, guides and friends who had pretty much packed self-reliance into their personal baggage; and the "passengers," paying clients who expected leadership and group regard to be included in the price of admission.

The passengers certainly had a point, but the factions were suddenly realigned when Joel Fogel pointed his tape recorder at John Yost and asked a leading question. John snapped, and vowed that if Joel didn't turn off the recorder at once, he personally would throw it in the river. "You're a pain in the ass," John sneered. At once the group split into those who supported John's brash put-down of Joel, and those who were put off by it all. John Kramer was the first to cast his vote, standing up from his place in the shade to walk over behind Yost in a gesture of support. I moved in next to Yost. Dick Moersch, with his evergreen goodwill, nodded his head in approval at the threat to toss Joel's recorder in the river, and seemed to grin in anticipation.

Larry Krasnow, who had just before the expedition agreed to invest in the SOBEK purchase of a Grand Canyon rafting operation, tried to bring his concerns back under discussion, saying that he felt Yost's attitude was insensitive and unsafe, and demanding an apology for the events of the previous day. Yost refused, and Julia went over and sat next to Larry. Most of the rest of the group were just nursing their beers and wondering how this little psychodrama was going to play out, when Joel turned to them and tried to suggest that another leader should emerge, perhaps himself.

"Opportunistic agitator. Take it away, Joel," Kramer responded with asperity. Nobody bit, and Joel seemed to acquiesce at last to a lesser role in this expedition than he had hoped for in his fantasies.

There was still some concern, however, that the haphazard philosophy of the hike could cause life-threatening problems downstream. Sam Moore tried to lighten the mood by piping in that he felt the worst-case scenario would be if we ran out of beer. Larry Krasnow didn't see the humor, and again complained that the SOBEK guides had displayed gross unprofessionalism and a dangerous "me-first" attitude. He said he had felt abandoned during the hike, and announced he was thinking of leaving the expedition at this point. "All I want is an apology," he insisted, eerily echoing Dr. David Gray's negotiating stance with Ken Warren at Yushu. The only viable option for Krasnow would be to spend the night in nearby Daqu at the Tiger Leaping Gorge Hotel, take the equipment truck back to Lijiang, then catch the scheduled "people's bus" for the three-day drive back to Kunming. Julia and Ken said that if Larry departed, they would consider going too.

But even as the plan was being aired, it seemed to evaporate: the prospect of being crammed into a seat constructed for the Chinese bum, and rattling for sixty hours down dusty mountain roads in a box of steel and tin packed with peasants, pheasants, chickens, and children, somehow seemed a poor alternative to the big rapids of the Great Bend. So, after another hour of deliberation, some soft encouragement from the guides, and a hot Spam lunch, nobody left. The fate that had befallen Ken Warren's expedition, its abandonment by four members, had been averted. Our own little mutiny was over, its fury spent. We rigged our boats where the river cut through the base of Daqu's fields, and the expedition, complete to the last man and only woman, floated downstream to a broad beach for camp.

The following day the river expedition would start in earnest. On our maps, which were old and now suspect, both the gradient and the canyon walls showed steep, with no villages for miles at a stretch. This was commitment. Once we shoved off and turned the bend, we were on our own. If we met with another Tiger's Leap Gorge, one perhaps uncharted because of its very isolation, there would be no road upon which to truck our gear around, and possibly not even a path for us to hike. We had heard rumors that two more Chinese rafters had died in this section, and we knew for a fact that no Westerner had ever been in these gorges at river level since Joseph Rock and Peter Goullart had ferried across it forty years earlier. This was truly going to be a first—and perhaps a last.

Luo had declined to continue rafting with us, citing sore feet from the hike. But we were loath to continue into this inaccessible, unknown stretch without someone in the party who could communicate with the villagers along the way. So, after some keen lobbying, including the key word *safety*, Zhong Jun, the thirty-year-old secretary of the mountaineering association of Yunnan Province, volunteered. He was an accomplished climber who had made it to within one thousand feet of the summit of Yulong Shan, but he had never been in a raft and didn't seem to speak more than fifty words in English. He didn't look happy as he wandered about the beach with a scowl, staring at a small pagoda perched on a limestone cliff across the river, perhaps his last contact with civilization for some time.

That night, as we tried to swallow our freeze-dried noodles and rehydrating succotash, John Kramer stepped forward to explain some of the dazzling geology we had witnessed while trekking through Tiger's Leap Gorge. John held a master's in geochemistry and mineralogy from Penn State, and he had decided to spend as much time as possible interpreting the makeup and movements of the earth in this extraordinary landscape. Several of us had asked Kramer to decipher the colors and codes we'd encountered, and rather than translate to each of us individually, he had agreed to a group lesson.

"These mountains owe their magnitude to two things: youth and India." He stood near our campfire, illuminated by the setting sun. At first hesitantly, then with greater confidence, he took us into his area of expertise. "Back when Gondwanaland was intact, all of South America, Africa, and what became India were one continent. Then, around eighty-eight million years ago, Gondwanaland broke up, and the piece of Africa we know as India shot north out of the southern hemisphere at the prodigious rate of a hundred eighty millimeters per year—about nine times faster than a fingernail grows.

"Finally, in the Eocene epoch about thirty-eight million years ago, it collided with Asia. The ocean that once existed between India and Asia was subducted, swept under the rug of Asia, as the heavy oceanic crust was sucked or pushed under the lighter Asian continental crust into a subducting trench. There was a coastal mountain range of volcanoes, an ancient Asian Andes, in Tibet, but India was light crust just as Asia was, so when it reached the trench it didn't dive, but collided with unimaginable force. The throat of the trench clogged, and the world's biggest mountain range was formed. I liken it to the gag reaction followed by nature's Heimlich maneuver, which coughed up the Himalayas.

"Now, if you can picture a map of Asia, you'll recall that Yunnan isn't behind the main line of impact, but off to one side. The bend in the structural trend of its mountains, which is also shown by the curving of the great rivers draining the Tibetan Plateau, is caused by the driving of India deep into the underbelly of Asia. If you plant your foot on a rug and push it across the floor, you'll see a series of folds develop that curve around your foot, just as the mountains of southwest China draped around India. If the rug were brittle, it would also tear, and a piece in Yunnan would start to rotate clockwise, opening rifts and initiating strike slip faults.

"India had tremendous momentum when it struck, and it continues to plow northward into Asia today, at the reduced rate of only fifty millimeters per year. So structural adjustments had to make up for the volume of at least nine hundred fifty miles of convergence since the Eocene collision. Some of the rocks went straight up, only to be eroded away—the higher they went, the faster they fell. Some of the material interpenetrated at medium depths, and some of it at great depth was under such pressure it acted like putty in a tightening vise and just flowed out of the way.

"Here in Yunnan, huge blocks of crust have spun clockwise out of the way at the surface, while being bolstered by new additions of plastic material at depth. The rigid surface rocks were stretched to the breaking point by this geo-tumor. Like the molting skin of an arthropod, it cracked. Huge blocks under pressure from below rose up at tilted angles, including keystone wedges called grabens—which seem to observers at the surface to have collapsed to form deep, broad valleys, but have actually risen at a slower rate than the blocks on either side. Geologists call this extensional tectonics, and consider it a precursor to the rifting of continents.

"The compound result of all this is a mix of stresses which cause slipping of previously folded blocks past one another with concomitant pulling apart. It's incredibly complex and fascinating for the geologist. Sort of a combination of lots of little San Andreas faults crossing the Nevadan basin and range, but in a folded terrain. Whew! But I see you're wondering where the Yangtze fits into all this," Kramer said, as if coming out of a personal mind warp, "so I'll try to wrap it all up.

"As should be obvious when you remember your mental map, the ancestral Yangtze used to continue southward, down the riverbed that is now the Red River going through Hanoi to the Gulf of Tonkin. At some time after India collided with Asia and mountain belts were draped around the convergence—perhaps when the geo-tumor began to grow and initiate tilting and rifting—headward erosion by a stream from the east was faster than that down the intermontaine valley of the ancestral Yangtze. This side stream began to cut across the divide of the Great Bend, perhaps assisted by a regional tilting, eventually eating its way down the old Yangtze drainage from north to south. It followed structural weaknesses in the rock, eating back and continuing to capture the flow of more and more of the Yangtze's eastern tributaries. Telltale 'barbed' tributary confluences pointing upstream are evidence of the former drainage direction.

"At Shigu it captured all the flow of the mighty Yangtze from Tibet, forever changing the river's course, and incidentally the course of human history in China. From then on the Yangtze bent towards the east, and followed the old course of its tributaries by heading north into the Great Bend, then south down another ancestral riverbed, then back again to the east. The outflow into the Gulf of Tonkin remained, but for a much smaller river system, the Red River or Hong Ha.

"By the way, in all likelihood Jade Dragon Peak and its adjacent mountains did not exist at the time of the capture of the main Yangtze, otherwise they would have formed an insurmountable barrier to the river. Their uplift probably occurred after the Yangtze, in full force, flowed eastward with enough erosive power to keep pace with the rapid uplift.

"In Tiger's Leap Gorge, the whole river runs along a huge fault called the Yangtze Fault. It's fairly common for rivers to do this, since the rock along faults has been crushed and is therefore easily eroded. Faults provide a line of least resistance to the forces of erosion."

"How long has the river flowed east, carving Tiger's Leap Canyon?" someone asked from the dark circle of listeners.

Kramer shrugged. "My guess is about eighteen million years. A blink in earth time."

The fire had died down, and glowing coals, red reflections of the stars above, now lit the quiet crew on our little beach at the terminus of Tiger's Leap Gorge. It required a herculean effort of the imagination to encompass the spans of time that Kramer spoke of. It brought our passage down the Yangtze into a different perspective.

Kramer's lesson was sobering, and we staggered through the thick sands of time to our tents.

Before launching on the brittle morning of Tuesday, October 27, Skip Horner gave an extensive safety talk, going over the use of throw lines and how best to move in the water in case of an unexpected swim. His trim tan body moved like a dancer's in demonstration, and made it look easy. Then he explained the most critical aspect of rafting big water: "highsiding," throwing one's full body weight onto the high side of a raft that's being pushed up towards a capsize. It could make the difference between life and death, he sternly warned; he seemed to be staring at Jon Ingleman, probably the least experienced boater in the bunch.

It was late morning, gear all secured and spirits rising, when we finally pushed off into the current and drifted inexorably around the corner. We passed several log chutes, where Yunnan pines, dragon spruces, and Chinese larch trees cut from above Tiger's Leap Gorge were trucked around the dangerous canyon, then sluiced down into the river, where they would float to mills downstream at Dukou and Yibin. The fact that the chutes existed at the head of the gorge we were entering caused some comfort—at least the logs could survive whatever lay ahead. The evening before, Yost, Skip, and Slade had compared notes, and judged the water flow in Tiger's Leap Gorge at between 60,000 and 75,000 cubic feet per second. They also agreed that the drop through the gorge was much greater than that shown on the maps;

hence, they reasoned, the gradient below Daqu had to be less. We hoped they were right.

For an hour the water remained smooth, though the walls of the gorge seemed to be edging towards one another, assuming a concave shape. If we came to an unrunnable rapid in here, there would be no way out: the canyon as conundrum. Despite all the power of rationales and topographics, I just couldn't shake the feeling of uncertainty about what we were doing and doubt about where we were going.

Then, at a western affluent, the canyon tapered for a bit, and the first rapid appeared. It was huge, a wave train of enormous breakers that looked like an exaggerated version of Hermit Rapid on the Colorado, one of the classic runs in Western whitewater. Below the rapid, high along the opposite cliff, I could see a set of full-sized logs, stripped clean of bark, pounded into cracks as though by a giant jackhammer.

After an hour of scouting, Skip and John Yost made the first runs, opting to take the bold route down the center. They rode the syrup-slick tongue into the maw, where they were dwarfed by the immensity of the waves. The sixteen-foot boats seemed to shrink, as in a science-fiction movie, as the glassy swells rose above them and pitched them to the edge of capsizing. John Kramer, in the back of Yost's boat, was catapulted over the duffel pile. The Yangtze pulled its punches, however, and the two rafts wallowed through and pulled into a small eddy, slightly the worse for the washing.

Sam tightened his spray skirt around his C-1 cockpit, ready to go next. He appeared unnaturally tall as he bobbed next to Joel, who was seated in his kayak. Slade asked Sam if he wouldn't rather be in the stabler craft, the kayak, for this upcoming challenge.

"If you meet your maker on a river, would you rather be on your knees, or on your ass?" Sam grinned as he pushed off into the current. He made a nearly flawless run, convincing us that even if he couldn't count rapids or tell a kilometer from a mile, he was at least a hell of a boater.

Next Jim Slade and I, piloting the last two rafts, pulled out into the main current. Having watched Skip and Yost get thrashed in the center run, we set ourselves up in a position where we could pull the boats laterally away from the largest waves, but the river was too, too powerful and had its own ideas. Once grabbed by the currents, I felt as if I were effectively out of control. I struggled to haul my oars through the thick water, cursing myself for letting my rowing muscles lay fallow for too long. It was all I could do to keep the raft straight as it barreled through the giant waves, but I managed to pull into the eddy without looking too ragged, and Slade pulled in right behind me.

Finally Joel Fogel, in the Perception kayak, readied himself. Just before he got in his boat, however, he took out his portable video camera, turned it on himself, and left a goodbye message to Coty, his Mexican wife, and his four kids by three different relationships. It was a theatrical gesture, but perhaps not without a touch of heart. Then he packed away the camera, paddled into the tongue, and entered his first major rapid on the Yangtze. Though he was rolled three times in the descent, he managed to right himself each time. His self-obituary had been premature.

Jubilant, he paddled into the eddy where the whole team was spiritedly preparing lunch and reviewing the first-met challenge on the Yangtze. Both John Yost and Gerrit had drawn blood in this initial adventure, on shin and wrist respectively; so, as is the privilege of those stumbling through unnamed territory, we decided to dub our initial cataract "First Blood." Looking at their injuries while puffing ruminatively on a Winston, Ken Jarkow smiled and said, "Shit happens."

The afternoon brought powerful currents, roiling boils, insurgent suckholes, twirling whirlpools, and two more big rapids. The second pounded a cliff on the west bank, yet offered a gorgeous beach midway through on the east side, ideal for our night's camp. So we skirted a huge hole, tugged out of the rapid, and parked beneath a high sandbank. Jim Slade had cut an exacting line through all the afternoon rapids, executing surgically perfect runs, so Jacques Vroom, who always wore a blood-red helmet as he rode the rapids, now started calling Slade "the Surgeon."

The twilight brought an unexpected light show, with brazen bolts of pastel shooting through the clouds and striking the peaks while the horizon lit up in a five-alarm sunset. I had seen the Aurora Borealis in Alaska, but that night the famous Northern Lights paled by comparison. When darkness finally draped the surrounding cliffs, Sam took out his Panasonic shortwave radio, and we all gathered around for what would become a regular nighttime ritual: listening to the world economic news on Voice of America. The news that fourth week in October 1987 was not good. The yen had dropped a record amount; the Hong Kong market had been frozen; the London exchange was in chaos, all in response to the record 508-point drop on the New York Stock Exchange that had occurred on October 19, Black Monday, the day we had arrived in China.

The faces around our little council dropped as well. I knew that many of our group were affluent, judging from their ability to come up with the money needed to help finance our expedition. Now I guessed from the frowns and sagging shoulders that while we had started the expedition with nine millionaires, we were now down to about six.

CHAPTER NINETEEN

Halloween Suite

> The conditions of conquest
> are always easy. We have but to
> toil awhile, endure awhile, believe
> always, and never turn back.
> —SENECA

Jon Ingleman woke up to pain. It was a familiar ache, but one he had not had for two decades. Twenty-one years earlier he had passed a kidney stone; now, here on the Yangtze, hundreds of miles and several days from the nearest hospital, he thought he was passing another. When daylight came, Jon sought out Dick Moersch, who gave him some Demerol from the medical kit. But Ingleman was clearly unhappy beyond the abilities of Demerol. His reasons for joining SOBEK on the Yangtze stemmed in large measure from the recent death of two of his friends, contemporaries who had died suddenly of heart trouble. Ingleman had embarked on a personal fitness program, including working out with weights and long bicycle tours, and as the trip approached he believed he was in the best shape he'd been in for years. Now, out of the blue, his health was jeopardized by a completely unanticipated ailment. He staggered back to his tent to endure his private pain.

Dick also attended to several blisters still festering from the Tiger's Leap Gorge hike. Breck's were particularly bad, and after a detailed examination Dick concluded that the abscess on his little toe required a rubber seal. There was no rubber seal in the trip's medical kit, but Breck had an inspiration.

"Anyone got any rubbers?" Breck called out. Several of us glanced involuntarily at Sonny, who ducked with a grin into his tent and produced several packs from his kit.

223

"Lubricated or non?" asked Sonny. Dick accepted a nonlubricated, and with a sly smile wrapped Breck's wound.

"Perfect fit," announced the doctor.

The morning also brought visitors from the village of Hang Ka, up on the canyon rim. Great traders that they are, the villagers brought down fresh foodstuffs from their gardens and pens to sell. After five days of freeze-dried, we were a ready and eager market, one shipped right to their doorstep. Ken Jarkow, a successful, wheeling-dealing member of the Manhattan garment industry, took on the task of bargaining, and secured assorted fruits, vegetables, three live chickens, and a goat, which the villagers slaughtered on the beach as part of the deal.

Refueled, we packed and moved downstream. Slade tied a cardboard box on top of his gear, out of which the feathers, claws, and beaks of the three chickens occasionally poked. As impossible as it seemed, the river canyon grew steadily narrower, until it seemed even thinner than Tiger's Leap Gorge; but it was deep and the gradient was low, so there were no equivalent rapids. Eddy fences, where an upstream current collided with the downstream flow, proved the greatest danger, grabbing the tubes of the boats and sucking them down, so that for a tense second water would pour into the rafts. A discolored ring marking the high water flow painted the cliff about fifty feet above our heads. Imagining the river at that level was frightening. Below the high water line, the limestone walls were fluted, scalloped, and polished like Carrara marble. Above the line, the dark walls arched upwards in a single, smooth sweep for nine thousand feet or more, almost twice the height of the Grand Canyon at just a third the width; in the high cleft above us falcons wheeled in the currents. John Kramer perched on the back of Yost's raft, happy and at home, taking notes and making sketches of the grand geology surrounding us. As we slid through this corridor, completely inaccessible except by river, we were seeing sights never before seen by Western eyes—geological dykes and faults, million-year-old metamorphosed rocks, unexplored side streams, unclimbed peaks, and Jim Slade rowing chickens down the river. It was poultry in motion.

Then, soon after lunch, a nightmare presented itself. The gorge pinched even more as we eased towards the chambered roar of a major rapid. We pulled hard against the current, but our strokes could only slow, not arrest, our forward movement. Less than three-hundred yards downriver we could see the spray from an exploding wave marking the entrance to a significant rapid; not far beyond the horizon line, a sheer wall interrupted the river's progress, no doubt sending the rapid into a screaming right-hand turn around a blind corner. This could be the circumstance we all feared: absolutely no way to row back upstream, the current too strong; absolutely no way to hike out, the walls too sheer. We hadn't seen or heard an aircraft since we launched at Shigu. In that sense, the area was more isolated than the Arctic. If the rapid proved to be a waterfall, or an unrunnable mess like Spam-in-a-Can, we were stuck. No exit.

The left wall sliced into the river like a meat cleaver; there was no way to pull over and scout on that side. On the right, a small landslide offered a slight mooring about two hundred yards above the rapid. We rowed with Talmudic caution; all six boats squeezed in, and most of us scrambled up for a vantage while Jon Ingleman stayed on a raft, still suffering from his kidney stone. Stretching our necks out over the river, we could see a nook just at the head of the rapid on our side. It looked as though it just might have room enough to pull in a boat, maybe two. Sam Moore, in his C-1, volunteered to take a look, and the rest of us watched from our outpost as he eased down the right wall and spun out of sight into the nook. Joel Fogel then followed in his kayak. For long minutes we waited, then Sam peeked out and hesitantly signaled us to run the rapid, pulling left to right. We tried to signal back the question of whether we could pull a raft into his spot, but he didn't understand and kept waving for us just to go for it.

Skip and John Yost went first, with Christian and John Kramer riding the backs of their boats. Slade and I stayed back on our perch, but we had asked Christian and Kramer to signal to us as they entered the rapid whether one raft, or two, or none, could squeeze into Sam's nook. It would help if we could pull in and survey before committing to the rapid.

As the two rafts slid down the tongue, Christian held up two hands—good news, we could park and scout. Then Kramer held up one hand, meaning just one boat could jam in; then Christian wildly waved both hands across one another, telling us no boats could make it. Then the two rafts fell off the planet, dropping around the corner and out of sight.

Slade and I waited to see if Sam would signal back that Skip and Yost had made it through safely. But Sam didn't even look back at us. Instead, he leapt into his C-1 and madly paddled into the rapid, plunging out of sight. What did it mean? Was he off on a rescue? Did one or both of the rafts capsize? In all the excitement, did he just forget to signal back? We decided to wait for Joel. He would let us know.

But there was no sign of Joel. We waited. Nervously, I clambered to a protected roost to release my bowels, and dropped my favorite deep-dish Sierra Club cup, which bounced off the cascade of hot rocks into the river. Slade also took the chance to rid himself of excess weight. Still no sign of Joel or his yellow kayak. Ten minutes. Fifteen. We couldn't wait any longer. We had to go for it.

Slade pulled out first; I was just a few strokes behind, so we could help one another if there were trouble. I was scared. I'd run thousands of rapids over a twenty-year career of river rafting, but never had I entered a major rapid of this size and power, in such an isolated canyon, blindly, without knowing the fate of those who had gone before.

As quick water grabbed the boat, I pulled like a demon to the right, then straightened the boat as we dropped over the horizon. An enormous souse hole waited to greet us, soaking us in white froth; then we punched through its far wave and emerged on the other side for a roller coaster ride down a series of haystacks. I tried to keep the heavy Media Boat straight as Breck bailed frantically; Slade, running a bit farther to the left just in front of us, was thrown sideways into one wave. The surgeon dropped his knife—his oar was ripped from his grip. With a lunge he recovered it, gained control of the boat, and pulled over to the right shore, where all the boats were bobbing, right-side-up.

"What took you?" Skip asked casually, putting away the camera he had been using to shoot our descent. Everyone was grinning, including our CIST escort Zhong, who suddenly seemed to be enjoying this rafting stuff. Even Jon Ingleman had a healthy glow in his cheeks; he said the rapid must have shifted his kidney stone so it no longer bothered him.

The only real danger had occurred when Joel had headed into the rapid without ever signaling back upstream. Just as he was about to plunge into the hole, he saw he had forgotten to attach his spray skirt, and as he struggled to seal it, he rolled over and was swept from his kayak. He was washed through the rapid sans boat, "like a toothpick in a toilet bowl," he later said. In his own notes he named the rapid "Fogel's Folly," and we saw no reason to change it.

The incident spooked Joel, and that night, as fresh chicken legs and a bottle of Jim Beam were passed around camp, Joel asked the various guides if he could ride on their raft for the rest of the trip. The Yangtze, he admitted, was more menacing than he had expected, its rapids beyond his skill. Everyone brushed him off: kayakers came on trips to kayak, and no one wanted to tie the bulky boat on the back of his raft.

Sam Moore took me aside and told me a little story about how Joel ordered his kayak for this expedition. It seems he had called up

Perception kayaks and asked for a yellow boat with two float bags—no length, no model, no specifications. It was comparable, Sam said, to entering the Indy 500, and then calling General Motors and asking for a red car with four tires.

Later that night Joel confided to Jon Ingleman that he carried a supply of Cup-a-Soup packets in his kayak, just in case he was run out of camp and had to survive on his own.

The next morning, sun flowed into the canyon and highlighted the gorge broadening downstream, with cornfields and small homesteads grabbing pieces of level land. His doubts banished by daylight, Joel reconsidered, and got back into his kayak. The going was indeed easier. There were rapids, half a dozen or so, but they were straightforward runs with easy routes between large waves. We made good time, and by noon we were at the top of the Great Bend, where the Wuliang Ho—probably one of the ancestral Yangtze channels that Kramer had told us about— flowed into the river. Our altimeter told us we were at 4,920 feet, over a thousand feet below our put-in. A high sandbank marked the Wuliang's entrance, and on top of it we spied Joel Fogel, who had arrived before us, sunbathing in the nude. He was obviously feeling more himself.

It was at this point that the north shore briefly defined the border of Sichuan, "the heavenly state," China's most populous and resource-rich province. We stopped in Sichuan for a few minutes, and wet our feet in the blue Wuliang; then we rowed back over to Yunnan, where the beach was longer and lower, more suited to a lunch stop. We set up our standard midday meal—tasteless Chinese crackers, unsalted (and increasingly sour) cheese, trail mix, fruit leather, and, thankfully, a huge hunk of Mr. Goodbar to share, courtesy of Gerrit Schilperoort.

We dined next to a small gold-mining operation, a primitive wooden sluice box at river's edge through which two villagers of nearby San Chankou were relentlessly pouring gravel and river water. This was, after all, the River of Golden Sands; it was the first of hundreds of gold-extracting maneuvers we would encounter in the coming miles, and with Black Monday just behind us, there was a temptation to dig in. The Chinese government has permitted private gold mining since 1975, when it reversed a twenty-six-year-old policy against the practice. In fact, in the early 1980s leader Deng Xiaoping encouraged gold mining by independent peasant miners such as the ones along the Yangtze in order to increase the country's hard currency reserves, needed for his ambitious industrialization and modernization plan.

According to Beijing's official figures, some 50,000 miners along the

Yangtze have panned, chiseled, sluiced, and sifted for gold ever since. But they are required to sell any gold they find to the government at 1,200 yuan per fifty grams—only about $320, about half the going rate on international markets and much lower than what black-market dealers in Hong Kong will pay ($950 per fifty grams). The discrepancy quickly led to increased smuggling. Rather than raise the official price, however, Beijing decided to "collectivize" the miners. Individuals are no longer permitted to mine gold, but must work collectively under the supervision of local authorities.

In our passage we had come across dozens of lone miners, and Zhong, whose English was tested as he gave us this information, let us know that smuggling was still very much alive. Once I understood the economics of it, I wondered aloud, "Well, what do you expect? With the gap between what the government pays and what a Hong Kong trader offers, who can expect a Chinese miner to work for such a dim sum?" Zhong smiled politely and wandered back to the lunch spread.

That afternoon we started the long slide down the southern leg of the Great Bend, continuing our magical glide through the spectacular and unknown canyons of the Jinsha Jiang. It was a magnificent surprise to discover this river, we agreed—comparisons with the Grand Canyon kept being made, and almost invariably the Arizona abyss came up short. It had the color, we acknowledged, and the history; but the Great Bend was bigger, deeper, steeper, and virtually unknown. Then, the next day, the topography changed dramatically: Where just miles before there were groves of pine trees, we now passed oaks and prickly pear; the limestone at river level gave way to black metamorphic volcanic rock, the remains of some ancient eruption; and the walls lowered and leveled back, allowing cattle grazing, sorghum fields, and full villages to tenant within the canyon.

The next morning, October 30, we stopped at the Naxi village of Jian Wan, and were able to purchase local beer brewed from the highland barley, *gingke*, plus several bottles of potent rice wine, potatoes, ten fresh eggs, bok choy, peanuts, pear apples, and the large bitter tangerines called *mitou*. We also picked out a couple of large pumpkins, for the next day was Halloween and we had vague plans to carve them into jack-o'-lanterns. But it wasn't enough for the flesh-starved members of the party: Ken Jarkow again found himself driving the bargain for a whole pig—cost, about $40—purchased from a flintlock-wielding hunter.

We weren't allowed to take pictures in Jian Wan, however; a

cigarette-puffing party official came scurrying out of the upper village and put an end to our socializing, still assiduously guarding his corner of the canyon in the Forbidden Zone. As John Yost brandished his oars to pull away from the village, the just-slaughtered sow strapped on his stern, a patch of water convulsed and flared white just a few yards from his right oar blade. A boom shattered the silence and echoed up and down the canyon. Party leaders upset with the capitalist pigs? The hunter with his flintlock and a change of heart? We all ducked, just in case, but surfaced when two Jian Wan villagers across from the blast started giggling and held up a stick of dynamite. They were simply fishing, the new, modern way.

"Shit happens," Ken Jarkow grinned. It was now the trip motto.

We made camp early that night near a village called San Ji An Guen, so as to be able to have sufficient time to prepare the pig. John Yost and Dick Moersch forced a stick up the pig's rectum and out his mouth, while the rest of the group hurriedly built a stone fireplace and stoked up a bonfire to create the needed coals. Curious villagers, some dressed in their finest Naxi dress (including the decorative *pan-tou*, a traditional headdress), wandered down to the beach to watch and offer their local handcrafts for our inspection—pewter pipes, sheepskin jackets, and the skin of a large spotted wildcat. The pig spun sluggishly on the spit, beer was quaffed, and Sonny started negotiating for a sheepskin coat. By nightfall, we were all porking out on the blackened sow, an orgy of grease, a beggar's banquet on the Yangtze, a scene from *Lord of the Flies*. The crowd of villagers around us grew larger and bolder. It was as if we had left behind Hotel California at last and checked into the Halloween Suite.

As the last bones were being picked, Joel, with several *mao-tais* under his belt, broke into a song and a sailor's jig, to the great amusement of the village children. Most of them had probably never before seen a Westerner in the flesh, and were no doubt astonished at his silliness. As the children broke into applause, Joel went into his next act, a Hawaiian love song, replete with paddling gestures and a hula. At first, we found Joel's antics a bit embarrassing, but somehow his childlike lack of inhibition, his spontaneous, innocent approach to cross-cultural enter-tainment, connected in a way that all our handshaking and protocol never had. At least his off-key voice and exaggerated hula were nonthreat-ening, even appealing, and struck some basic chord.

Joel's discombobulated song and dance routine prompted several giggling, wide-eyed gamines to link hands and return his gesture by performing a circle dance while singing a lively folk tune in high-pitched voices. We applauded in genuine appreciation, and they repeated the performance. The singing went on and on, the dancing round and round, more children joined in, and the songs reverberated up and down the canyon until the group collapsed in laughter.

It was time to show our stuff. The round-eyes gathered behind our kitchen table, and went through our repertoire of songs; then we launched into a spirited version of "Jingle Bells" for our little audience, followed by a ragged round robin of "Row, Row, Row Your Boat." Our manly, tuneless voices—Julia's was drowned out by the vulgar boatmen— contrasted starkly with the high, tinny singsong of the Chinese children, but it all sounded just fine to us.

Breck, a bit *mao-tai*ed himself, tried to instruct the Chinese children in "Row, Row, Row Your Boat," so they could sing along. They proved to be quick studies, and the resulting intercultural chorus sounded melodic, almost practiced. This prompted Breck to go a step further, and he came up with an impromptu Top Ten to teach the children, including Van Morrison's "Gloria" and Chubby Checker's "Let's Twist Again," all with accompanying body movements. The Chinese loved it, and parroted back Breck's every chorus with near-perfect renditions. They then taught us to sing some of their favorites, and we quickly proved to be not nearly the students our young comrades were. Kramer broke out his harmonica, a middle-aged Chinese man pulled out his *lu shen*, a musical gourd pipe, and we had dueling banjos, Yangtze-style. It quickly became a riot of singing, an international hootenanny.

The cultural exchange continued deep into the night, as we learned an assortment of songs of which we knew neither words nor meanings; and the Chinese learned bits of "Louie, Louie," "America the Beautiful" (to which Sam responded with "Dixie," demanding equal time), the theme from "The Beverly Hillbillies," and perhaps the highlight of the evening, a rousing, hand-clapping round of "My Baby Does the Hanky Panky."

As we crooned and lilted towards the midnight hour, Dick Moersch and Jon Ingleman stepped forward and offered a clean, capering version of "Goodnight Irene." We took the cue and said goodnight to our new friends. For that one night we had all been part of the same riverside community, soaring with the same feelings of happiness to be alive.

Ultimately we had one man to thank. Perhaps he was a buffoon, the trip jester, with an ego beyond imagination, but Joel Fogel had had the pluck and temperament to explore the river of foolishness that runs through all cultures. While the rest of us were ready to explore imposing landscapes, we were too timid to be ourselves. Joel had no such timidity. It had been a remarkable evening, and we had Joel to thank for it.

Had there been any early risers, they would have seen a large green squash, pierced by a Tekna river knife, as the centerpiece on the commissary table the next morning. It was only appropriate: it was Halloween, the last day of October. We'd had our treats the night before, but so far—knock on wood—had missed the tricks.

We didn't think our luck would last. The villagers of San Ji An Guen had told us through Zhong that there was a rapid downstream, a big one. At 11:30 A.M. we pulled into a village on the left bank called Hung Men Kou that overlooked a rapid of the same name. At first we made jokes about it, that only hung men would run it; but then, the more we looked at it, the more we knew the metaphor cut both ways: it could just as easily hang us.

It was easily the biggest rapid we had encountered below Tiger's Leap Gorge, nearly half a mile of white terror, beginning with a hole that could swallow the Dragon Throne and its entourage, and ending with a series of spiky tail waves that looked like the back of a Chinese dragon. For over an hour we nervously paced along the rocky shore scouting this Hydra, and finally decided there might be a run if one entered the tongue pulling towards the left bank like death was chasing. With enough power and the correct timing, in theory a boat could crash through the lateral wave that created the wall of the tongue, and skim past the megahole on an expressway down the left. In theory.

I didn't feel comfortable with the split-second timing—there was just one trough in the wall, which a speeding boat would have to hit exactly. Nor was I certain I had the strength to punch through the wall, even at its weakest point. So I opted to photograph and to walk. Skip Horner, who even at forty was in great shape, and one of the most talented whitewater boaters I'd ever seen, thought he could make the pull and volunteered to go first. Julia wanted to ride, but Skip didn't feel she had the strength or experience to be his crew for such a dangerous run, and he diplomatically denied her passage, choosing Sonny instead. John Yost said he would follow, and told his riders—the two doctors, Dick Moersch and Jon Ingleman—he figured a 75 percent chance of making it through the plotted course right-side-up. The kayak and canoe were carried around. The other two rafts, Jim Slade's and the Media Boat, would wait and see.

With a row of still and video cameras lining the eastern bank, Skip entered the tongue, pulling like a big dog; Sonny Falack, who had capsized twice in Skip's boat on an exploratory expedition on Pakistan's Indus two years before, rode the bow, his black wet suit silhouetted against the awful white of the cataract. Furiously, Skip pulled, but the water was king, and the raft couldn't quite make the mark. It struck the wall of the lateral wave beneath the target, and rode up on its comb, a long white plume that feathered down into the edge of the hole. Skip was on a collision course. He took a quick, deep stroke to straighten his boat for impact, and crouched like a cougar ready to lunge.

The raft slammed into the rolling white rampart, twisted, then kicked up on its side, hurling Sonny into the boiling currents. With split-second reactions Skip threw his body up against the overturning boat, and his momentum and weight seemed to arrest the flip. The raft hung as though flash-frozen for an eternal second, then flopped back right-side-up. Sonny, who had grabbed a rope when going over, pulled himself in, and Skip grabbed the oars, regained control, and piloted the boat safely through the rest of the rapid.

It was an impressive show, and I had turned to express amazement to Jim Slade that the raft had not capsized, when Slade pointed to an overturned raft entering the rapid's tail waves. It had to be John Yost's boat. We had been so intent on watching Skip's miracle run that we'd missed Yost's. He had entered just seconds behind Skip, had failed to punch through the wall of water, and had capsized in a rolling wave above the abominable hole. The raft had fallen over on top of the two bow riders, and the upstream oar snapped like a chicken bone across Dick Moersch's head. Yost and his passengers were swept smack through the middle of the worst recirculating hole on this stretch of the Yangtze. And though a dozen expedition members were situated on shore just twenty yards across from the hole, more than half missed the flip entirely.

Both Yost and Moersch had been in capsizes before, Yost several times. Instinctively they swam for the left eddy, the closest and largest, reaching it four hundred yards below the capsize. Kramer was stationed in the shallows with a rescue line, which he successfully tossed to Dick Moersch, pulling the doctor to safety. Yost swam to Skip's boat and was safely pulled in. Jon Ingleman, however, had never been in a capsize. When the raft flipped over on top of him, he was sucked down deep, spun like laundry, then spat up below the hole, thirty feet downriver from the raft.

Instinctively he started swimming in the direction he was facing, towards the right, and he kicked and pumped his arms, but the powerful current kept carrying him further downstream. Then he was sucked into a second giant hole, and went under for what must have seemed like an eternity. Finally he popped up, obviously tired, but the river was showing no mercy, and dragged him on towards the distant bend.

Later, he remembered the thoughts that came to him as he struggled in the grip of the hostile current:

While down there I thought, "Please don't let this hole be a keeper, or I'm going to drown!" When I came out I was gasping for breath. I couldn't believe what I saw ahead: endless, giant rollers. How could I get through that and still be breathing? I tried to swim but was helpless, like a twig in a torrent. Down into a trough I slid grabbing for breathers, looking up at walls of water. I'd get buried in a wall, and wait for it to spit me out, to begin the process again. I was in serious trouble. I was helpless, gasping for breath, and my arms and legs were beginning to go.

Far away on the left bank I saw Kramer with the signal asking if I was okay. I signaled "No!" I knew there was no way a throw rope could ever reach me. My only hope was to get to the right bank which was so far away . . . I was totally exhausted and gave up swimming. I just tried to shove my jacket down so my mouth would be above water. I would never give up. I realized the river power might drown me regardless of my will. I thought of J. D., my son. Why did I do this? I can't breathe! Was I going to die?

Waves were rapidly sweeping me towards the cliffs on the right. I tried to get out of the main current. No use. I wondered if I would get dashed into the cliffs. Would I have the strength to get into an eddy? I tried feebly for two eddies. No way. I swooshed by the cliffs out into the middle again. I knew my only hope was a kayak rescue. I looked upstream and saw Sam two hundred yards away. I took heart, then felt despair when he was gone. I remember feeling rage, anger, at what I'm not sure. It may have been at myself, possibly the river, probably my absolute helplessness against the incredible power of the river. Because I was in such oxygen debt, I became dizzy. I was afraid of blacking out and drowning.

Sam Moore, in his C-1, did make it to Jon, and pulled him over to Skip's raft, where Jon—ashen, limp, barely conscious—was hoisted over the gunwale, crumpled into the boat, and retched. "You're a horse!" Skip yelled at him as he rolled around the bilge. "Most people couldn't have survived that." Then he was taken to shore, helped out of the boat, and treated for shock.

After the near-disaster of Yost's flip, the remaining boatmen looked at the rapid with renewed respect. Slade found a sloppy, unsporting, but probably safe entrance over a small pourover next to the left bank. A cheat run, sure: but a run, and a way to avoid that hole. First Jim Slade, then Dave Edwards took the cheat route, just in case.

The whole of the expedition reunited as everyone pulled in for an early camp on a broad beach a couple of miles below Hung Men Kou. Jon staggered off and sat by himself. After a time, I wandered over and talked to him. I asked him what he was thinking about when he was in the water. The near-drowning experience was one I felt I could share, as it had happened to me fourteen years before on the Baro River in Ethiopia. By way of reply, Jon reached into his wet gear bag and took out a Hallmark plaque showing a papa bear holding his baby bear who's flying a kite. The baby bear is saying, "I love Daddy."

Jon told me his son, J. D., had given him the plaque several years before. When, three weeks before the expedition, J. D. had asked him not to go on the expedition because he feared his father would die Jon packed the plaque as a reminder that his son wanted him back.

"All I thought of was my son, and how I had promised I would walk around any dangerous rapids. I thought of how I was going to die, and let my son down. I thought of how devastated he would be without me. It broke my heart. I asked myself, Why did I do this stupid thing? Why was I foolishly wasting my life on some macho misadventure? The thoughts were unbearable to me. I love my son more than anything in the world."

Jon's confessions were sobering. He was forty-five, divorced, a loner form Fort Wayne, Indiana, the least experienced member of the expedition. He had kayaked West Virginia's New River, canoed the Boundary Waters, hiked the Swiss Alps, and bicycled through England. He wanted a grand adventure, a test, a chance to be involved in something "historic" before it was too late. Jon, like all of us, wanted to explore more than a river on this trip: he wanted to explore himself. And with the capsize, he'd been sucked down into darkness and spun around his own axis. "Those who go beneath the surface do so at their own peril," wrote Oscar Wilde, but he neglected to mention the reward that can come with the peril.

Jon Ingleman discovered in the darkness beneath the surface a new light, a lightness of being. To approach death, yet draw away, allows an up-close look at the limits of mortal existence. He had crossed a wilderness and found a reason—the reason explorers, climbers, rafters, and even dentists from the Midwest take the risks they do: the chance for validation and growth that comes by confronting death, and that makes living all the more meaningful and worthwhile. Jon Ingleman, that Halloween, had been baptized as an adventurer.

It was a strange camp that night, the dark side of Halloween. A turquoise pool, mineralized water from some unknown source, nestled invitingly at the base of the mountain wall behind us. Offered a chance to bathe in relative peace, we soon turned its waters milky and sour with our eager libations. At dusk, a mighty blast of cold wind came up the canyon, feathering the tops of the dunes with fans of biting sand. Cat tracks, large pads the size of a fist, pocked the beach downstream from the kitchen, and clustered around a small burrow in the cliff face. A feeling of isolation permeated the camp, but it was not without an element of threat that seemed to echo from the water's turmoil not far upstream at Hung Men Kou.

CHAPTER TWENTY

The Last Rapid

I lifted up my eyes to the
mountains and clasped my hands
and invented a clumsy prayer that went:
Please let me come back.
—PAUL THEROUX

The next day, Jon Ingleman was back on the horse, riding in Jim Slade's raft as we rowed through a series of intermediate rapids. After one challenging stretch, Joel paddled over to Jon and congratulated him for getting back in the raft after his ordeal of the previous day. "It's one thing to run dangerous rapids if you're ignorant of what the consequences could be; it takes courage to do it when you really know," Joel praised Jon. Then he paddled away, perhaps having revealed a bit of himself. My opinion of Joel Fogel was undergoing a gradual change. There were some things about him I could never accept, nor forgive; but I had to give him credit, he was a more complex man than I had known.

Early in the afternoon we reached the first bridge since before Tiger's Leap, a cabled, wood-planked road span at the town of Sidu. This was supposed to be a resupply stop, but we had been making such good progress through the Great Bend that we were two days early, and our supply truck had not yet arrived. Still, though we had plenty of food and no real need to check in with our CIST land crew, Sidu was the largest town we had come to since Shigu, and we decided to take a few minutes to check it out.

The town had its charms, the most immediately apparent of which was a riverside restaurant featuring cold beer and hot spicy Sichuan beef, which was immediately adopted by the crew for several savory hours. Sidu was built near a major copper mine, and was blessed with a small hydroelectric plant and thus electricity, a luxury the villages upstream had been without. Several of us decided to remain behind and recharge the video-camera batteries, so while the rest of the crew took off in three boats downstream, planning to camp at the first beach of any size, Ken, Dave, Joel, Breck, and I checked into the Yangtze River Hilton, a dank room with four steel beds and a single bare lightbulb beneath the restaurant.

We then set off to explore Sidu. I was eager to see more of daily life along the river in the Great Bend. The citizens were wonderful, inviting us into nearly every home we passed. In one, a man with thick glasses sat in the back of a grim room hunched over a ledger sheet, an abacus on the far end of his desk, and a Casio electronic calculator in the foreground. Sidu, it turned out, was very much a town in transition, caught between two worlds, one dying, the other struggling to be born.

I wandered up a hard-packed red dirt road, past rows of poplar and willow, and stopped to look into a long concrete building called a *pingfang* that seemed to be a dormitory for the mine workers. Immediately, a young man with a guitar grabbed my arm and pulled me into his room, where his portable tape player was blaring a disco version of "Don't Rock the Boat." Down the hall another boy pulled me into his cubicle to show off his etchings, coal line drawings of landscapes, self-portraits, Vladimir Lenin, even a nude of a Chinese woman, something I had never seen in more progressive Chinese cities such as Shanghai.

My tour continued to another dorm room, one featuring Mozart and Michael Jackson, hot peanuts and sweet brandy. It was getting harder to believe we were in a remote canyon in southwest China. Then, a boy took me by the hand and led me up a long stairway to a small park, where twenty townspeople sat on the edges of their folding chairs watching—a television. It was the Thirteenth Communist Party Congress, being broadcast live by satellite from Beijing to this outpost that in many ways looked as though it had been lost in a time warp. As we sat there in the park, deep in the Great Bend, a thousand miles away Deng Xiaoping was stepping aside as his party's leader after a tumultuous decade of change.

The coup de grace came, however, during dinner back at the restaurant. We were wolfing down helpings of Chinese sturgeon, the famous Yangtze fish that dates back 140 million years and grows to as much as ten feet and one thousand pounds along this stretch of the river. Despite its age, it tasted fresh, and despite the ambience defined by a table of locals hawking and spitting in the overture that is China's phlegmatic serenade, the meal was thoroughly satisfying. During seconds, a teenager came over to us and uncurled his palm. There, scrawled in jiggly letters, were the words: "Go to the cinema."

Cinema? Movies in this place? It seemed impossible, but the day had been full of impossibilities. We followed our usher across the bridge, up a steep path to a mud-walled *hutong* (compound), paid our 2-cent admission price, walked through the portal created by a curved stone lintel set over stone posts, and found ourselves standing in an open-air theater. Watching a silent super-8 war movie were five hundred sunflower-seed-munching Chinese who were unconsciously supplying a soundtrack of sputum. We couldn't quite figure out the plot, but the Westerners were the bad guys, and whenever one was shot, the crowd cheered and someone threw sunflower seeds at us. We decided not to wait for the ending, and beat a hasty retreat to our hotel.

After an early breakfast the next day, we floated down to rejoin the main group, and continued downriver with no official resupply—but with fresh fruits, vegetables, and two cases of beer from Sidu. In quick succession we ran two major rapids, Man Lo Tan and Qin Jia Tan; by midafternoon we arrived at La Zi Tan. It was here, we were told, that two Chinese had drowned last year. La Zi Tan, like other rapids before, presented a nasty-looking hole across its middle with a cheat slide down its side. Downstream the current pressed into a flat wall of limestone, and we could easily imagine a high-water run, such as the Chinese must have taken. The boat would flip in the hole, the old water-soaked kapok life jackets would fail to keep their wearers afloat, the desperate swimmers would be hurled into the impassive wall. . . . Further on, we could see the river funnel into a tight gorge, and with the suspicion that life could be nastier still just beyond our sight, we decided to take the cheat run, pull in for camp, and set out to scout the gorge by foot.

It was a thousand-foot climb to the first plateau above the river, and six of us bushwacked our way upward through patches of stinging nettles, then traversed downstream to see if we could proceed, or if we might have to call it quits and hike out. But the hike showed us only a smooth green ribbon of river below, none of the treacherous rapids we expected from the narrowing canyon. After a couple of miles, we came to a village. Through sign language, we asked over and over again about rapids downstream, and the village elder kept shaking his head. "*Bu, bu.*" No: La Zi Tan was the last rapid, he seemed to say with emphasis. The last rapid between his village and Jinjiang, the bridge beyond the bottom of the Great Bend where we hoped to take out. The Last Rapid.

This was great news. We wouldn't have to abandon the gear and trek out, we could float home and float home victorious. We had taken the best shots the Yangtze could throw us and emerged from the Great Bend intact, ahead of schedule, and with food to spare.

Back at camp, we found the rest of the group lying on the beach, getting a lazy tan. We told them the good news, then broke out the beer and prepared a feast from our stash of potatoes and chili. It was time to celebrate. We had the dubious distinction of being the first nonfatal expedition on the upper Yangtze. Suddenly La Zi Tan didn't look so threatening, the hole in its center looked runnable, inviting even. Some of us speculated on runs down the glassy tongue into the long, curling wave that rose and broke and fell just twenty yards in front of our beach, then into the big water below, pulling away at the last moment from the fateful wall. . . . The beer tasted better with each bottle, washing away our cares.

The morning after, heads ringing from the merrymaking, we took another look at the rapid across from our camp. The bank was ribbed with watermarks, proof that the flow was dropping. The rapid still looked runnable, if anything easier than it had the day before, but we would have to portage a boat back upstream if we wanted to run it. Would the thrill be worth it? Breck, John Yost, Skip, and Julia were still enthusiastic about the prospect, but Julia said she wouldn't ride with Breck or John—she didn't trust their boating skills. I passed on the run, thinking the fifteen seconds of whitewater excitement wasn't worth the heavy labor of carrying the raft and rowing frame upstream. Jim Slade concurred. Then Breck and John Yost, heads now clearing, threw in the towel for the same reason.

That left Skip, a true whitewater junkie. He was still tempted, but Julia demanded that if he made the run, she be in the boat. "I paid as much as anyone for this trip, and I wasn't allowed to ride through Hung Men. Just because I'm a woman doesn't mean I can't do it. So if you go, I want on." That was enough to make Skip pass as well, feeling it would be the easiest way to maintain expedition harmony.

Meanwhile, Sam and Joel in their easily portable hard-shell boats still hadn't decided. When Dave Edwards rowed my boat down the cheat run of Hung Men, Breck had positioned himself in the bow and used one of Sam's canoe paddles to help propel the boat. When the raft tumbled over the sharp waterfall, Sam's paddle had snapped. It was his lucky fifty-eight-inch blue spruce and mahogany-veneered Kober, the one that had seen him safely down rivers in Chile, Nepal, and Mexico, and he wasn't happy about its loss. Now, without his charmed paddle, Sam wasn't ready to tackle the hole that may have killed two Chinese the year before.

That left Joel. He studied the rapid while the rest of us loaded the rafts, then announced he was going to make the run. He passed out his portable video and two still cameras, and made sure everyone had their own cameras at ready, then carried his kayak upstream like a cowboy carrying his saddle. He disappeared behind a boulder that marked the entrance to the millrace, performing whatever prerapid ritual he needed to do. After a few minutes we heard him call out, "Here I come. Get the cameras ready."

Then, with a series of Andy-Devine-steering-Jezebel-down-the-mountain whoops and hollers, he came charging down the chute on his yellow steed, and dropped straight into the middle of the hole. The wave seemed to close its sharp knuckles on Joel, then he shot out the top and slid down the backside of the claw, his yells of triumph echoing through the canyon. It was a sensational show, and I found myself applauding. For all Joel's vanity, he did possess a certain kind of courage, a willingness to put his pride and life on the line in pursuit of a goal—even if that goal smacked of personal glory. For the moment, I admired Joel. Maybe he had been a lousy kayaker, but he had come to boat the Yangtze, and he had learned along the way. And this morning, he was the first man ever to kayak this rapid.

As we loaded up the last of the gear, we began the daily ritual of raft roulette, distributing eighteen rafters among the four rafts. The optimum number of passengers for rafts of our size was four, including the guide, but because of our uneven number, two rafts every day had to carry five. As we readied for boarding, Julia came down to my boat and asked if I had room. I said no, as four others had already made claim to spaces. I watched her as she asked Slade, then John Yost, and finally Skip. He too, like the others before him, shrugged his shoulders and said he was full.

It was obviously impossible for all four rafts to be full without Julia, and the scenario suddenly struck her in the worst way. She turned her back and burst into tears. Dick Moersch saw her first, and bounded over to comfort her, assuring her it had surely been just a mistake. And it was: it turned out Gerrit had committed to my raft as well as Slade's, and when he crawled onto mine he had neglected to tell Jim. Skip had thought Zhong was riding with him, but discovered otherwise when we counted heads. It was an innocent error, but it was easy to understand Julia's bout of paranoia. She was the "odd man out," the only woman traveling with nineteen men, as far from home as an American can get, participating in a dangerous sport for which she had little experience. Whether the rest of us, wrapped up in the heavy baggage of our male psyches, would have had the guts to show our emotions in a similar situation was doubtful. Julia dried her eyes and jumped onto Jim's boat.

That morning we drifted downstream on a river we believed had dealt us the last of its fire, past willowy waterfalls that traced graceful white lines down the fever-red canyon walls. But just before lunch, the river suspiciously pooled, and around the next sharp turn there was another rapid. We ran up to scout it, thinking it must not be significant, the villagers would have told us if it were, but scouting just the same. Surely *this* must be the last rapid. It was a rapid all right, but it looked like a huge wave train with no keepers, the perfect situation for a "photo opportunity." Skip, still restless from having to pass on the rapid that Joel had run earlier in the morning, decided to take the amusement park ride down the middle.

Earlier in the morning the subject of hubris had come up in Skip's boat—the fatal flaw of the classic hero who believes he can do no wrong and thus strides boldly into disaster. Some of his crew remembered a slightly flawed feeling, a disease in the moment, as Skip confidently rowed into the heart of the current, setting up for the center run. As big Jacques Vroom sat on the duffel in back, armed with his video camera, and Jon Ingleman nervously braced next to him in the bow, Christian looked down the rapid as they entered and said, "Jesus, that fourth wave looks huge."

They blasted down the center and rode up and over one big breaker after another, hooting and hollering like broncobusters. Then, as they slid into the trough before the fourth wave, the raft slowly torqued sideways, and Skip muttered, "Uh-oh, looks like a big one." The boat rode up the face of the wave, then stalled for a long second as Christian rode the high tube and Jon, still unaccustomed to highsiding, sat on the lower one. Jacques's big frame held down the stern, and that was all it took: suddenly the raft was over.

"I knew I should have been thinking about my young son, like Ingleman did," said Christian later. "But all I could think about were my feet. The water sucked off one of my sandals, and when I surfaced I thought, Damn, now I'll have to wear those frigging tennis shoes that ruined my feet in the gorge hike. Then the black sole of my sandal floated to the surface just a reach away. I grabbed it and used it as a paddle to help swim the boat to shore." The water was forgiving, and crew and raft were safely ashore in less than a minute. Jon Ingleman, however, had by now picked up a reputation. He was called Aquaman from then on. And some started calling the rapid Hubris behind Skip's back.

Not long after lunch, we passed beneath a bridge, an isolated link in the middle of an uninhabited landscape. A solitary truck roared out of the denuded hills as we approached, kicking up a trail of yellow dust, and rattled over the rusted chain-link span as we floated beneath it. In one of Joseph Rock's early articles about the river gorges of Yunnan, he noted that in the whole length of the Yangtze course, as of 1926, there was not a single bridge, with the exception of "the imposing structure at Tsilikiang, one and a half day's journey southeast of Likiang." The article's accompanying photo showed the bridge we found in the middle of nowhere, halfway down the last leg of the Great Bend. It was only later that we realized the location of the bridge corresponded to the take-out point for the Chinese expeditions of the year previous. We had at last reached unknown waters on the Yangtze.

The current continued to speed us downriver, into broad shallow stretches punctuated by holes and boulder gardens, but the assurances of the villagers that there were no more dangers lulled us into complacency. Fortunately Sam Moore resumed his role as probe, canoeing ahead to scout the river. About 4:30 we rounded a sharp bend to find Jim Slade perched on a bluff, madly waving us to shore. We made the cut, pulling into a narrow eddy buffeted by a powerful current, and climbed up to see what all the arm waving was about. A couple of hundred yards downstream the river plunged over a steep chute into a vicious confusion of crosscurrents, holes, and boils. Farther down, a series of standing waves rose and fell, receding into the distance like a train ride to hell. Jim had been suspicious of the accelerating pace of the river, and when he rounded the bend he saw Sam Moore paddling like a desperate man for the left bank. Except for Jim's lucky suspicions and Sam's scouting, we would have floated into the worst rapid yet—one that well may have been the Last Rapid for us all.

Glumly, we looked around—this had to be camp for the night. We had been blessed by large sandy beaches, hospitable neighbors, and balmy weather, but here we were stranded on a rocky bluff high above a churning current, misfortune mocking us with its rough laughter just downstream. Those of us who would be piloting boats spent the waning hours of the day scouting the rapid from all available vantages. The mad water threw rainbows all around us. For what seemed like an eternity I stared at the flux and flow. I didn't know it at the time, but this was the only unrun rapid we could encounter. I could see no clean run, nor any way to cheat. Portaging was impossible, as cliffs cut sheer to both banks. It looked like a white whirligig of earthly horrors. I wondered if we had

been spared real difficulties thus far only to be forced to abandon the run
and hike out so close to our goal. The Last Rapid had proven chimerical;
this camp was our Last Chance.

Meanwhile, Ken Jarkow, who through the course of the trip had
become ever more mellow, didn't even look at the rapid. "Shit happens,"
he shrugged when I started to tell him about the horrors ahead. He spent
the twilight reading Tom Clancy's *The Hunt for Red October*, and
seemed about as calm as a seasoned intelligence operative facing a driver's
test. Larry Krasnow likewise had tenderized, in fact seemed to be having
the time of his life as he hovered over the campfire telling jokes. Dave
Edwards tried to get into the act with a joke about two nuns in a bar, but
couldn't remember the punch line. In another corner Jon Ingleman was
reading John McPhee's classic, *Coming into the Country*. Knowing this
Last Rapid was nigh (or *was* it the last rapid?), I couldn't read a book or
tell jokes; I could barely write in my notebook. And certainly I couldn't
face the freeze-dried meal that was shaping up to be some sort of chili, a
sure added insult to intestinal injury. The night was polished to a sheen
and the breeze was warm. The moon was waning, and a huge ring
encircled it, promising rain in the coming days. I fell asleep with the
rapid's low roar leaking into my tent.

After a quick breakfast, for the first time on the trip, everyone struggled
into either tight-fitting wet suits or the looser, more colorful dry suits. A
rheumy-eyed farmer wandered down from his field to watch us load up
for the rapid, which he said was called Ma Wei Tan. He looked to me
like a spectator at Evel Knievel's Snake River Canyon jump—someone
secretly hoping for the worst. I watched as a bright butterfly landed on Jim
Slade's wrist, and for several seconds refused to release as Jim shook his
arm violently. Jon "Aquaman" Ingleman came down to the rafts to see
which one would take him, and Skip looked up and crossed his fingers as
though warding off a vampire. Jon's white-bearded face dropped, then
Skip broke into a broad grin and waved Jon on board.

The run was going to call for a strong, sustained pull across the river
to the opposite bank, where a rough tongue slid sloppily over boulders
into a string of holes that could easily fill us with water and possibly flip
us, but that fed into a side current that missed the hungry heart of the
rapid. Still not feeling confident about my strength, especially rowing the
Media Boat, heaviest and slowest of the fleet, I asked Dave Edwards if he
wanted to row. "Yes, yes," he answered with alacrity. It had clearly been
tough on Dave, an excellent river guide, to sit in the back of the raft with
his cameras during most of the expedition while someone else rowed.

Now, he could shake the sticks in a major rapid, as he had done in Hung Men, but this time he wouldn't, in fact couldn't, cheat. Every possible run went through the wild wave train at the center of the rapid.

Dave's adamantine arms seemed diesel-powered as we crossed the main current and reached the side channel that dropped into the first hole. I hung on in the back of the boat with one hand gripped around a duffel strap, the other holding a waterproof Nikon above my head. I was tossed around like a rag doll as we foundered through a picket fence of sharp boulders and soggy holes—and then we rode the current past the wave train. Six, eight, ten of the monsters reared up, each one higher than the last, the tallest some eighteen feet. Twelve, fifteen, nearly twenty huge waves in all paraded off our left bow, like a legion of soldiers at attention, bidding farewell to the fools who challenged the Great River.

Another mile on, and suddenly it was over. The right bank jutted out in a rocky shelf to almost touch the left wall, and we slid through the turbulent twenty-yard channel that marked the end of the gorges of the Great Bend. We were at last slow boats in China, drifting through a landscape of mud-and-wattle homes, placer mines, water buffalo, golden hills, and blue-suited children clustered on the muddy beaches, waving and shouting in friendly welcome.

As we sailed down this great vein towards the heart of China, Joel paddled up to my raft, rested his arm against the rowing frame, and looked up to ask, "Would it be correct to say we've navigated some of the biggest rapids on earth?"

I had the feeling Joel was fishing for a quote he could use in articles and presentations, but I answered truthfully. "No," I replied. "The Zaire, which runs over a million cubic feet per second as it falls off a steep escarpment, has rapids much, much bigger than anything on the Yangtze."

"How about we've paddled the toughest rapids in Asia?"

"No. The Brahmaputra has a steeper gradient and more water."

"Oh. Well, thanks." And Joel paddled off towards the raft a few hundred yards in front. We watched as he visited all four rafts. Later that evening the guides compared notes and found Joel had asked everyone the same questions, and in each case had been answered in the negative. Somehow, though, everyone was pretty sure that nothing would stop Joel from telling the story the way he saw it.

We camped that evening at a wide bend of the river, across from a town called Dome, the largest we had seen since we left Daqu ten days earlier. The people here were connected to the outside world by a road we could see winding through the far hills. While we were setting up camp, Joel wandered off to explore our little spit of land, and returned a few minutes later, proudly leading a half dozen men. There was something odd about his new friends, odder even than their shabby clothes and unkempt hair would suggest. There was a strange look in their eyes, a bold glee that made them seem wilder than any of the tribal people we had encountered in the more remote reaches of the gorges. As Joel introduced them to his river companions, he told us he had found them working as gold miners and living in caves, just over the bluff.

"Great, Joel, thanks for sharing your friends with us," someone remarked. The more we saw of the six men, the more they seemed like outcasts, village idiots or exiles, the troglodytes of Dome. There was probably no room for them in the society the New China was building, but that didn't stop the effervescent Joel Fogel from greeting them as friends—and inviting them into our camp. They eagerly peered around our campsite, at the strange nylon tents rising from the sand, purple and green sleeping bags, anthracite-black flashlights and yellow Walkmans, the expensive toys of a material culture. Slowly, the realization dawned that there would be nothing to stop these outlaws from returning to camp late at night and just helping themselves. Even Joel soon realized his mistake, and by maneuvers subtle and not so subtle we encouraged the troglodytes to return to their caves, secured our loose gear inside our tents, and hoped for the best.

But Joel was on a roll, back among strangers where his mad enthusiasms could once more be appreciated. As the strange half dozen wandered away, smiling at secret thoughts, a small flat barge floated across the river. A greeting party waded ashore, composed of a nervous young man wearing a pink sweater beneath a blush-plaid suit, his white shirt buttoned to the top, and two very pretty teenage girls. The man identified himself as an English teacher, and even though he was the first English-speaking person we had encountered in three weeks, we took pity on his students: his language skill was dreadful. Haltingly, he explained that the two girls were his students, and they were excited to meet real Americans and hear how they spoke.

Once it became clear the teacher and his students were just there to gawk, most of us returned to our camp chores. Not Joel: he took an avid interest in our visitors, and tried to communicate with them. After a while Breck wandered back to where Joel was crouched in what seemed like a negotiating session with the young teacher and his beautiful students. Suddenly Breck yelled, "Fuck you, Joel," and I dropped what I was doing and hustled over to the scene.

"What's the matter?" I asked Breck.

"Joel is trying to convince the teacher he should let the girls come with him. He says he'll pay for them to come to the States, go to school, and live with him."

"Yeah. What's wrong with that?" Joel retorted, suddenly angry at our intrusion. "I've had fourteen exchange students from all over the world!"

"You're full of bullshit, Joel," Breck said.

"Fuck off," Joel cried at Breck. "It's none of your business."

"You fuck off," Breck returned.

"No, you fuck off." And on it went for a few more rounds, until Skip stepped in and yelled for them to back off and grow up.

Joel went off to his campsite to sulk, leaving the three Chinese smiling stupidly, unable to understand what had just happened. I was initially repulsed by Joel's behavior, an act that seemed the ugliest of the ugly American, more juvenile than anything he'd done to date. But as I put up my tent and looked over at the two girls, they flashed back shy smiles, and I started to reevaluate. Maybe Joel's impulse was not so abnormal: who wouldn't be attracted to the beguiling smiles of exotic foreigners? It was Joel's actions that crossed the line. Where most of us operated more or less within the unwritten rules of protocol, Joel seemed to live by his own rules, in his own dominion. In some cases this trait was admirable—it was, after all, the mark of a true explorer, someone who refused to accept conventional boundaries and dared to go beyond. Yet Joel seemed to warp this vitality.

Still, I suddenly found I could fathom it. For a decade and a half I had transferred to Joel my deep guilt about an unnecessary death on a river in Africa. But ultimately I had to blame myself—for being attracted by what he stood for, for allowing myself to succumb to the dangerous bait of ego in exploration, for letting Angus MacLeod get into my boat. I looked over at Joel and saw an overpolished mirror of myself.

Ever since I met Joel he had been trying to validate his existence with incessant photos, films, and videos of himself in extraordinary environments, doing extraordinary things. But didn't we all enjoy the moment when a camera was pointed at us, didn't we all brandish our best grin and relish the final product? Of course, most of us pretended we didn't care if we appeared in a video or a magazine. Most of us pretended we wouldn't want to snatch up a beautiful Chinese girl and take her home. But Joel had shed false modesty and shame, and was able to act the ego-starved child that exists within us all. It could be repugnant to see Joel in action; but it was, in some way, comprehensible. I could never forgive Joel, or myself, for what had happened fifteen years before. But I could finally accept it.

As a strangely subdued Joel stooped to unpack his duffel, I walked over to his distant encampment. "It's all right," I said, looking down at him. "I understand." He looked up at me, then smiled tentatively. I walked back to my tent and began to unpack my own gear. A few minutes later I glanced up to see Joel again talking with the two girls.

As we moved downstream the next morning, the river broadened. For the first time in our two weeks on the river, the sky was overcast. A sprinkling of rain fell, then evaporated. A wind began to press upstream. We had to turn our backs to it and lean into our strokes to make progress. Many river guides, it seems, have an outlook reflective of the way they row—facing upstream, looking at all that went before, their backs to the future as each stroke is pulled. They look to the past, at rough currents long since smoothed, living a life that disappeared decades ago. There is romance and adventure in the long ago, and a boatman's arms, with each stroke of the oars, reach out to embrace what has passed, while pulling the boat to an unseen future.

As we eased away from the Great Bend of the Yangtze, and into the final eastward turn that set the river's course for the coming two thousand miles, this attitude seemed appropriate. We were leaving behind a Yangtze unchanged for centuries, the Yangtze we had dreamed about, and it had been more than our midnight visions could have conjured. Now it moved away from us, looking like a sepia-colored daguerreotype in the flat light of midday. Ahead, behind our backs, loomed the Fujichrome Yangtze of tomorrow—the huge dams, arching bridges, massive agricultural projects, crowded towns and cities, leading ultimately to Shanghai with its 13 million souls. But that wasn't the world we had come to see, and we would end our odyssey at the Jinjiang Bridge, the span that marked the entrance to the river's future.

At noon on November 5, we took our last few strokes into a mud bank at the base of the Jinjiang Bridge. True to form, Mr. Cao and Mr. Luo were waiting with San Miguel and, its bold red-and-white logo familiar even in Chinese lettering, Coca-Cola. Our altimeter read 3,800 feet, meaning we'd dropped almost half a mile in elevation since our start at Shigu. The bounding river that we had ridden through "the land of stars and horses" was now flat and slow, dirty and old. It was heavily populated from here on out; in its lower reaches it passed through the most productive and densely populated region in China. We had passed through the last of the true wilderness of the Yangtze; we had run some of its best rapids, and yes, we had walked around those in the depths of its mightiest gorge. We'd seen a river and a region that had occupied our dreams for years, and by doing so, we'd achieved a goal. We hadn't conquered the river, if that meant running a river without ever taking a boat from the water, as the Chinese had tried to do, as Ken Warren so badly wanted. But we were certainly not defeated.

The sort of linear purity that persists in mountain climbing just doesn't exist in river exploration. The purpose isn't to descend at all costs; nor is it to be the first to vanquish a series of rapids. The objective, I believe, is to discover new truths—about our environment, about the peoples we meet, about those with whom we travel, and about ourselves. Jon Ingleman did that profoundly. I think Joel Fogel did it too; and I realize now that I did, even on this "last great first." We didn't come, see, and conquer; but we learned, we shared, and we gently touched a handful of distant lives during our brief journey through the Great Bend of the Yangtze.

Index

921
BAN

Bangs, Richard, 1950-

Riding the dragon's
back.

11837

$29.95

DATE			